INNOCENCE

(Revivaltime)

INNOCENCE

The True Story
of Steve Linscott

Gordon Haresign

Zondervan Books
Zondervan Publishing House
Grand Rapids, Michigan

INNOCENCE
Copyright © 1986 by W. Gordon Haresign

Zondervan Books are published by the Zondervan Publishing House
1415 Lake Drive S.E., Grand Rapids, Michigan 49506

Library of Congress Cataloging in Publication Data

Haresign, W. Gordon.
Innocence: the true story of Steve Linscott

1. Linscott, Steve—Trials, litigation, etc. 2. Trials (Murder)—
Illinois—Maywood. 3. Trials (Rape)—Illinois—Maywood. I. Title.
KF224.L49H37   1986   345.73'02523   86-11164
ISBN 0-310-43801-2   347.3052523

Unless otherwise noted, all Scripture references are taken from the
New International Version (North American Edition), © 1973, 1978,
1984, by the International Bible Society. Used by permission of
Zondervan Bible Publishers.

Printed in the United States of America

87 88 89 90 91 92 / CH / 10 9 8 7 6 5 4 3 2

To my wife, Nancy,
and daughters, Carin and Gayle,
who have patiently and lovingly endured
the brunt of my involvement
in the unfolding drama
of Steve and Lois Linscott

CONTENTS

PREFACE

I was at a Sunday evening church service when I learned that Steve Linscott was in trouble. The police, I was told later, had accused him of rape and murder. I couldn't believe it. Steve had been in my classes at Emmaus Bible College. He was a serious student, and I had enjoyed his class participation.

Two months before, after returning from a fruitful summer ministry in Maine, Steve had invited me to monitor his spiritual growth. As an elder at River Forest Bible Chapel, I gladly accepted the honor and, as a result, developed a keener, closer interest in him.

When Steve was arrested, one thought flashed through my mind: A person is presumed innocent until proven guilty beyond a reasonable doubt. *Beyond a reasonable doubt!* Both the police and the press seemed to be presuming Steve's guilt until he could prove his innocence.

During my ten years as director of Emmaus Bible Correspondence School (probably the largest school of its kind in the world), I witnessed the rapid growth of a ministry that offered serious Bible study for thousands of prison inmates across North America. The results were exciting, though the moral conflicts were, at times, agonizing. Students frequently shared their stories with the instructors. While many prisoners readily acknowledged their guilt, others asserted their innocence. I soon learned that not every inmate who claimed to be innocent *was* innocent; still, I was alarmed at the number of complaints about questionable practices used by authorities, slipshod investigations, withholding of evidence, and unfair treatment.

We often hear stories about convicts who, after several years of prison, are released because their innocence, unexpectedly, belatedly, has been proved—*beyond a reasonable doubt.* Such mistakes cannot be casually written off, not when lives and families and principles are involved.

"I didn't do it," Steve told me. And I believed him. Steve and Lois needed help, assurance, and love. My wife, Nancy, and I gave them as much as we could. Soon, others followed our lead. The Steve Linscott story is an amazing record of how God worked through hundreds, possibly even thousands of people in accomplishing a desired end.

As the case began to draw national attention, Steve and Lois asked me to write their story. I felt honored but reluctant. I considered myself inadequate, having never attempted to write anything like this before. But I also felt exceptionally qualified. I had witnessed the Linscotts' despair and brokenness; I had felt their heartaches and borne their sorrows; I had prayed, wept, and hurt with them; I had been involved in the case from the beginning and spent countless hours following leads and looking for suspects. Probably no one was as informed as I was about the case.

Because of my intimate involvement and my outrage at the injustices I perceived, it has been difficult for me to be objective. Yet I have tried. I have had to remind myself that the standard of "beyond a reasonable doubt" should apply to the prosecutors of a case as well as the defendant.

It is my prayer that this book, dedicated to the cause of justice, will help lead to a public outcry for reform in our judicial system so that once again we can refer to it as the fairest in the world.

ACKNOWLEDGMENTS

I sincerely acknowledge my appreciation of all who assisted in the production of this book. Several helped type my original manuscript—from handwriting that at times was hardly legible. Tom Decker unhesitatingly provided copies of legal briefs, willingly read the manuscript, and made invaluable corrections, particularly from the legal standpoint. I am deeply indebted to the editorial staff at Zondervan who saw potential in the book. My special appreciation, however, goes to Judith Markham and Bob Hudson who helped make the book what it is. Both are skillful editors. They knew what they wanted and guided me through several drafts. Last, but by no means least, I express my gratitude to Steve and Lois Linscott. Not only did they provide much information, they helped check the accuracy of it once it was written. This is their story. Without their experiences, request, and permission, *Innocence* would not have been written.

1
The
Dream

It was early fall. The trees were beginning to show their colors, and the days were noticeably shorter. The chill in the air was a welcome relief after one of the hottest summers on record. The Oak Park schools were back in session, and the community had settled into its autumn routine.

The 1980 presidential election was just a month away, and the candidates were vigorously campaigning. Challenger Ronald Reagan was traveling through the Northeast while President Jimmy Carter was wooing voters in Michigan. Chicago's Mayor Jane Byrne was planning a huge Monday rally for the incumbent.

Overseas, the Persian Gulf conflict continued. Iraq had broken a cease-fire agreement, barely twelve hours old, and the bitter war with Iran resumed. The Iranian hostage crisis was entering its three hundred and thirty-fifth day.

In the early hours of Saturday morning, October 4, Steve Linscott awoke and looked at his watch. It was 2:00 A.M. Like Nebuchadnezzar, the Babylonian king in the Book of Daniel, he had been troubled by a dream. As he lay there, he tried hard to dismiss it from his mind.

He had dreamed of a light-complexioned, square-built (but not muscular) man with short blond hair, about five feet, six inches tall, wearing reddish-brown pants and an off-white terry-cloth T-shirt with two horizontal reddish purple stripes across the chest and a single stripe on the arms. At first the man seemed friendly as he talked with someone nearby whose face remained blurred throughout the dream. Behind him, to his left and slightly below head level, a yellowish light softly glowed. Farther to the left stood a couch, which helped create the impression of a peaceful living-room scene.

But suddenly the man's attitude and facial expression changed. A sense of foreboding entered the dream. From behind his back he produced an object and held it before his companion with a leering smile. Steve described the object as some sort of weight or counterbalance, like the pendulum of a grandfather clock. How quickly the scene changed! The atmosphere became ominous.

At this point Steve awoke for the first time. When he went back to sleep, the dream resumed where it had left off, but it was more vivid. Unexpectedly, using the object pulled from behind his back, the man attacked. The assault clearly surprised the victim.

No doubt stunned by the initial blow, the victim appeared to offer no resistance but had an air of passivity, first falling onto hands and knees, then to a crouching, and finally to a lying position. The assailant continued to rain blows mercilessly upon the victim's head and body. His movements were quick, ruthless, and brutal. Blood splattered everywhere. It was gruesome.

14

Awake once again, the vividness of the dream still with him, Steve suddenly thought he heard a noise in the front room—like the rustling of paper. Dressed only in his undergarments, he leaped out of bed, and with the outside streetlights providing sufficient light, he checked the living room. Finding no cause for alarm, he walked around the small apartment and tried unsuccessfully to shake off the dream. All was well, so he returned to the bedroom he shared with his wife Lois. Through the open doorway he saw that two-year-old Katherine and ten-month-old Paul were sound asleep in the adjoining room.

Later, after Steve's dream, Lois was awakened by their baby's cries. Steve too heard the cries and stirred slightly, but his subconscious mind told him that Lois would respond to Paul, who had developed the habit of waking up each night and crying between the hours of one and three. He was still not weaned. Sometimes when she rose, Lois looked to see what time it was, but this night she did not look at her watch. Once she had changed, fed, and quieted the baby, Lois returned to bed and snuggled up to her husband.

As Steve looked at Lois, he was struck by the contrast between her tranquillity and the tumult of the dream. He thought through the bizarre dream again, then lay back, and once more fell asleep. Around four o'clock, hearing the dog bark furiously, he rose to see if someone was at the door. Finding no one there, he returned to bed and slept soundly until awakened by the patter of Katherine's feet as she came into the bedroom.

For the next hour or so the young couple played with Katherine and Paul. Since it was Saturday morning, both parents could afford to relax and enjoy the time together. As Steve romped with his two children, he never imagined that his dream would turn into a living nightmare, haunt him for years to come, and become a unique instance in the annals of American criminal history.

2
Headed for Trouble

For Steve and Lois, the journey to Oak Park, Illinois, began in early 1974. Steve, then a student at the University of Maine, was home in Ellsworth, Maine, for the weekend. His mother, Teresa, looked at him and said, "Steve, it'd be great if you could meet one of Debbie's new friends, Lois Beverly. A wonderful girl! If she were Catholic, she'd be a saint one day."

Steve just laughed at his mother's constant matchmaking.

Around the same time, his older sister Debbie had told her friend Lois, "I'd love for you to meet my brother—even though he's an atheist." She chuckled.

Steve met Lois for the first time during another of his weekend visits. When Steve first saw Lois, with her long black hair and homespun attractiveness, his heart leaped.

"Mom's right. Don't be surprised if one day I marry that Beverly girl," he said to his sister.

"I doubt she'd want to marry you!" Debbie joked. She couldn't believe her brother would be attracted to someone as religious as Lois, who was the daughter of former missionaries to the Bahamas and who had a deep personal commitment to Jesus Christ. She was outgoing, friendly, bright, attractive—but seemingly out of reach because of her Christian principles.

Five months passed before the two met again. In the summer of 1974 Steve had just finished his sophomore year. One night Lois and her brother Dan planned to go bowling and dropped in on the Linscotts to invite Debbie to go with them. When they tried to persuade Steve to join them, he declined; he had promised to stay with his handicapped sister so that his parents could go out.

Lois thought it remarkable that a young man would be so willing to take responsibility for his sister. As for Steve, that night he decided that he would call Lois for a date before the end of the summer.

He made another decision that evening. Steve realized that he was at a crossroad in his life. Born into a military family in Newport, Rhode Island, he was three when his parents moved to Cuba; five when they moved to Freeport, Maine; seven when they moved to Norfolk Naval Base in Virginia; ten when his father retired as a chief radioman after twenty years in the Navy. Soon thereafter the Linscotts had settled in Ellsworth, forty-five miles south of Bangor where his father took a job with the Federal Aviation Administration as an air-traffic controller.

It was time for another change, Steve decided. College had made him aware of his need to examine his values and set adequate goals. Courses in existentialism and eastern religions had made a deep impression on him and stirred him to search more diligently for the real meaning of life.

"I knew my life was empty," he later admitted to me. "I

17

longed for real satisfaction but didn't know how or where to find it. In my heart I knew that eastern religions and mysticism didn't provide the truth I was looking for. In my continuing search for truth I had turned to literature and read as widely as possible. None of the classroom lectures helped make things any clearer; they just added to my growing confusion. Answers to basic questions eluded me. Where did I come from? Why am I here? Where am I going? These are questions that every honest philosopher has asked since the beginning of time."

At school Steve had been active in extracurricular activities. As a freshman at Machias College, he had played basketball, become an active member of the Newman Club and the choir, joined the nationally known college service fraternity Alpha Phi Omega. In his sophomore year at the University of Maine, he had played intramural tennis and basketball, and worked at menial jobs during the weekends. During the intervening summer he held two jobs, one of which continued through most of the school year.

Steve had enjoyed school. Grappling with life's problems was challenging, but his studies left him exhausted and his search for philosophical truth left him confused. It wasn't surprising, therefore, that he decided to leave school and join the United States Navy. It was the change he needed.

A month before leaving for boot camp, Steve asked Lois for a date. In reply, she invited both Steve and Debbie to accompany her family and several friends to a Christian movie. Although he went, there was little time to talk.

A few weeks later, on the eve of his departure, Steve impulsively dropped in on Lois, only to find her and her brother leading a youth social. He stayed for a while and asked many questions about the Christian life, but since this was a "fun night," most of his questions went unanswered. He left the meeting early to finish his packing. He had no sooner arrived home than the phone rang. He immediately recognized the voice on the other end. His heart pounded. It was Lois calling to say good-by. Seizing this unexpected opportunity, he asked permission to correspond with her. And that was the beginning of their relationship.

Steve excelled at boot camp. He was selected honorman of his company, and in a letter to his parents, his commanding officer wrote, "This selection is based on individual performance of duty in all phases of basic training, including leadership, initiative, military bearing, sportsmanship, response to orders, general cleanliness, qualifications of a good shipmate and high overall scholastic standing."

One time, while home on leave, Steve was able to spend time with Lois. "Steve, read the Bible," she said as they parted, "then write and let me know what you learned." The correspondence with Lois continued to deepen their friendship, and he took advantage of their relationship to ask questions arising from his reading of the Bible.

From the tone of his letters, however, Lois had the impression that Steve was becoming less receptive to Christianity. At one point she thought seriously about ending their correspondence—and their relationship; instead, she prayed for him. She had no idea how much Steve was struggling, searching, and reading the Bible as he grappled to find the answers to life's questions.

One evening in the base library Steve poured out his discontent in a letter: "If there is a God, why would He allow human tragedies?" he asked. Steve couldn't finish the letter. It was late. And he was tired. Gathering his notes and the partially written letter, he returned to the barracks.

That night, as Steve lay in bed, he weighed all the arguments he had heard from Lois and her father, Roy Beverly. Roy was an aggressive preacher of the gospel, but Steve refused to be intimidated and was determined to find the answers for himself.

The next morning he awoke earlier than usual and went to the coffee shop on the base. Here is how Steve described what happened next: "Apart from a cleaning lady, I saw no one else; all the tables were empty and clean, except one. It had a few dirty dishes and some paper on it. For some reason I chose to sit there and placed my school books on a chair, figuring that the lady would clean it before I got back with my coffee and donut.

"But the previous occupant was at the counter getting more coffee. When I returned to my table, I was surprised to find another sailor there. Embarrassed, I began to move my books, but the stranger invited me to stay. I did not know it then, but he had been praying that God would send someone with whom he could share his testimony. *I* was the answer to his prayer!

"I had prided myself on being able to absorb scholarly works on Buddhism and existentialism. But somehow I could never make sense out of the Bible. This man could! He talked—while I just sat there and listened, amazed. In the process, the stranger answered questions that had taken me years to formulate. Suddenly I knew that God was reaching out to me, for only God could know the things that troubled me and could provide the answers when I needed them most.

"The realization of God's existence struck hard. I struggled only an instant before swallowing my pride and then, silently, I admitted that there was a God, that God was reaching out to me in love, that I was a sinner for having rejected God's love for so long. I believed in my heart and then quietly, as the man continued talking, asked Jesus Christ to be my personal Lord and Savior. The peace that flooded my heart and mind was unbelievable. It was as if a mountain had been lifted off my shoulders."

The sailor invited Steve to a Christian ranch the following day and placed a Navigator booklet, "Beginning with Christ," into his hand. The booklet dealt with several of the major doubts that assailed him in the first hour of his new life in Christ. To Steve, that was further confirmation of the reality of the experience he had just had. Instinctively, he knew that something great had happened to him. The date was November 24, 1974—the day before Thanksgiving.

That evening Steve read the very negative letter he had begun to write to Lois the night before; then, skipping a couple of inches, he related what had just happened. He wrote that his soul had experienced a "gentle embarrassing happiness."

In college Steve's search for understanding and truth had only frustrated and confused him; his mild experimentation with marijuana and the four or five times he had taken pills had brought only fear. Now he had found the answer to his deepest needs.

Lois could hardly believe it. Overwhelmed with joy, all she could think of to respond was, "This *is* a miracle!"

In his next letter, Steve related how, a couple of days later, he had been invited by a number of his buddies to a marijuana party. They waited for him to change. As Steve pulled off his shirt, the Navigator booklet fell out of his pocket and landed on the floor with a loud slap. He hadn't yet told his friends that he was a Christian, but when he saw the booklet on the floor, he instinctively knew what to do. He declined the invitation.

He was learning about the practical guidance of Christ.

When Steve graduated from radio school in San Diego, he returned to Ellsworth for a short break before commencing his first overseas post. By now he and Lois were very close, and they were trusting God to guide their relationship.

After a few days together, they flew in separate directions—
Lois to Italy for a short-term mission project, and Steve to
Japan for a two-year tour of duty.

In Japan, Steve was assigned to the admiral's staff of the
Seventh Fleet. After another investigation, more extensive
than the one in radio school, he passed the highest checks for
top-secret crypto security. On many occasions, while aboard
the U.S.S. *Oklahoma City,* Steve prepared messages for the
admiral himself, and his work helped contribute to the unit's
earning the Meritorious Unit Commendation.

Off-duty hours were spent at the Overseas Christian
Servicemen's Center (OCSC) in Yokosuka where he was
stationed. Many servicemen have been blessed by this
international ministry, and Steve was no exception. The
center became his "home away from home," where Bible
study, prayer, and fellowship with other Christians became a
routine and a delight.

Steve's enthusiasm was now leading others, including
his own mother and some of his siblings, to the Lord. There
were those, of course, who told him that his "one-track"
mind was irritating and that life consisted of more than
"talking about Jesus." He shrugged off these remarks and
determined that his life would back up his words. On board
ship, believers would often meet for Bible study after the
evening meal. Soon Steve was accepted as the teacher, and
those he discipled, in turn, began leading others to Christ.

As Steve's first two-year stint in the Navy was drawing to
a close, he wrestled with a big decision: Should he stay with
the ship, which meant more months at sea, or should he
accept an assignment to Guam?

With a two-week leave coming up, Steve was eager to
see Lois after almost a year's separation. So he flew to
Maine—with a diamond ring in his pocket.

Steve proposed. Lois accepted, and the wedding date

was set for February 23, 1977. This helped simplify Steve's decision about his next assignment. At Guam they would have the time to build a solid foundation for their marriage.

Steve and Lois discovered many opportunities for Christian service in Guam. They became active in a church fellowship, served on the local committee of Child Evangelism Fellowship, and became involved with Campus Crusade for Christ. Steve coordinated Navigator Bible studies and became a part-time announcer for the local Trans World Radio station, the largest missionary radio outreach in the world. Lois, who had attended nursing school and obtained her licensed practical nurse certificate before they were married, found work as a school nurse on the island.

After three months, Lois became pregnant, and the parents-to-be enrolled in Lamaze classes so that they could be together when the baby was born. The birth was an emotional experience for Steve as he stood in the delivery room on June 12, 1978, and watched Lois deliver their beautiful baby girl. They named her Katherine.

With his tour of duty almost completed, Steve began to think seriously about preparing for full-time Christian work. He sent partial applications to Moody Bible Institute in Chicago, Illinois, and to Prairie Bible Institute in Alberta, Canada, and complete applications to Multnomah School of the Bible in Portland, Oregon, and Emmaus Bible College in Oak Park, Illinois. Before he could complete his applications to Prairie and Moody he was accepted at Multnomah and Emmaus. Steve chose Emmaus because, he believed, that was where God wanted him.

Like most schools, Emmaus asks its applicants to provide references from a pastor, a teacher, and a friend. Steve's references were outstanding. Concerning his home life, one friend said, "Steve and Lois, along with their daughter, Katherine, provide a very warm Christian atmosphere. . . .

They have a good, harmonious relationship." Steve's pastor reported, "His growth and maturity in Christ are very inspiring and substantial." All the references noted that Steve responded well to authority and worked well with others. All felt he had enthusiasm and sincerity. "He studies the Word and applies it," said one. "Steve is single-minded and goal-oriented. He is extremely honest and has a desire for holy living and is deeply committed to Christ."

Their correspondence with Emmaus Bible College had led the Linscotts to contact Jim and Marge Chesney, from whom they planned to rent a small four-room apartment on the third floor of their large house on West Washington Boulevard in Chicago. The Chesneys were looking for a couple to become part of their extended Christian family. With their three boys, they occupied the first floor. Jim, formerly with Youth For Christ, was now a student counselor and athletic coach at Oak Park River Forest High School. Marge was a school teacher. Another Christian couple, Randy and Susan Murphy, already lived on the second floor.

On March 30, 1979, after five years of service, Steve received his discharge. The Linscotts returned to Maine, packed their things in a small U-Haul trailer, hitched it to their Mazda coupe, and headed for Oak Park, Illinois.

The great Chicago fire of 1871 was largely responsible for putting Oak Park on the map. When Chicagoans swarmed out of the city in search of new homes, this small village experienced a population explosion. Today, tree-lined streets, stately homes, and excellent facilities make Oak Park one of the more fashionable suburbs. Expressways link it to the outside world, and each day railroads whisk thousands of commuters to and from Chicago's Loop. The world's busiest airport is only twenty-five minutes away.

Oak Park has been the home of many famous men: Frank Lloyd Wright, the father of modern architecture; novelist Ernest Hemingway; Percy Julian, the famed black chemist; Edgar Rice Burroughs, Tarzan's creator; and Bill Kurtis, former anchorman for the CBS morning news. Today it boasts one of the finest educational systems in America. In 1976 the village won recognition as an All-American City. The racial and cultural mix of Oak Park makes it one of the few cities that can claim to be successfully integrated. Its chief drawback: the increasing crime rate.

Steve and Lois had their first encounter with Chicago police soon after their arrival. The area in which they lived was noisy—people often screamed at each other and car horns honked through the night. Tenants in the next-door apartment building regularly tossed their garbage into the Chesneys' backyard.

One evening as the new arrivals looked out of their third-floor window, they saw one car force another to the curb immediately below them. A man then jumped out of the first car, climbed into the other car, and began beating its sole occupant—a woman. Acting on impulse, Steve immediately called the police. The man emptied the contents of the woman's purse onto the pavement and continued beating her until the police arrived. Fortunately, the woman was not seriously harmed.

The high crime rate also affected them personally. Returning from church one Sunday, Steve and Lois discovered that their home had been broken into and burglarized. Gone was Lois's diamond ring. Their stereo was missing, and so were the Christmas tree and their presents to each other. It was no consolation for Steve and Lois to learn that the Murphys and Chesneys had suffered even greater losses.

But in the midst of their pain God brought real encouragement. The Linscotts received an anonymous gift of five hundred dollars to help cover the loss. To them, it was a sign that God does care for his children.

In spite of these difficulties, their first year in Oak Park was a positive and enriching experience. Steve loved the classroom; the faculty was everything he had hoped for, and their ability to teach the Word of God and relate it to their own lives was both an incentive and a model.

Saturday mornings were spent at the famous Pacific Garden Mission on State Street in Chicago, where Steve joined other students from Emmaus and Moody Bible Institute in ministering to the servicemen and others who found a haven there. Many came from the nearby Great Lakes Naval Base to find fellowship with committed Christians.

Steve remembers counseling a fifty-five-year-old black man whose life had nearly been destroyed by alcohol. Steve explained the gospel with clarity, he thought, and how Jesus could free people from their bondage.

"What do you do," the man asked, "as you walk across a hot desert with parched throat and lips, ready to die? Suddenly, you see a bottle in front of you, and as you stoop to pick it up, you discover it's whiskey!"

"My friend," Steve responded, "Jesus offers you living water. If you drink it, you'll never thirst again. Remember this: God loves you and Christ died for you."

All of a sudden a deep sob broke from the man, and he asked if he and Steve could pray together. With great joy in his heart, the man received Christ as his personal savior, and now he and Steve are brothers in Christ.

One of the other great miracles that God worked at this time (January 1980) was the birth of Paul Mark Linscott—a little brother for Katherine!

Just before the end of the school year, Steve heard about the Good News Mission, an international ministry providing chaplains and other services to the inmates of penal institutions. Headquartered in Arlington, Virginia, the mission had been providing comprehensive chaplaincy programs across the United States for over twenty years. In an effort to expand its operations, the Mission had recently acquired a house in Oak Park, which became known as the Austin Center and provided a local headquarters for the organization and its five chaplains. Its main purpose was to provide a rehabilitation facility—a halfway house—for ex-offenders who had committed their lives to Christ while in prison.

Two Emmaus students, Roger and Charlotte Savage, had been managing the property for the past year and functioning as houseparents, but they planned to leave during the new school year.

Steve, with his strong background in discipling young Christians and with a growing family to care for, immediately expressed interest in the opening.

Roger Savage encouraged him. "You would be able to minister to inmates of penal institutions in a variety of ways, and the property manager can also live there rent-free."

Since the Chesneys were selling their house on Washington Boulevard, this seemed to be the perfect time for Steve and Lois to consider a change. So Steve pursued the possibility.

He met with the five chaplains, got the job, and finalized arrangements for his family to move into the Austin Center after their summer vacation. Steve's only concern was that the neighborhood was reputed to be even rougher than the one they presently lived in.

Steve and Lois spent the summer in Maine, where Steve became involved in the ministry of a local church, shared the preaching, and led a midweek Bible study on the life of Joseph.

27

During this ministry, Steve developed strep throat, which kept him confined to bed for several days. While he was sick, he had a strange premonition. He saw himself involved with the police during the coming year, with his studies interrupted.

This was not the first time he had had a premonition—there had been others when he was younger—and each premonition became a reality. What this one meant, if anything, he had not the slightest idea. Maybe he and Lois would witness another incident from their window. But Steve knew the future was in God's hands.

In September, with a heavier course load than the previous year, Steve was extremely busy. The first quarter was intense. He responded well to the challenge, worked hard, and stretched himself to his limits.

The ministry at the Center was enjoyable too. Hosting dinners and helping to lead Bible studies were exacting work but exciting. The chaplains had told the Linscotts how pleased they were with the spiritual growth of the residents. Ministering to them, keeping up with studies, and caring for his family left Steve with little time for anything else.

But the neighborhood continued to be a concern. The Linscotts never got used to seeing bright-colored Cadillacs and other large cars pull up outside the apartment house diagonally across the street. Prostitutes strolled out and casually entered the cars. The drug traffic was obvious. Day and night the action went on, and many times during their first month at the Center, Steve and Lois were awakened by the honking of horns—pimps trying to attract the attention of street solicitors.

Steve would hurry home from school as soon as his activities and duties were completed. Not only did he find it easier to study at home, but Lois felt safer with him around. By October the Linscotts had settled into their new routine, loving the work God had given them, and troubled about the lost souls in their neighborhood.

Fortunate is the neighborhood with a concerned Christian like Steve in its midst. The Oak Park police would soon say otherwise.

3
Tragedy
in the Night

Karen Ann Phillips surprised her classmates one evening during the summer of 1980 as she sat under hypnosis in her astrology class at the Temple Kriya Yoga in Chicago. She said that she believed that she would die a violent death. While in a trance, Karen also stated that in a previous life she had been a nun in Germany and had been murdered. In this particular class, such disclosures were not unusual.

Karen was an attractive, vivacious young woman, five feet, eight inches tall, weighing about 125 pounds. Flowing brunette hair rested on her shoulders. Her eyes were alive with a sense of adventure and a love of life. She was born in Forest City, North Carolina, on April 29, 1956, attended local schools through high school, and spent two years at North Carolina colleges before transferring to Aurora College in Aurora, Illinois, forty miles west of Chicago. In the spring of

1979 Karen graduated with a bachelor of science degree in biology.

Planning for a nursing career, Karen enrolled at the Rush Presbyterian Saint Luke's .Medical Center on the outskirts of Chicago's inner city and moved to a one-room apartment on Austin Boulevard in April 1979.

While Karen was still a student at Aurora, a friend introduced her to the Temple Kriya Yoga. In time, all Karen's friends were associated with this Temple in one way or another. Contradictory reports exist concerning group sex, drug use, and strange religious rites by some who have attended the Temple.

At the Temple Karen met Helen Palella. The two became good friends and attended the Temple's astrology class together. According to one report, Helen believed she too had been a German nun in a previous life, had known Karen then, and had also been violently murdered in that incarnation.

By the time the new friendship with Karen was forged, Helen had become a Swami, or priestess, in the system and was one of its most active members. The Temple offered classes for members at various levels of involvement, and Helen was a teacher for the highest level. Enthusiastically, she began exposing her new friend to the religion and in due course persuaded her to study for the "priesthood" too.

Karen studied hard and read widely about such subjects as mind control, thought transference, and dream telepathy. She practiced yoga and transcendental meditation, developed an interest in holistic health, and concentrated on developing her inner life. When she moved to Oak Park in April 1979, she was already well initiated into Temple activities.

By the fall of 1980 Karen was fanatically devoted to the Kriya Yoga religion. In fact, she contributed a large share of her student loan to the Temple and did not appear too concerned that she was sinking into debt in the process.

Karen's closest male friend was Jerry McDuffie, a college professor in North Carolina. When Karen talked to friends about her out-of-town fiancé, it was generally assumed she was referring to Jerry. On several occasions when Jerry visited Oak Park, he accompanied her to the Temple and sat in on some of her classes on mass hypnotism, reincarnation, mysticism, and mind transference. Sexual activity among members and drug use to heighten religious experiences were openly discussed at the sessions Jerry attended.

Jerry was not impressed. He told Karen that he didn't like her involvement in the Kriya Yoga religion and that she was spending more money on Temple activities than she could afford. Some of the members struck him as "hard-core drug addicts," and he wanted to shield Karen from this type of exposure. He feared that Karen was naïve. "Be careful of the bad elements in society," he warned repeatedly, aware that on one occasion Karen had allowed into her apartment a complete stranger who had approached her on the street, asking to paint her portrait.

Jerry believed that Karen had developed an unreasonable attitude toward the Temple; she would not listen to or accept any criticism of its system. He feared she would try to rehabilitate some of the drug addicts and endanger herself.

Karen did not completely ignore Jerry's advice. Aware of the dangers of the Austin neighborhood, she considered moving into an apartment-sharing arrangement with another woman and the woman's boyfriend—in spite of the fact that this man had made sexual advances toward Karen.

Ultimately, Karen's commitment to the Temple resulted in a growing rift between her and Jerry.

At approximately 7:00 on Thursday evening, October 2, Karen knocked on the door of her new neighbor, Peter Pohlot. The two had become good friends in the three weeks they had known each other. "Would you like to play cards?" she asked when Peter opened the door. For the next two hours they played several games of Master Mind and several games of cards.

Afterward, Peter accompanied Karen to her apartment. He needed to press some clothes and Karen offered her iron. Peter returned to his apartment to do the ironing and brought the iron back about 10:30 P.M. When Karen opened the door, she had the telephone receiver in her hand and was still talking to someone on the other end—probably Jerry McDuffie. She and Jerry took turns calling each other every few days, and Jerry remembers calling Karen around that time that very evening. "Don't call tomorrow night. I'll be at the Temple," Peter heard Karen say into the phone.

Jerry thought it strange that she didn't want him to call. Usually she went to the Temple each Friday evening for her astrology class and was home by 10:00. It had become their routine for him to call at that time on Fridays. But he decided not to probe. "I'll call Saturday morning," he said.

On Friday, October 3, Karen went to school as usual. Her class that day on "Clinical Rotation for Community Health Nursing" began at 8:30 A.M. with a pre-conference session. At 3:30 P.M. the class met again for a post-conference.

Judith Voeller, professor in the Department of Community Health Nursing, never saw Karen again after the session ended at 4:30. Later she told police that Karen had seemed upset that afternoon. When Judith had asked Karen if anything was troubling her, Karen had responded, "No, everything's all right."

Phyllis Nash, a nursing student who worked with Karen in the clinical rotation course, drove Karen home at about 5:00.

Karen then drove to the parking lot a block and a half away from the Temple and went to class. There she met Cathy Ruffer, one of the people whose life frequently overlapped Karen's. Cathy too was a nursing student at Rush Presbyterian and a member of the Temple. The astrology class met every Friday evening from 6:30 to 9:30. It had begun six months earlier with about a hundred people, most of whom dropped out. When the class resumed after the summer recess, only about forty people were still enrolled, and interest continued to wane throughout the fall. By October 3, only ten students remained in the class.

When Jean Gersten, another member, arrived at the Temple around 6:00 that evening, Karen was already there, standing behind the juice bar that served nonalcoholic beverages, fruit juices, tea, and vegetarian foods. After each class it was customary for students to go to the office, collect cassette tapes of the lectures or special assignments, and then leave. That evening Jean left before Karen.

Instead of hurrying home after class for her customary phone call from Jerry, Karen stayed at the Temple to complete her duties at the juice bar. She knew that she would be later than usual that night, but the reason is unclear. Did she simply want to put in extra time at the juice bar, or was she planning to meet someone?

At 10:00 Karen stopped by the reception desk. Margie Strall, the part-time receptionist, was still there finishing some clerical duties. Margie had worked at the Temple for the past four years and was allowed to park her car in front of the building. As she often did, she offered to drive Karen to her car in the parking lot a block and a half away. At first Karen accepted but then decided to walk when Margie told her that she would be another fifteen or twenty minutes. When questioned later, Margie said, "Karen appeared impatient this evening."

34

At about 10:15, Helen Palella, who had been in Karen's class that evening, tried to call her. She got no response. She tried again about fifteen minutes later. At 10:30, at about the same time as Helen's second call, Dolores Jones, who lived across the hall from Karen, heard someone run through the hallway. Could it have been Karen making a dash for the phone in her apartment? In her haste, could Karen have left the keys in the door and thereby allowed an intruder to enter?

Karen picked up the receiver and talked with Helen for about twenty minutes. She told her friend how much she had enjoyed the class that evening and made a date to pick up Helen the next morning at 11:00 A.M. to go to a flea market.

There seems to have been a lot of activity at the apartment house that night. Peter Pohlot reported he had spent the evening with a friend watching television until 11:30. Howard Jones, another neighbor, returned from his evening shift around midnight. He remembers finding the outside door of the apartment house open—unlocked and standing ajar—and thinking at the time that this was most unusual. The entrance was always kept locked so that a visitor could only gain entrance if admitted by a resident. There was no buzzer system.

Perhaps Karen herself left it open in her haste to reach the telephone. Or perhaps she left the apartment later and absent-mindedly forgot to close and lock the door on her return. Since her car doors were left unlocked, it is also possible that she went out and was abducted as she returned.

Mohammed Azadegan, who lived in the apartment next to Karen's, entertained a cousin and his girl friend until 12:30 that night. About 1:00 A.M., above the noise of his television set, Mohammed heard voices and a pounding noise in Karen's apartment. He reported that there were two voices, and they seemed to indicate some sort of argument.

As the pounding continued, Mohammed became concerned. He ran to Karen's apartment and knocked on her door. Immediately the talking and pounding ceased. There was a hushed stillness. No one answered. He waited a full minute and returned to his own apartment. Immediately the voices and pounding resumed. Turning on his television set once more, he watched the news for another half hour and fell asleep.

Next morning, when Karen was more than half an hour late for the appointment, Helen was annoyed. By 12:30 she was worried. Karen was never this late! If her car had broken down, why didn't she call? Had she had an accident? Was she hurt? Helen finally dispatched her husband, Dominick, to investigate the problem while she stayed by the phone in case Karen called.

Dominick had his instructions: He was first to check the road in case Karen's car had broken down. Then he was to see if perhaps it was still in the driveway. Maybe it had failed to start and after working on it for a while, Karen might have decided to take a bus or a taxi. When he arrived at Karen's residence, Karen's car was still in the driveway.

Dominick walked up to the apartment house and knocked on Mohammed's door. It was around 1:00 in the afternoon, just twelve hours after Mohammed had first knocked on Karen's door. Mohammed thought Palella's first question significant: "Did you hear any strange noises last night?"

By this time Peter Pohlot had come down from his apartment to express his concern. After calling his wife to let her know that Karen's car was still in the driveway, Dominick asked Mohammed to stand on Peter's shoulders and peek through the window of Karen's apartment.

"The gas burners on the stove are on," Peter called down. That was all he could see.

This was a matter for the police.

Kenneth Wiese of the Oak Park Fire Department was with the 611 Rescue Squad that day. He was assigned to investigate the locked apartment at Austin Boulevard. He arrived around 3:00. After examining the outside of the building and seeing no open windows or doors, he used a short stepladder to reach and force open a window. In the living room he found the battered body of a young woman lying face down in a pool of blood on the carpeted floor. Except for a turquoise nylon nightgown wrapped around her upper torso, the woman was naked.

A short time later, firefighter Wiese opened the front door to allow the waiting ambulance crew and police into the apartment. From the hallway, Karen's friends could see her body lying in the middle of the living room floor. Dominick Palella slumped to the floor and covered his face with his hands.

4

"Behold, the Dreamer Comes"

It was midafternoon on Saturday, October 4, 1980—the day after his strange dream—when Steve Linscott looked out his window and noticed a fire truck, an ambulance, and several police cars parked across the street. "An accident," he said to Lois.

Earlier that day, Lois had entertained a group of women for a luncheon at the Austin Center. After the guests had left, Steve and Lois began tidying up. They were in the kitchen washing dishes when there was a knock at the door. "You go, Steve," Lois said.

Two Oak Park police officers were at the door. "We are making a routine call and investigating a murder of a young woman near here," they said. By this time Lois had followed her husband to the front door. "Did you see or hear anything unusual or suspicious ... around 1:00 in the morning?"

"No, we didn't," the Linscotts responded.

"If you think of anything, no matter how silly, please let us know. Also check your neighbors in case they heard or saw something."

"This neighborhood is rougher than we thought," Steve murmured as the police walked away.

That evening, just as the police had requested, Steve called together the residents of the Center and told them of the murder, sharing the scanty information given to him by the officers. No one had seen or heard anything suspicious, but they promised to keep their eyes and ears open. Steve said he believed the murder had occurred in the adjacent building. (In reality, it had occurred two buildings away.) Then the dream of the previous night flashed through his mind. *Could it have any connection?* he wondered.

The next day, Sunday, was busy. There were three church services during the morning and evening, and studies to pursue in the afternoon. During an afternoon break, Steve discussed his dream with Jim Saucerman, a thirty-year-old counselor who had been at the Mission for two years and who, like Steve, was a student at Emmaus Bible College. Jim's response was, "Dreams have been used to solve crimes before. Your dream might have some significance. I think you should tell the police."

Police officers and evidence technicians searched the victim's apartment and scoured the area for clues. In a clump of bushes, five to ten feet north of the front of the building, they found a blue tire iron with a reddish-brown substance and some hairs on it. Six weeks later, after the forensic tests had been completed, this tire iron proved to be the murder weapon.* The murderer had probably tossed it into the

---

*The possibility exists that a table lamp in the apartment may have been the murder weapon. A reddish brown substance on the lamp was never checked by the police.

bushes while leaving the apartment. Did the northerly location betray the direction of the murderer's retreat? The Linscotts, it should be noted, lived to the south.

The police examined the victim's body and observed multiple wounds, abrasions, and bruises. They noted the strange position of her fingers: the index finger and thumb of the left hand were joined together to form a circle, and the remaining three fingers were extended. The fingers of the right hand were in a similar position but not quite so pronounced. A number of hairs had stuck to the palms of her hands. The hands were "bagged" with polyethylene bags and secured with rubber bands to preserve evidence. Hairs (later identified as a mixture of Caucasian, Negroid, and animal hairs) were found on the bedsheets, which were then stripped from the bed and parceled. Sample strands were taken from the victim's body and carefully placed in envelopes that were then sealed and initialed. A sample of blood was recovered from the carpet with a swab. A kitchen knife was found lying on the kitchen counter and a T-shirt was observed on the bed. Panty hose lay on the floor next to the bed.

The police found that the back door to the apartment was locked from the inside and secured with a chain. The front door was examined and no visible signs of forced entry were found. On the following day, however, when other officers returned to the scene of the crime, they noticed, to their chagrin, fresh jimmy marks on the door and wood shavings on the floor. From the floor beside the shavings they recovered Caucasian and Negroid hairs. Had these been missed the previous day? (The police reports indicate that these were not there the day Karen's body was found.) Or had the murderer returned after the murder had been discovered? If so, what was his intent? These questions were never answered.

The apartment was processed for fingerprints and four "lifts" were obtained. (Almost a week later the evidence technician returned for an additional fingerprint search. This time he lifted ten to fifteen prints from the victim's front door and door jamb.)

Pictures were taken of the body and the apartment. The room was small, twelve by fifteen feet. The furniture, arranged in a U-shape along three walls, consisted of a bed and a two-tier nightstand on which stood several religious pictures, candles, an incense burner, and several pieces of incense.

There were also a trunk, a desk, and a stereo. A television and a table lamp had fallen to the floor, indicating that there had been a struggle. Apparently, the turntable, with a record on it, was still revolving when the police arrived. Jerry McDuffie later mentioned that Helen Palella told him that the record was "prayer music." But this seemingly important information was not included in any police report, communicated to the defense lawyer, or raised by the prosecution in the trial proceedings.

The body of Karen Phillips was taken to a nearby hospital and then to Cook County Morgue where a medical examiner carried out an autopsy. Dr. Donoghue identified sixty-six evidences of injury, thirty-two above the shoulders, and concluded that Karen died of beating and strangulation. The abrasions and bruises on her arms and hands seemed to indicate attempts at self-protection. The head wounds indicated that a heavy metal object had been used to beat her. Of the nine injuries to the victim's head, seven were lacerations. Of the remaining two wounds, the first was described as being four inches long and in a large crescent shape; the other was described as a large bruise. In addition to stab wounds to the head and right side, there were cut wounds made with a sharp object on her lower middle back and right

41

side. After carefully examining the body, the medical examiner also took hair, blood, and swab samples, which were transported by the police, with the rape kit, to the crime lab in Maywood, Illinois.

Early Monday evening Steve and Lois went for their customary walk, during which they discussed the murder that had been reported in the Monday October 6 edition of the *Chicago Tribune*:

WOMAN FOUND FATALLY BEATEN

Oak Park Police Sunday were investigating the apparent murder of a 24-year-old nurse's assistant, who was found bludgeoned to death with a blunt instrument in the bedroom of her first-floor apartment . . .

Karen Ann Phillips was found by police Saturday afternoon bleeding from a head wound. She was pronounced dead on arrival at West Suburban Hospital in Oak Park. Her body was transferred to the county morgue.

Police were alerted by a friend of Miss Phillips after she failed to show up for a shopping trip earlier in the day. There were no signs of forced entry into the apartment and no weapon was found, according to police.

Police said Miss Phillips possibly knew her assailant. However, police had no suspects or motive in the slaying.

Miss Phillips, who lived alone, worked at the University of Illinois Medical Center.*

The news report, it should be noted, was not entirely accurate. Karen Phillips was not a nurse's assistant, and the police had told the *Chicago Tribune* that a tire iron had been

---

found *in* the apartment. This was reported in an out-of-town edition the following day.

As Steve and Lois walked through the neighborhood, he told his wife about the strange dream. He wondered whether he should report it. "What do you think?" he said.

"Well, they'll probably think it's silly," Lois chuckled, "though they did say that if we could think of anything, no matter how silly, to let them know. It certainly couldn't hurt."

Lois and Steve concluded that, at worst, the police would simply file the report away; at best, the description of the assailant in the dream might be useful.

Steve discussed the dream with another student, Carlos Craveiro, who was one of the most "street wise" people that Steve knew. Carlos was more circumspect than Lois but thought that it might be worth mentioning to the police. After discussing the dream with several other Christians at the Center and receiving no negative responses, Steve decided to call.

That evening, in the investigations office at the Oak Park Police Station, Detective Robert Scianna was with his partner, Ronald Grego, and his supervisor, Joseph Mendrick. They were interviewing Helen Palella. At about 9:30, a telephone call interrupted their conversation. The caller said, "You'll probably think this is silly, but I had a dream, apparently on the same night as the murder. Do you want to hear it?"

"Sure," said the officer.

"Well ...," and Steve related it in detail.

"Why don't you write it down, and we will drop by and pick it up later," Scianna told Steve.

Steve complied, feeling it was his civic duty to do so. He was impressed that they were sufficiently interested in his dream to want to come over and pick up his statement. *It may be important*, he thought.

Detective Scianna and Sergeant Mendrick called at the Austin Center shortly after the call and collected Steve's written account of the dream. The statement read:

I had a dream Saturday evening in which I saw a man bludgeon a person to death.

The man was blond haired, fair features, the hair was short; the man is square-built, not muscular but good size. About 5' 5" to 5' 7" wearing terrycloth, short sleeve shirt with two or three narrow horizontal lines across the chest. His pants were brown (dark) or reddish brown. The man was easy going in character and was at ease with the person.

The person struck seems to me to have been struck while lying down or crouching and to have been hit on the head (the side) (possibly on the right hand, though I'm not sure).

The person struck seems not to have given a lot of resistence [sic]. She has an air of acceptance or peace. She clearly wasn't expecting the attack. I note this from the change in the person attacking, as he was calm and at ease with the victim before the attack, and quick and brutal during the attack. The person was struck a number of times. The last impression I have of the attack was the bludgeon striking bleeding flesh and a lot of blood flying. The person struck seems to me to be black, though I'm not sure.

Secondary impressions are of the attacker in the first stages, the quieting stage, the easy going stage as having a light on behind him and to the left as I see him, and lower than his head. It makes a soft glow in the room. I can't get any impressions on the rest of the room except that it seems to be a living room, a couch seems present to the left of the light.

As I dreamt, the first stage was very clear, but I woke up as I sensed a change come over the person, and I tried to shake off the dream and go back to sleep. I went to sleep again and dreamt of the attack. After this I awoke and was very disturbed because of the vividness of the dream. I thought I heard a noise in our front room of our apartment and so I got up and went out and came back and went to sleep.

Concerning the second stage of the dream, the attacker is striking down on the victim. She is below his waist and then below the knees and does not give much resistence [*sic*] to this attack.

Note that in his account, Steve first refers to the victim as a "person" but later used the word "she." He maintains that in his dream he was unable to determine whether the victim was a male or female and that his use of the word "she" was the result of his hearing about the murder. By the time he had reduced his dream to writing he knew that the victim of the actual murder was a woman from at least two sources: the police and the *Chicago Tribune*. Note also that in the dream the victim appeared to be black, and the setting was a living room with a couch—details that have nothing in common with the actual murder.

The following day, Tuesday, Scianna and his partner Grego visited the Fourth District Circuit Court in Maywood and consulted with State's Attorneys. It was agreed that Linscott would be called to the police station for interrogation. That afternoon, Scianna telephoned Steve and told him that they had been talking to a dream expert and wanted further information. Steve agreed.

The next afternoon, as Steve drove into the police parking lot, he felt a little foolish, but not apprehensive. There was a sense of pride that he might help solve a crime.

News of the murder had been carried in two or more newspapers and was a topic of conversation in the community. By the time Steve agreed to be questioned about his dream, he had already been exposed to media coverage and rumors about the murder. The extent to which this information was to color his impressions of the dream in the hours of questioning remains unknown.

Inside the police station, Steve was led past a table where another man was having his rights read to him. "That's routine!" said one of the officers. "He's just had his house burglarized and is making a statement." A few minutes later, concluding that it was just a formality, Steve agreed to have his rights read to him.

After settling into Cokes and amiable conversation, the officers asked Steve a few routine questions. The environment was nonthreatening; in fact, the officers seemed almost apologetic. Then they focused on the dream. Friday had been a normal day at school, Steve told them. After working on his car briefly in the afternoon, he did his homework assignments. In the evening, he studied and then socialized with some of the residents at the Center. Lois had gone to bed around 10:30 P.M. and was asleep by the time Steve joined her about thirty minutes later.

The police asked question after question about the dream: What was the location? Could he describe the room and its contents? They inquired about the assailant: his background, temperament, personality, description, sex life. "Get into his head," they said. "Give us your impression of what he's like." They asked about the murderer's motive for visiting Karen and killing her. So Steve speculated. They wanted to know how he entered the apartment; whether he felt any guilt and desire to confess; if so, to whom he would go. They were interested in his present whereabouts and whether he would kill again.

The detectives asked about the victim, her background and education. They asked Steve if he psychically knew her housekeeping habits or her religious interests. They wanted to know if she knew her assailant and why she let him into her apartment. "From the dream, I would say that . . . ," Steve consistently—and unwittingly—responded as he tried to extract from his dream as much speculation as he could.

"Do you know anything at all or did you get any impression from your dream as to what kind of background she had?" one of the officers asked.

"No, I didn't," Steve replied. "I thought she was not a crude person, but just kind of maybe somewhat educated, somewhat intelligent—at least high school and beyond, a little bit." It was a calculated guess, and Steve was wrong. Karen had a bachelor of science degree in biology and was in her *seventh* year of post high-school education.

The dream was dissected and analyzed. Steve answered questions, many of them leading questions, with his impressions from his dream. He did his best to cooperate. His psychological studies during his university years were useful now, he thought, as he tried to "get into the murderer's head" and think through his possible thoughts and motives, as he had been asked. Steve's responses were open and frank.

"Okay, during your dream do you dream that you also are being splashed with the young lady's blood as the man is striking her? That you could have gotten blood on yourself? Did you attempt to protest or intervene at all?" the police asked Steve. "And did you see boots in the dream?"

Steve thought hard for a moment. "Just maybe a thought that kind of comes; he might have had some kind of heel boots on or something with a little larger high heels."

When the police officers told Steve they were interested in his dream from a psychic standpoint, he believed them.

47

Finally, after nearly three hours of questioning, the interview concluded, too late for the Linscotts to attend their evening Bible study group in the home of John and Evelyn Montgomery.

The police had done their job; they had coaxed Steve into talking freely about the dream. The information was then passed on to State's Attorneys at Circuit Court the next day.

Steve was unaware that a net was being drawn around him.

That evening, as Steve related the experience to Lois, she was alarmed. "What if the police regard you as a suspect?"

Steve laughed. "That's not possible!"

But the next day, in his course on Paul's Epistle to the Romans, Steve's mind wandered back to the interview. For the first time, he realized that their line of questioning was intended to implicate him. A distressing chill shot down his spine. Unnerved, he decided to break his pledge to the police not to discuss the case and confided in Chaplain Russell Stroup, director of the Good News Mission operations in the Chicago area. A retired military chaplain, Russell Stroup counseled inmates at jails and prisons in the area. Chaplain Stroup advised Steve not to talk any more than was necessary, but he did not seem alarmed.

"Let me know what happens, Steve."

"I will, Russ."

When Detective Scianna called that afternoon, Steve came straight to the point. "Does the tone of your questioning indicate that I am a suspect?"

"No!" Scianna replied and quickly added, "Will you write down any questions that you might have and bring them here to the station? We also want to make a composite sketch of the assailant in your dream."

Steve's mind whirled. "That's reasonable! That's originally what I thought would help—and assumed would happen," he replied. Though leery, Steve still wanted to help. "One more visit and it'll all be over," he said to Lois.

Serious police investigation of other possible suspects ended, in effect, at this point. To date, no police officer has interviewed any of the residents of the Austin Center to verify Steve's story or to investigate their movements on the night of the murder. Considering the nature of the Center—a half-way house for ex-convicts—the failure to interview any of its residents is hard to understand. Furthermore, since 83 percent of all murders are committed by family, friends, or acquaintances of the victim, the Temple and Karen's own apartment building would seem to have been the logical places to begin a detailed investigation. The police seemed to have done only routine checks at these places. No investigation was done on the Chicago side of Austin Avenue and many residents on the Oak Park side were neglected. The police never returned to question any of the neighbors who were absent at the time of the original call.

Nor did the police question a known rapist who lived six blocks from Karen's apartment—a man who may have known her. This man already had a considerable criminal record, and within the next few weeks he committed several crimes in Oak Park and other suburbs. Around the time of the murder, he was receiving psychiatric treatment. During the weekend of the murder somebody broke down the rear door of his landlady's home three different times. It is quite probable that he was responsible. When the Oak Park police chief was offered a file of evidence that might link this man to the murder, he rejected it.

At 6:00 on Friday evening, Steve returned for more questioning. Later in the interview, Scianna and Grego were joined by Assistant State's Attorney Jim McCarter. Had Steve known how long he would be at the station he would never have gone.

For an hour and a half Steve struggled to describe the "dream assailant" for a police artist. His struggle was not with the dream, but with the artist's attempts to bend his descriptions. After several attempts, the artist finished with what he called "something in the ballpark area." Steve noticed that the police artist looked at him often, and not surprisingly, the sketch bore some resemblance to Steve. *Did Scianna lie to me?* Steve asked himself as once again his suspicions were aroused. Later, the artist added eyeglasses, sideburns, and a mustache—a move that caused the sketch to look even more like Steve but prevented its admissibility in court.

Scianna and Grego explained that they would also like to go over the dream "just one more time."

"All right. Just once more, quickly," Steve said.

Again the police read Steve his rights. "No, I do not wish to consult a lawyer or have one present," he responded. "I have absolutely nothing to hide."

"Why don't you explain how the dream began, every-thing you can remember," Scianna said and added, "Well, I just—it's remarkable how you can—how helpful this is to us; and that's the reason we're going over it again. What I'd like to do now is maybe dissect the dream a little bit—little by little—and get your impressions. The last time you had some pretty strong impressions where you helped us in our investigation of this crime, and I was hoping maybe we could go through this again, if you don't mind."

It never occurred to Steve to question Assistant State's Attorney McCarter's presence in the room. His casual dress belied his official status. Besides, Steve hardly knew what a State's Attorney was.

Once again, Steve reviewed the dream. All the while he was torn between his new suspicions about their methods and his sense of obligation to do whatever the authorities asked. He certainly didn't want them to think he had anything to hide. Fortunately, these interviews were taped and are now part of the public record; the quotations that follow are actual transcriptions of these tapes.

As the officers' questions continued, Steve found it harder and harder to give specific answers: "I don't even know if that's—I don't really know. . . . I don't see it that way really. . . . I sort of see it like that she expected him, you know—she would expect that he would be there—no problem. . . . Maybe not even that. I'm not sure. I really— okay, my impression . . . I'd say no, she isn't unhappy that he'd be there, you know. Maybe he came by to pick something up or something—I don't know! . . . I don't know! . . . Maybe he was selling Amway or something."

Then Steve decided to ask the question that burned in his mind: "Something . . . bothered me a little bit yesterday," he said. "Do you suspect me of this crime?"

There was a long pause. Then all three men tried to speak at once. Assistant State's Attorney Jim McCarter answered, "We don't suspect you. At this point, what we are looking at is from what you know. If we have to present you as a witness, we have to be able to eliminate you as a suspect. Okay? Obviously, you know, you should know yourself—you are the key to this case and what you have provided for the investigators is just, you know, it's invaluable at this point. But, it's not too often that this type of evidence develops. And how many times have you heard of this type of evidence? There are instances of this which makes you, you know, certainly makes you unique that you can experience something like this. But in order to bolster your creditability we have to eliminate you completely as any possible suspect, so if someone is arrested they can't turn around and say: I didn't do it, he did. That's what we are after right now. Plus, obviously there has not been—no one has been arrested for that murder. Obviously by the investigators talking to you they may be able to jog something in your memory, which can give them a clue. That's what we are attempting to do at this point."

The investigators tried to set Steve's mind at ease, suggesting that he had some psychic talent that, combined with his psychological studies, could help solve the crime. Steve relaxed. The men seemed sincere. At one point when Steve introduced the gospel, Detective Scianna openly discussed his own personal problems with his Catholic faith but suggested that maybe God had a purpose in this interview.

As their questions continued, however, Steve became more uncomfortable: "Yeah, well, to be honest with you, I kind of wonder at your motives sometimes," he blurted out. "Well . . . I keep . . . trying to think along with you guys as you're talking, but your line of questioning still might be trying to implicate me, as far as having a split personality or something."

Grego was the first to respond. "Maybe we're doing it unknowingly, you know, we're just in conversation. . . . It's just a slip of the tongue—I'm sure that's all it's meant by. But, would he feel easy with us?"

"If we had a lead on you, you know, these officers wouldn't be sitting here without handcuffs, you know," McCarter responded. "And you wouldn't be walking out of here shortly or whatever. . . . But, I would ask you this, you know: would you be willing to do certain things and that would be to give us a sample of your blood. A sample of you saliva and a sample of your hair. Also, there's one other thing. Would you allow the officers to look in your car?"

Steve agreed. He had nothing to hide. But he had another question: "Do you mind if I talk to . . . with a counselor at school or something like that—an older person, more wise?"

"In all fairness to you I think you should talk to that person," Assistant State's Attorney McCarter responded.

"I don't mean to talk to him now," Steve said. "Like tomorrow! . . . [It's] 11:30. Let me call my wife. . . . I'd like to call my wife."

That very evening, unknown to Steve, Lois was having visitors of her own: two plain-clothes policemen and Senior Assistant State's Attorney Jay Magnuson. They told her they were consulting with a psychiatric professional in California and wanted to question her about Steve's dream life. They were friendly and put Lois at ease. They plied her with questions about herself and Steve, and they looked around the Austin Center with her permission, though without a search warrant.

Normally cautious, Lois was unusually trusting in allowing these men into her home. She even accompanied one of the officers upstairs to their second floor apartment and showed him around. *Policemen are different*, she told herself. *They are the epitome of honesty.*

The visitors asked about Steve's religious experiences and possible drug use. In response, Lois told them the story of the most dramatic conversion to Christ she knew— Steve's. But at the mention of her husband's preconversion drug experimentation (which had been mild) the officers pricked up their ears. They also asked to see Steve's gym shoes and carefully examined the tread. Were they trying to match a telltale shoe print left in the victim's apartment or the surrounding yard? No further mention was ever made of the shoes.

After the officers left, Lois was worried. *Why was Steve being kept so long?* she wondered. Each time she called the station she was given the same answer: "He won't be long; we're almost finished."

Lois called Chaplain Stroup around 10:30 and shared her fears.

Around 11:30, after insisting that he be allowed to call and refusing to cooperate otherwise, Steve finally got through to Lois. It was then that he learned of the visit of the officers.

Lois relayed a message from Russell Stroup: "Leave immediately; don't get any further involved." But the officers continued to detain Steve.

According to Steve, Scianna said, "You're not going anywhere," pushed Steve, and took his keys and wallet.

"Get a lawyer! I want to speak to a lawyer!" Steve demanded.

"Is there anybody else you would rather speak to?" the detectives asked, insisting that lawyers were very difficult to reach at this late hour.

"Okay. Chaplain Stroup," Steve said.

Between 12:30 and 1:00 in the morning, Russell Stroup arrived at the police station. Still sleepy, he was escorted through the security doors and led to an empty room. He was shown pictures of the murdered girl and encouraged to convince Steve to furnish blood, saliva, and hair samples. Then he was given a few minutes alone with Steve.

"What's the situation, Steve?"

"They apparently want me to give some samples to them, Russ. They won't wait until tomorrow lest I sleep on it and call a lawyer. They lied to me Russ! They did suspect me. They were at the house asking Lois questions behind my back."

54

"You don't have anything to hide," Russ assured him. "Give them what they want, and then let's get out of here." Since Russ was an older, experienced man who knew the correctional system, Steve respected his advice.

Between 1:30 and 2:00 A.M., Steve, Russ, and Officers Grego and Scianna then drove to West Suburban Hospital to obtain the samples that the police still insisted were needed "to eliminate the suspect."

On the way, one of the officers pointed to a white stucco frame house two doors north of the Austin Center. "There it is, Steve. That's where it happened!" Steve was surprised. He and Lois were under the impression that the murder had taken place in the large brick apartment building adjacent to their own home.

At the hospital Steve provided the samples and watched as they were placed in envelopes. But, Steve maintains, they left without sealing the envelopes in his presence.

Back at the station, Russell Stroup and Steve watched as the police searched Steve's car. A few days earlier the Linscotts had been driving to the grocery store when their daughter Katherine stood up in the car and balanced herself on the hump between the bucket seats of their Mazda. In the process she caught her hair in the overhead dome light. While she cried, Lois gently extricated her. Apart from a few tears, she was unhurt, but several strands of hair were caught in the light fixture. Carefully, the police retrieved one long light brown hair from the light and placed it in an envelope.

The police instructed Chaplain Stroup to remain in the reception area while Steve was hustled into the fingerprint room and then back to the interview room. By now it was between 2:30 and 3:00 in the morning. Twice, Steve asked to have Russ present, but his requests were denied.

In the interview room, Grego said, "Steve—I'm going to say my piece, okay. You've cooperated with us as much as you can, as much as you say you know, okay. I'd like to think that you were the person that needs this help, okay. My partner and I and everyone else is convinced that you killed this young lady, okay."

"You're kidding," Steve exclaimed.

"I'd be more than happy to give you any help that I can give you, okay. The evidence that you gave us tonight—will convict you!"

"What evidence are you talking about?" Steve interrupted.

"If you would just let me say my piece, okay?" Grego continued. "The evidence that you gave us tonight will convict you. If we have to come back and get you with an arrest warrant, the judge will now see that you do not request any help. . . ."

"You're barking up the wrong tree! Analyze the evidence! Analyze your evidence first!" Steve shouted.

"It will be analyzed," Grego shouted back, "and when we arrest you with this evidence, it's going to come back that it's you and it's going to come back and show everybody that you don't want any help. We're more than happy to give you help, more than happy."

"I'm requesting on tape that I request Chaplain Stroup."

"You sit here. . . ." Grego screamed. "We're not asking you anything, we're telling you what we know. Now, just sit there and shut up—nobody's asking you questions. You're going to be arrested for this."

Detective Scianna then vented his accusations on Steve. "I'm going to go down the points, you want to analyze the evidence. Don't say anything, because I don't want to hear anything," he shouted. "I don't want you to say anything. When you want to say something you tell us and we'll get a counselor for you. I don't want to hear nothing from you. Don't say anything, just look." Scianna held up the gruesome pictures of the murder victim and crime scene, but Steve refused to look.

"You want evidence," Scianna continued. "What is that? That's a boot. This is a living room setting. This girl is on her hands and knees. This is where she was being beaten about the head with a blunt object. This is a blunt object. Let me get the picture out. What does this mean? This passiveness in her fingers? Is she wearing anything? Seven blows to the head. Where did I hear that? Maybe one or two glanced off the shoulders. Where did I hear that? Well, that's pretty, let's count them. That once was a pretty girl. Okay, descriptions— what's a description we have on the offender? Let's—let's see a composite picture. Does this look like anybody in this room?" Steve glanced quickly at the police artist's drawing.

"Hey, some guy drew that—I told you it wasn't what I [saw]!" Steve retorted angrily.

"Yeh, well, the guy drew it?" Grego interrupted scornfully.

"Who has a shirt that matched the description you told us?" Scianna immediately went on to say.

"I wonder if you guys will be apologizing once we analyze that little bit of information I gave you tonight. . . . If you are wrong, I wonder if you will!" Steve remarked as the shock and bewilderment of the forceful accusations increased. The hour was late and he was tired, emotionally drained. Already, he had been at the police station and the hospital for more than eight hours.

"Steve, we won't be apologizing, Steve," Scianna replied. "Let me tell you what we're going to be doing. Steve, let me tell you something. In your tapes, you said this man would have to come forward when the time was right."

Steve lashed back at Scianna. "If I for a minute thought I was the guy I would walk right in and . . . say, hey—I wish to be prosecuted!" With this, Steve stood up and made for the door, but the police officers prevented him from leaving. "Why are you keeping me from the door?" Steve shouted at them.

The heavy-set Grego took over once again. "I want to tell you—I want to tell you why she died," he said, slowly but emphatically. "She died with you beating her, because she was a religious person. She died—you said in your tape that she died passive. You didn't know why. She offered no resistance. Her fingers are held with her thumb to her index finger in both hands."

Scianna interrupted. "She turned to God," he said.

Grego continued. "This is her religious prayer to God in her temple that she goes to."

"She turned to God," Scianna repeated.

Grego said, "The reason she wasn't screaming or fighting is because she was doing breathing exercises, preparing herself for death. For a religious person preparing herself for death while she's being killed from a somewhat, supposedly, another religious person."

Exasperated, Steve said, "I never met this girl before."

"Maybe you have never met," Grego surprisingly conceded.

It was now Scianna's turn to assume control. "Steve, you have to live with it. You have to."

"I don't have to live with anything, gentlemen," Steve responded emphatically.

"Yes, you do," Scianna said.

Grego then interrupted. "You cannot live with this, Steve, it's going to eat your heart out."

"I don't have to! It's not eating my heart out at all. I have absolutely—I'm innocent, guys, you know [that]. I want to see the counselor!" Steve cried out.

"The chances of you dreaming this dream," Scianna began, but Steve interrupted.

"Hey, I don't know what the chances are."

"This is not a dream; this is a murder. This is no dream to this girl—she is dead," the accuser retorted.

"I realize, I realize that," Steve responded in an exhausted tone.

Grego took over. "You're discovered, because you called us—you told us you did it only in the third person. That's why you're discovered. If you never called us, we would not have known where to go. You came forward to us. You want help. You want God to give you penance, you want to be redeemed by Him."

"Ha, that's pretty unbiblical!" Steve interjected. "My [points] are biblical, you know. You're telling me I need penance and penance is, you know, some tradition made up seventeen hundred years ago."

"I'm not quoting anything from the Bible, okay?" Grego responded.

Scianna spoke again. "I guess the game isn't over for him; he still wants to play games."

"I am not playing games, guys!" Steve was becoming more frustrated.

Scianna said, "Now, I'm finished. You know, you had your chance, you live with it, Steve. God help you. I don't know how you're going to do it, Steve. You live with it, not me."

"Sir, I don't have to live with it—I've got no convictions of it!" Steve retorted, meaning to communicate that he had no conviction of murder because he hadn't killed anyone.

At this point Grego took over once again. "Steve, you're not strong enough to live with this. This will be on your mind. You're not going to be able to sleep tonight and you're not going to be able to sleep tomorrow night—not knowing when we're going to knock on your door."

"Well, I've had quite an experience today!" Steve exclaimed.

"You have been quite an experience. You are going to get the electric chair. The judge is going to see—you have no remorse in your soul. It's embarrassing to what you did. It's a vicious crime, but it's embarrassing. Your wife will become embarrassed, your chaplain will become embarrassed. It's very embarrassing, very embarrassing."

Steve sat there, shocked and bewildered. "Sir, I have absolutely no recollection of what you're telling me is actually something that I've done," he finally blurted out.

"Could you have been sleepwalking? Do you sleepwalk?" Grego quickly responded.

"Sleepwalk? Well, I never sleepwalked in my life, that I know of."

"That you know of. Could it be sleepwalk? It happens— I'm asking you, could you sleepwalk?"

"I'm not going to admit to anything," Steve replied, then changed his mind. "I'll say no; I couldn't have sleepwalked."

"Fine! Fine! Fine!" Grego exclaimed as he continued to put more pressure on the tired and bewildered young man. "You got out of bed, why you went over there at that time, I don't know. You saw her in the neighborhood; she was—"

"Good grief!" Steve interjected. "Why somebody should let me in that I have never met before?"

"How do I know you never met her? I don't know that."

"No, you don't. That's true!" Steve interjected, but Grego continued.

"A very attractive girl, a very attractive girl. You wanted to talk to her. Okay? You went in there whatever time it was, you say 1:00—I never said 1:00—you told me 1:00."

"Unless you doctor those tapes, it's on the tapes," Steve shouted. Later he remembered that when the police first alerted Steve and Lois to the murder in their neighborhood, they had said that the murder took place about 1:00 in the morning.

"Steve," Grego continued, "I just cannot understand. Okay? You yourself told me. Okay? No matter how much of a shell you want to get into. Okay. I'm not going to doctor anything. I'm just saying what is on my mind. Okay? You were the one to—you were the one to come forward. This man wants to have his sins forgiven. Did you or did you not, say that? We spoke about that earlier today."

"You were asking about my physical impressions of this person," Steve replied. "If I had seen you in a dream commit murder and I would try to think—get inside your head, what would you as your sort of person do? You don't look like a person that goes around doing a lot of vicious acts, commonly and every day. So I would probably say, yes, this guy would probably be eaten out inside, and that's what I was trying to give you."

"Do you think there is any reasonable man alive today who for the first time in his life commits a murder and is not sorrowful for it? A reasonable man. Is there such a person that would not be sorry for killing an innocent person?" pursued Grego.

"If the person did the murder, you know, and it takes an awful lot to lead up to somebody to go and kill somebody. . . . Why would a person just walk up and start killing somebody?" Steve asked.

"You want me to tell you why I think you killed her?" Grego responded. "You were attracted to her. Okay? You liked her, you saw her, and you wanted her. You went over there, you got in the apartment, you spoke with her, you talked about sex. You found out there was going to be no sex—willingly, so you beat her to death and you beat her and you struck her. That's why she was killed—that's why she was killed, because she would not give you any sex. I know that, you know in your own mind, Steve. You can tell me everything you want. You can think in your first person, your second person, or your third person. I have been a policeman for twelve and a half years. I have dealt with all kinds—all kinds."

Steve just sat there, utterly dumfounded. "Have your say," was all he could utter.

Grego was not finished. "And you wanted sex from her, she did not give it to you willingly. So, you attacked her. That's why you killed her. That's why, because you became enraged."

"I couldn't have killed any person, never!" Steve shouted.

"Okay, this interview is over," Grego concluded.

Steve stood up to leave. "Sit down, you're not through yet," Grego screamed.

"I request a counselor!" Steve shouted back.

At that point Scianna switched off the tape recorder.

At about the same time as the hospital technician was taking hair samples from Steve's head and body, two police officers, Leahy and Dvonch, together with Assistant State's Attorney Colin Simpson, returned to the scene of the crime. It was the late hours of October 10 or the early hours of October 11, as one officer later testified; he could not recall the exact time. The officers wanted one further piece of evidence—the blood-soaked carpet. Much later, Steve heard that his hairs had been found on that carpet. Since the section on which the body had lain was all that the police officers really needed, they cut this out. After collecting a set of venetian blinds, a glass fragment from outside the building, and an orange card from the bathroom mirror, they returned to the station.

For the next eighty hours the physical evidence taken from Steve was locked in the evidence room of the Oak Park

Police Station—*with* the items (including the carpet) recovered from the crime scene. It wasn't until Tuesday, October 14 (three or four days later), that Officer Tony Muglia transported all the evidence to the crime lab in Maywood.

Grego had said, "The evidence you gave us tonight *will* convict you," How did he know? Was Steve being framed?

Lois had no idea what was happening. She had called the station repeatedly without a satisfactory response. Her last call was around 3:30 in the morning. "I'm calling again to find out when my husband is coming home," she said.

This time Senior State's Attorney Jay Magnuson was put on the line and immediately identified himself as one of the men who had visited her earlier that night. "Mrs. Linscott," he began brusquely, "your husband is a very dangerous person. He has three personalities! We are sending him home to you, and we want you to have a long talk with him. I want you to call me as soon as you can—we don't want another victim in this area. We are sending him home. Have a long talk with him and call me back."

Lois, shocked and shaken, couldn't believe her ears. *What a bluff this guy must be,* she thought. *He certainly wouldn't be sending Steve home if he really means what he says.*

At the station Russell Stroup waited patiently in the foyer until Steve was finally released, about 4:00 A.M.—ten hours after Steve had first arrived.

Tired, emotionally battered, confused, and bleary-eyed, Steve drove back home. For the next thirty minutes he told the story of his ordeal to his wife, Russell Stroup, and a few residents at the Center. Steve had originally scheduled an all-night prayer meeting for that very night. Carlos, Jim, and another friend named Les had stayed up all night praying with only one short break—when Carlos and Jim visited the station to glean information. They all prayed for Steve now.

Lois never called Assistant State's Attorney Magnuson. She didn't need to—she knew her husband too well. And it was fortunate that she didn't because Magnuson, in time, would personally lead the prosecution against Steve.

Like Joseph in the Bible, Steve had dreamed a prophetic dream, and the Oak Park police, like Joseph's brothers, had said, in effect, "Behold, the dreamer comes."

5

Numbered with the Transgressors

When Steve awoke late Saturday morning, October 11, after his night-long interrogation, his head throbbed. His mind still swirled from the accusations. The pain and anguish that surged through his body were relieved only by occasional moments of numbness. As he recalled the night before, his body shook with the realization of its stark reality.

Slowly he tried to sift his thoughts. *Why was I so stupid?* he asked himself. He regretted that he had not listened to Lois when she had first become alarmed. *How can they possibly think I'm a suspect?*

As Steve lay in bed, he recalled his premonition a few months earlier. It had come true; he had become involved with the police, and his studies had been interrupted. The only thought that cheered him was that once the evidence was analyzed he would be eliminated as a suspect.

The next day, at the end of the Sunday evening service at River Forest Bible Chapel, Ron Baines, a friend of the Linscotts, stood up and made an announcement to the congregation of over a hundred people. "I have an urgent prayer request," he said. "Steve and Lois Linscott are in *very* serious trouble and need our prayers at this time. . . ." Their church friends would mean a great deal to Steve and Lois in the months ahead.

Despite the interrogation, Steve and Lois still believed that the police would examine the evidence and realize they had made a mistake. Yet Steve couldn't get one of the officer's comments out of his mind: "Somewhere, someday, when you least expect it, we'll show up and arrest you. Don't ever forget that!" With this in mind, Steve called Dr. Dave Reid, one of the instructors at Emmaus, to alert him to the situation and to seek his advice.

Dr. Reid listened to the story and, recognizing the seriousness of the situation, recommended that Steve seek an appointment with the school president, Daniel H. Smith. Steve was granted an interview with the dean of education who later conferred with the president.

President Smith recommended a Christian lawyer, Frank Kannelos, a former judge who had returned to private practice. The faculty was then informed of Steve's plight, and prayers were quickly offered on his behalf.

On Wednesday evening, October 15, Frank Kannelos heard Steve's story from beginning to end, and Steve retained him as his lawyer. "Call me immediately if the police contact you again," Frank advised. "And say nothing until I get there."

Steve saw no reason to alarm his parents. They had called after Steve's first interview to let him know that the

Ellsworth police had informed them that their Oak Park counterparts were checking on his record. "There's nothing to worry about," Steve had told them.

But Steve was concerned. If the police did arrest him, he would need thousands of dollars for a defense. Since he and Lois were accustomed to thinking in terms of ten and twenty dollar bills, the cost of legal fees seemed astronomical. *I didn't do anything wrong—so why should I have to pay to defend myself?* Steve asked himself. *God wouldn't allow such a test if we couldn't afford it!*

As the weeks passed, Steve heard nothing more from the police. *Much ado about nothing,* he thought.

Meanwhile, rumors of Steve's "guilt" began to circulate in the community—rumors that led to further discussion of the case by some of the Emmaus faculty and the elders at the River Forest Church, who, though supportive of Steve, wanted to know the truth.

"Steve, did you do it?" asked Dave Glock, Dean of Education at Emmaus.

"No, I didn't," Steve responded emphatically.

The concern was healthy. Over the next few months, as friends, elders, and faculty members questioned Steve from every conceivable angle, his transparent honesty never ceased to amaze them. They were convinced of his innocence. Not only was such a brutal crime inconsistent with his lifestyle and love for people, they concluded, but he lacked the opportunity and a motive.

Steve and Lois were glad for their friends, for people who understood them, believed them, and stood by them. In fact, throughout the entire ordeal, not a single friend deserted Steve. In every instance friends grew closer, more supportive, more faithful. And the circle of friends grew larger.

These friends struggled with Steve as he searched for

answers to his questions: What was the purpose of this trial? What lessons was God trying to teach him? Why are the innocent allowed to suffer? The questions forced him to his knees in prayer.

One answer that came was that God was teaching him to develop more consistent times of fellowship with himself. Even for Bible-school students who constantly study the Word, this lesson needs to be learned and relearned.

One day a carton of books was donated to the Austin Center. In it Steve found a Christian classic—*The Imitation of Christ*, by Thomas à Kempis. As he began to read it, with its amazing challenge to holy living, he knew that he was in need of the kind of discipleship and commitment discussed in the book. He set the book aside when he realized that God wanted to do—needed to do—a lot more work in his life before he was ready for that kind of holiness. Steve began to pray that God would accomplish His purposes for his life and prepare him for the mission field.

Then Steve began to read biographies of the great missionaries like Hudson Taylor, who opened up the interior of China to the gospel, and David Livingstone, who took the gospel to Central Africa. These great men of God challenged him to even greater commitment and spurred him on to increased involvement with people. *Lord, I feel so unworthy*, Steve prayed. *Prepare me for the task you have for me. Get me ready, Lord.*

God has his ways of forging character. He often exposes people to and takes them through the fires of affliction. God's ways are perfect. Never will he cause his child a needless tear. And Steve needed to learn that.

During this period God's purposes became more visible to Steve through his instructors at school. Dr. Fish's course on Second Corinthians revealed the endurance the apostle Paul displayed in his many sufferings. Dr. Reid's course on the Gospel of Mark renewed and strengthened Steve's faith. The incidents of Jesus walking on water and calming the sea constantly filled his mind and challenged his spirit.

Still, the thought of useless suffering was frightening. He wondered, *How do false accusations fit into the picture? And what does God have in store?*

Six weeks passed. The school quarter was winding down; term papers were due; final exams were just a couple of days away. Steve looked forward to good grades and the next quarter's courses, for which he had already enrolled. Thanksgiving break was just a few days away. "After the pressure of studies and all we have been through, it will be great to relax with you and the kids," Steve told Lois.

On the Monday evening before Thanksgiving, the elders at River Forest Bible Chapel met for one of their regular meetings.

"How is Steve Linscott doing?" someone asked.

"Fine!" someone else responded. "I was just speaking to him yesterday and he was telling me it's more than six weeks since his problem with the police. He's heard nothing further from them, and he's pretty much dismissed the entire incident from his mind. He said there was nothing further to worry about."

Another elder, his face solemn, spoke up. "I've picked up from sources close to the police that they're looking for one final piece of evidence before arresting him. They just need to prove that Steve knew the woman. From what I understand things look extremely bleak." There was a shocked silence. A short discussion followed, and the elders paused, bowed their heads, and, one by one, prayed.

The next day Steve had his final examination on Romans. Rising earlier than usual, he put in an hour or two of

69

additional study and reviewed his memory work. He ate a quick breakfast with the rest of the family, and snatched a twenty-minute quiet time.

During these sessions with the Lord, Steve had been reading and meditating on Paul's letter to the Ephesians. That morning Steve read Ephesians 6:10–20. Verse 12 seemed especially appropriate, so he reflected on it for a while: "For our struggle is not against flesh and blood, but against the rulers, against the authorities, against the powers of this dark world and against the spiritual forces of evil in the heavenly realms."

As Steve prayed and committed himself to God for the day, a thought struck him: *It is not men and their devices that threaten a believer in Christ, but the Devil and his schemes.*

Steve said a quick good-by to Lois and the children, and left the house for his exam on Romans.

He did not see the two cars parked outside.

The previous Wednesday, November 19, Mohammad Tahir, a forensic analyst, had completed his first tests on the physical evidence obtained from the victim, Karen Phillips, and from Steve Linscott. Tahir was employed by the Illinois Department of Law Enforcement's Bureau of Scientific Services in the Maywood lab.

By Monday, November 24, the police believed that through these tests they could link Steve to the scene of the crime, even though one test actually revealed negative findings. With these tests in hand, plus cassettes of the taped interviews, the composite sketch of the assailant in Steve's dream, and other documents, Detective Scianna visited the Maywood Circuit Court to secure a warrant for Steve's arrest. In the months to come, those tests would cause a firestorm of controversy.

Judge Boscoe listened to the charges, heard and examined the evidence, and signed the warrant. Scianna then returned to the Oak Park Police Station to make arrangements for Steve's arrest the next day.

About two blocks from home, as Steve drove slowly and quoted his Romans outline from memory, he saw a flashing red light in his rear-view mirror. He knew he had not committed any traffic violation, so, unalarmed, he pulled his car to the curb. As he did so, he recognized the occupants of the car—the same two who had harassed him at the police station. His heart sank. *More harassment,* he said to himself.

The officers got out of their car. Scianna stood back while Grego came to the window. "You're under arrest," he said and ordered Steve out of the car.

"I'd like to see the arrest warrant," Steve responded, appearing calm. Inwardly he shook.

"It's in the car," Grego replied.

Steve parked his car and got out. As he turned back to the police car, Grego slapped handcuffs over his wrists. The harsh truth struck him: he was being arrested for murder. For a moment he stood motionless, unable to think or speak.

As he dropped into the back seat of the police car, the warrant was shown to him. His heart pounded as he read the charges: rape, three counts of murder, armed violence. When Steve asked why a tire iron was mentioned, he was told that was the weapon he had used to murder the woman.

"I don't know anything about it," he said. Steve did not even know that a tire iron had been used *or* that a rape had been committed. He was puzzled and remained silent the rest of the way to the police station.

At the station Steve was taken to the same room where the earlier interviews had taken place. The officers went through his belongings and took him to another room for fingerprinting and to have his picture taken. Officer Scianna sensed his humiliation. "That's a process we take all criminals through," he said.

"I'd like to speak to my lawyer," Steve said.

His request was ignored at that time. Only after being locked in a cell for what seemed like an eternity, was he taken to the office and permitted to call his lawyer.

Frank Kannelos was startled. Just minutes before, he had talked with Lois on the phone and was told that nothing had developed. Frank had concluded that the police were no longer interested. Now Steve was calling from jail. Frank promised to see him the next day in court and reassured him that he would also call Lois immediately.

But before Frank was able to call, Officer Grego had called Lois. "Mrs. Linscott," he said, "we have your husband here under arrest on charges of murder and rape."

"How long have you had him down there?" Lois asked, fighting hard to maintain her composure.

"Since 8:15 this morning."

"What! And you're just now, four hours later, letting me know!"

"*Hey lady!* We don't owe you a thing! You should be thankful I ever called," Grego replied. "If you want to see your husband, you'll have to come over within the hour."

Fortunately, Carlos Craveiro had just returned from school and, after helping Lois deposit her two children at a friend's home, drove her to the police station. As she was being led to see her husband, Officers Scianna and Grego intercepted her. They escorted her into a small room. "Before you see your husband we want to talk with you, Mrs. Linscott."

"I want to talk with *you*," Lois retorted. "What is the evidence against my husband?"

"His sperm count matches that of the murderer!" the officers responded, searching her face for any telltale reaction.

"That's ridiculous! Let me see my husband!" Lois pushed past them into the hallway. "Where is he? I want to see him!"

The officers opened a door. Sitting across from a large desk, Steve sat quietly, looking exhausted and pale. Lois was allowed a couple of minutes with him while Detective Scianna sat about two feet away, watching them intently. As she waited for him to leave, she burst into tears.

Steve took his wife's hand and said sadly, "He's not going to budge, Lois. We'd better learn to communicate in this type of situation. Be strong. Don't forget to talk to the lawyer. Even though we are separated, we will not be robbed of life." Steve hesitated for a moment, uncertain what to say next. Just one more thing needed to be said, "I love you, Lois!"

"I love you too, Steve!" And Lois left the room. As she walked from the station, tears rolled down her cheeks.

Steve was led back to the investigations office. In the presence of Scianna and Grego, instead of remaining silent as Frank Kannelos had advised, he posed some questions to Sergeant Mendrick. Eighteen months later Mendrick brought them up in the trial.

"What would happen if someone came in and confessed to the murder of Karen Phillips? Would I be released today?" he asked.

"If someone came in and confessed to the murder of Karen Phillips, we would have to check out the confession to see if it contained facts only the murderer or police would have known. We would have to try and substantiate these facts through some form of physical evidence," the police officer replied.

"Well then, do you believe that some people could possibly have insight into the future or dream about the future?"

"Not in your case, Steve! Because hairs matching yours were found in the murdered girl's apartment. If you didn't kill her, why were your hairs there?"

Again he thought of the comment six weeks earlier: "The evidence you gave us tonight *will* convict you." Remembering his reading of Ephesians 6:12 that morning, Steve said, "Well, if my hairs were in the apartment, the Devil must have put them there!"

When questioned about that statement, Steve gave a theological response: "There are two forces in the world today: the forces of good and the forces of evil; the forces of Jesus Christ and the forces of the Devil."

When the officer asked if there were books to back up his claim, Steve replied, "Dozens."

Steve was then taken to another meeting with Mendrick at 4:00, and his rights were read to him again: ". . . Anything you say may be used against you. . . ." But in spite of his lawyer's instructions, Steve could not keep quiet. He sincerely believed that *anything* he said would only strengthen his case, and he wanted to convince them of his innocence.

The officer immediately zeroed in on the dream. This was obviously his intent for the meeting. In his subsequent trial testimony eighteen months later, Mendrick related some of the conversation: "Since your dream was so vivid, is it possible you thought you were dreaming, but were actually in the girl's . . . murdered girl's apartment? Something like an LSD trip where the mind is watching the body?" Mendrick asked.

The question was absurd. Referring to his prayer time earlier that day, he said, "No, because I checked out my subconscious in the morning. I also checked my right arm to

74

see if it was sore, because the person I saw hitting the girl in the dream hit her so many times, he might have had a sore arm in the morning; and I certainly didn't. Also, the murderer would have had a lot of blood on his clothes, and I didn't own clothes like the person in the dream."

"Did you check your clothes for blood in the morning?"

"No! But if there was blood on my clothes, my wife would have seen it and asked me about it," Steve replied.

After the interrogation, Steve called his parents in Maine: "Mom, I've got some rough news. It's not the kids, or Lois. . . . No, there's no accident. I've been arrested for rape and murder. There's been a big mistake! You know I'm innocent." There was a stunned silence at the other end.

"Well, son, did you do it? Did you *know* the girl? Did you ever see her before?"

"You know that I didn't do it!" Steve responded, and he told his mother the whole story.

"Steve never told me a lie in his life," his father remarked later. "And one time, I wanted him to kill my old dog, but he wouldn't even do that." Paul Linscott was very supportive of his son and promised that he would mobilize help immediately.

After the phone call, Steve was shown to his cell. He had no idea what time it was because his watch had been taken from him. "Let me know if you need anything," Sergeant Mendrick said. The sudden concern surprised Steve, but he appreciated the thought.

Scianna was not so kind when he visited a little later. Although he did not show any hostility, it was evident that he was convinced of Steve's guilt. "It's unfortunate for you, but I'm convinced we have the right man," he said with a serious look on his face.

Wisely, for once, Steve said nothing. That night he slept on a metal bed, alone in the cell. As part of the routine, his shoelaces and belt had been removed—just in case he tried to hang himself. An officer sat outside the cell all night and watched him.

The next day, two incidents brought a measure of comfort to Lois. The first was an article in the *Chicago Tribune* that featured a former Baptist deacon and Sunday school teacher who had been convicted of two rapes. The article described how he was released after spending five years in prison for crimes that the prosecutors now claim he did not commit. This man had been identified in a police line-up by the two victims and was then sentenced to prison for two consecutive terms of fifty and ten years. He never doubted his innocence. He rejected a plea bargain which could have released him on parole after eighteen months. The prosecutor admitted to "completely and absolutely believing what those women had said."

The tragedy of such cases lay in what is not reported in the paper. Usually, mistaken identity alone cannot result in a conviction, no matter how sure the witnesses are. So it is not uncommon for prosecutors to argue that physical evidence— blood, hair, and saliva—fails to *exclude* a possible suspect, when, in reality, they are simply proving the often unreliable nature of that type of evidence.

The second incident that encouraged Lois was a mysterious, anonymous phone call. The caller sounded emotionally upset and extremely agitated. Lois estimated his age between forty and fifty. Speaking in a deep voice, without an accent, he introduced himself as "the Sarge."

"You mean from the Oak Park Police Department?" Lois asked.

"Where else do you think?" he shouted.

"Our lawyer has told us not to talk with you."

"Wait! Don't hang up—*don't* hang up! Don't you care that I can help you?"

"Well, yes, but *who* are you? What's your name?" Lois's head spun as she tried to collect her thoughts.

"What! Do you think I'd risk telling you who I am? No way! Well, I'll tell you. I'm the Sergeant-at-Arms of the Democratic Convention in your ward." (A later check revealed that no such person exists in that ward.) "Does Steve have a good lawyer?" the man asked.

Lois hesitated for a moment, uncertain what she was getting herself into. "Well, yes," she replied.

"Well that's good! If he has a good lawyer he'll be okay! You have nothing to worry about," he continued. "He didn't do it! I know he didn't do it!" He sounded somewhat relieved.

Lois brightened up considerably. "We also have God! He *will* vindicate Steve."

"Are you religious then?"

"I suppose you'd call it that."

"My wife and children are religious, but I'm a Jehovah's Witness."

"What's your name? Where do you live? What's your number? How can you be so sure my husband didn't do it?" Lois asked excitedly.

The mysterious caller evaded these questions, and after reassuring Lois once more that Steve would be all right if he had a good lawyer, he hung up.

What did the call mean? Was it just a freak? Did the caller really know something? Had Lois just spoken to the killer of Karen Phillips? Did he, after reading that morning's article about Steve's arrest, feel a twinge of guilt that an innocent man had been arrested? Lois immediately reported the call to Frank Kannelos and later to a number of close friends. Acting on advice received, she narrated the conversation onto a cassette tape that would be preserved for possible future use.

Earlier that day, Lois had delivered some clothes to Steve. He was transferred to a holding cell where he and Lois were able to talk, briefly, under that ever-watchful eye of Detective Scianna. They embraced quickly, not knowing when they would have another opportunity. After assuring Steve of her prayers and that several people were willing to testify on his behalf, she left, uncertain when they would be that close again.

Lois was not the only visitor that morning; five chaplains from the Good News Mission called. Their presence, friendship, and prayers cheered Steve. Chaplain Rick Gavenda said, "Steve, remember Joseph!"

At 9:30 that day, Steve appeared before the chief presiding judge at the Fourth District Circuit Court in Maywood. This was the first time Steve had ever been in a court building in his life. The State explained their charges while Frank Kannelos listened. He said very little because he had practically no knowledge of Steve, and in any event, he too had been caught by surprise.

Steve was terrified. He understood none of the procedures and felt utterly humiliated. He only knew that he was being treated like a criminal. He sat, handcuffed, in a room with about eight other prisoners, including a couple of women. Some of the people talked about the crimes they had committed. One woman told how she had "blown away" (that is, shot and killed) her boyfriend in an outburst of anger. The reason: he had slapped her.

Steve was so shaken that when he had an opportunity to speak before the judge, he nervously said, "I have two kids ages three and two, and have been married a year."

Fortunately, Lois was able to straighten out the record. The judge denied bond. For an entire week, Steve didn't even know what that meant.

After the hearing, Steve was allowed a few minutes with his lawyer and Lois. After kissing Lois on the cheek, Steve, still handcuffed, was led through a maze of corridors to a large holding tank where two steel benches were bolted into the concrete floor. The room was filled with men and smoke. Some of the men were "on the new" like Steve; others had been brought from Cook County Jail for their court appearances. As soon as Steve entered, the questions began: What were the charges? Who arrested him?

After a while, the men were handcuffed in pairs and taken to the buses that waited to take them to jail. The windows of the buses were barred and cages separated the prisoners from the guards. The women in the front of the bus were the object of obscene comments and verbal abuse. As Steve sat quietly and tried to maintain his composure, he thought about Lois and the kids.

He remembered the previous day when he had quickly kissed Lois good-by and started out for school. Yesterday, he was a Bible student. Today, he was on his way to jail.

Steve was learning what it was like to be numbered, like Christ, with the transgressors.

6
Will
Iron Gates Yield?

With a population of forty-five hundred, Cook County Jail is one of the largest in the country. Located on Chicago's south side at California and Twenty-sixth streets, it rises impressively above the surrounding buildings. The structure is an odd combination of old and new. Its modern half forms a vivid contrast with the older gray-stone buildings, which were constructed nearly half a century ago. Security towers rise above the massive walls that are ringed with barbed wire.

Overcrowding is a major problem. Seventy thousand people are processed through the institution each year, some of whom are quickly released when charges are dropped or bail is granted, while others have to wait a year or more for their trials and sentencing. The average stay is six weeks.

The jail is divided into six sectors. Each prisoner is assigned to a sector according to the charges against him.

Division Six is reserved for the most dangerous criminals—the murderers and rapists. This division is filled with tough and violent men, many of whom will stop at nothing to satisfy their desires—even in jail. They survive by intimidation and threats; they form their own rules and seek to dominate the lives of others. In this division, homosexual rape, beatings, and murder are not uncommon.

In Division Six Steve would be an easy target. Scianna and Grego understood this; they had once told him, "You'll be raped."

During that first day of processing at Cook County Jail, a guard made the notation on Steve's record that he was shaking and seemed nervous. Steve, of course, was scared stiff. At about 4:00 in the afternoon he was allowed a five-minute phone call to Lois. Until then, Lois had no idea what had happened to him after the hearing.

Minutes later Chaplains Steve Thompson and Chuck Haley of the Good News Mission visited Steve. Their encouragement strengthened him and did much to put him at ease. They outlined ways they would help both Steve and his family. Steve Thompson promised to call Lois immediately and tell her that he had seen him.

Later that evening Chuck Haley also telephoned Lois. "I've just left Steve surrounded by several of the best Christians in the division," he reported. "Maybe the authorities don't realize this, but Division Six is experiencing more spiritual revival than any other division in the jail."

Lois was relieved—especially after the horror stories she had heard.

She was even more relieved to hear that two weeks before Steve's arrival, the toughest gangleaders and troublemakers had been moved out of the wing. God was answering prayers.

At about 7:00 that evening, Steve reached Wing 2H in

Division Six. To his amazement, he was shown to an empty cell, which he had to himself for a few days. The cell was off to one side out of the stream of traffic and was quieter than most. Steve needed this to get his thoughts together and reflect on all that was happening.

In the days that followed, Steve learned to appreciate small blessings: Mail started to arrive. The chaplains visited regularly. Carlos Craveiro, in his capacity as resident counselor at the Austin Center, had unrestricted movement in the division and visited Steve as often as he could, sometimes as late as 11:00 at night. He brought books and letters, and relayed messages.

Steve was grateful to be in the wing that had the strongest Christian community in the jail. Since his arrest, Steve had found it hard to pray and almost impossible to minister to others—two things that otherwise came naturally to him. But with the encouragement of the other Christians, Steve was able to work on his spiritual discipline.

The Christian inmates on Steve's wing were not afraid to witness and could tell the gospel in a way that got attention. They wanted to keep the laws of God and not do the brutal things they once did. Some of the most toughened men had been miraculously saved there by God's grace. Wing 2H could have been one of the worst jails to live in; many, including the police, felt it still was. But things *had* changed.

On one occasion, seeing the respect that Steve commanded on the wing, a new inmate, who was already used to "jail-house power," asked him who was "holding the wing down." Steve told him, "Jesus." The Christians, he explained, outnumbered the "gang-bangers," and the rest were just not "hooked up."

Tragically, many of these men were hearing the gospel for the first time.

Vincent was a good example. He was placed in Steve's

cell after a few days; he was Steve's "celly." Vince was destitute, nearly friendless, and seemed to have been completely cast out of society. Even his mother thought jail was the best place for her son; there, at least, he would be safe and provided for.

Being able to read and write set Steve apart from most of the inmates. He helped Vince write letters to his girl friend, who, as it turned out, was neither faithful nor friendly—but she was all Vince had. When Vince said that he wanted to write the "right kinds of things to her," Steve read to him from the *Living Bible*'s rendering of 1 Corinthians 13: "If I had the gift of being able to speak in other languages without learning them, and could speak in every language there is in all of heaven and earth, but didn't love others, I would only be making noise. . . . Love is very patient and kind, never jealous or envious, never boastful or proud, never haughty or selfish or rude. Love does not demand its own way. . . . There are three things that remain—faith, hope, and love— and the greatest of these is love." That so deeply touched Vince's heart that Steve eventually had the joy of leading him to the Lord.

As Steve's ministry at the jail expanded, he had the thrill of leading two more men to Christ. It was hard, though, to minister to others when he felt that he was the one that needed to be ministered to.

On December 3, *Oak Leaves*, a weekly Oak Park newspaper, carried an inaccurate report of Steve's arrest. It claimed that the crime had been "solved": "The suspect was arrested . . . as he was about to enter his car parked outside his home," Detective Scianna was quoted as saying. The article said that Scianna and his partners, Detective Grego and Sergeant Mendrick, recognized Steve's license-plate number. They immediately arrested Steve and charged him with first degree murder, rape, and armed violence. Scianna stated that Steve did not resist arrest and was not armed at the time of his capture.

The insinuations hurt. The article implied that Steve was dangerous, that he was suspected of having a weapon, and that, while on the run, he had been spotted by exceptionally alert detectives. The truth was that Steve had never left the area and that the police knew his whereabouts all the time.

On the day after the *Oak Leaves* article, a Cook County grand jury indicted Steven P. Linscott of Oak Park on charges of murder, rape, and armed violence. The police and State's Attorneys contended that the physical evidence led them to believe that Linscott was the person they were seeking. What physical evidence? Hair evidence is, to say the least, unreliable. No reputable expert, on the basis of normal forensic tests, would dare say that a particular hair came from a particular head.

Also at this hearing, Frank Kannelos withdrew from the case, citing irreconcilable differences. A public defender seemed the only option. The appearance was consequently continued to January 9 to give the Linscotts time to find a new lawyer.

Lois immediately began to collect the names of defense lawyers. She visited several who were willing to consult with her, but the fees were high. They were asking for retainers of between $10,000 and $30,000. Acting upon advice, Lois contacted the Christian Legal Society in Oak Park, and she was given the name of a Christian criminal lawyer in Wheaton, Illinois. She made an appointment.

With renewed hope, Lois set out for the interview. The drive should have taken her only forty-five minutes, but after battling rain and mechanical problems, she arrived at the lawyer's office much later. Then the lawyer refused to talk to her without a $50 payment to cover the hour-long consultation. She was devastated. She had come without her checkbook. She argued, but the lawyer stood his ground. "I have been burned by Christians before," he said. "I have to eat too, Mrs. Linscott!"

Lois returned home, discouraged and hurt.

Soon after this, Steve's father, Paul Linscott, arrived from Maine. He had come with the name of a defense lawyer who had been recommended by a prosecutor in Ellsworth. "He's one of the best," Paul was told. So Paul and Lois visited the fortieth-floor offices of Arthur J. O'Donnell in downtown Chicago. And they were impressed. O'Donnell was in his late fifties, although his white hair made him look a little older. He was debonair, well dressed, and had a confident, aggressive, boisterous flair. He had handled many murder and rape cases.

O'Donnell asked for a $10,000 retainer. After talking to at least five other lawyers on the phone, Lois realized that $10,000 was a fair price, even though she did not know how she and Steve were going to afford it.

To help pay the retainer, Steve's father dug into his meager resources. A close church friend also lent $5,000 toward the defense and another young couple lent $2,500. Finally enough money was collected to retain O'Donnell. Much later, a misunderstanding developed: the Linscotts believed the sum represented the total fee. In reality, O'Donnell claimed, it barely covered the "out of the pocket" expenses. Eventually, the fees were paid for, in part, by the "Linscott Defense Fund," which was established by the River Forest Bible Chapel. It is probably a blessing that Steve and Lois did not know what the final, heavily discounted bill would be. Otherwise, he would have thrown himself on the mercies of a public defender.

The first hurdle facing O'Donnell was the procurement of a bond hearing. Bail had been denied, but O'Donnell was confident that, with a proper presentation, it could still be granted. Steve, his family, and their many friends prayed that this would be accomplished before Christmas.

Although Steve was not out on bail, he was not alone. Friends visited, wrote, and prayed. The telephone was near at hand, and Steve used it whenever he needed to talk.

His closest friend, however, was Lois. She seemed to be filled with a spirit of love and ministry, and supported her husband unreservedly. Repeatedly and emphatically, she would tell people, "He didn't do it! I know he didn't!" and people were impressed with her sincerity. When Steve was hurting, it was Lois who lifted his spirits. Steve was amazed at the way God strengthened his wife for their ordeal. She was truly "worth far more than rubies."

But with all his wealth of friends and supporters, Steve was especially aware of God's presence. As he prayed and read his Bible, he knew that God was there with him.

One day, Carlos brought him *The Imitation of Christ,* the book by Thomas à Kempis that he had left unfinished after the first interrogation. The book challenged him—and broke him—just as it has done with countless others in the centuries since it was written. Attracted by the book's uncompromising call to holiness, Steve began to fast, sometimes two or three times a week for as long as thirty-six hours at a stretch. He prayed eight to ten hours at a time.

I wonder if I am doing right or just acting selfishly, praying that God would deliver me from jail and from this terrible ordeal, he once asked himself. Then he recalled Jesus' story of the woman who constantly pleaded her case before the unjust judge. In the end, she was rewarded for her persistence. Hers was the kind of prayer that got results. So Steve persevered.

86

He realized that God had not abandoned him, that God still loved him. He saw that God had permitted this ordeal for a purpose—a purpose, however, that was still unclear. Was it to gain his attention or affection? Was it to teach him that nothing could separate him from the infinite love of an almighty God? Not even disappointment or sorrow, loneliness or hunger, imprisonment or false accusations? At one point, when Steve felt he could sink no further in his miseries, he abandoned himself to God and to His will for his life. The struggle was far from over, but he was beginning to learn what it meant to have nothing else in the world but Jesus.

Steve Linscott was arraigned Monday, December 22.

As Steve sat in a back room with the other prisoners, two bailiffs entered. "Is there a trial today?" one bailiff asked the other. He was asking because the courtroom was unusually crowded.

"No, I don't think so."

"Who has all the support? What kind of case is it?" And the other bailiff went to inquire. Steve said nothing. He realized that his friends were gathered in the courtroom, and he was grateful.

At the arraignment hearing O'Donnell asked that bail be set at $100,000. If granted, $10,000 (10 percent of bail) would secure Steve's release. But a prosecutor for the State argued that no bail should be granted. Referring to Steve's statements about the dream murderer in the taped interviews, she told the judge, "He said he would do it again." She said that if the judge granted bail, it should be set at $1,000,000. Steve's supporters gasped.

O'Donnell told the judge about Steve's background and exemplary record, and produced two character witnesses.

87

One of them was John Montgomery, president of Central Educational Network (a division of Public Television). O'Donnell again asked that bail be set at $100,000.

Judge Boscoe considered the evidence and the arguments, and decided to grant bail—at $450,000. Steve's father had already planned to mortgage his home for $10,000, but where would they find the 10-percent fee of $45,000? Steve would not be able to spend Christmas with his family.

Shortly after Steve was taken back to Cook County Jail, Lois and the children went to stay with John and Evelyn Montgomery. John, who was a character witness for Steve at the hearing, has been in the field of education for all his professional life, serving several years as a school principal and working for Public Television. John was an elder at River Forest Bible Chapel and taught a college-and-career Bible class. As vice-chairman of the board of trustees of Emmaus Bible College, he felt a particular concern for the reputation of the school.

But despite the Montgomerys' love, care, and friendship, Christmas without Steve would be depressing.

The Oak Park Police Department, in the meantime, was beginning to feel the pressure of the community's growing support for Steve. Steve's friends and supporters contacted Chief Wilbur Reichert to protest Steve's arrest and urge a continuance of the investigation, which had ceased with Steve's arrest. Stamped across Steve's police file were the words, "Arrest Closes Case." The police were in a bind. A renewal of the investigation would be tantamount to an admission of doubt and could invite litigation against the department. Nevertheless, with mounting pressure from the community, the Oak Park police unofficially admitted that another suspect might have been involved.

But in spite of this admission, the police continued to ignore their leads. On December 3, for instance, near Fox River Valley Shopping Center (not far from the school that Karen Phillips had attended in Aurora), local police were investigating the rape, deviate sexual assault, and robbery of a local woman. Through a composite sketch, the assailant was identified. He was already well known to the DuPage and Kane Counties' law enforcement officers. This man was also well known to the Oak Park police because he had been involved in two recent incidents—a rape and an assault (though the charges were later dropped). It was also known that at the time of Karen's murder he was living in Oak Park—six blocks from her apartment.

According to one victim's testimony, this man had beaten her and threatened to kill her, telling her that he had raped and killed other women, some of whom he had thrown into the Fox River. The Aurora police had, in fact, recovered the bodies of several women from the river. There was no doubt that he was violent and emotionally disturbed. Although his police file was thick with numerous reports of investigations, the police had found it difficult to "nail" him. Now was their chance.

On December 4, the Aurora police called their Oak Park counterparts and instructed them to arrest the suspect. Two days later, when detectives from Aurora arrived to pick him up, the Oak Park officers said, "Let us know whether he is a *secretor* or a *non-secretor.*" They clearly had the Karen Phillips murder in mind.

Six weeks later, when the test results were known, the Aurora police called to say that the suspect was a secretor. "Then that rules him out," the Oak Park police concluded.

Steve Linscott, like 20 percent of the population (and like twelve thousand other residents of Oak Park) is a non-secretor. This simply means that the enzymes in Steve's blood are not secreted into his body fluids, such as saliva, perspiration, and semen, and that it is impossible to determine his blood type from examining these fluids. The blood type of non-secretors can only be determined from an analysis of the blood itself.

In a forensic report dated November 19, Mohammad Tahir indicated that Karen Phillips's blood type was ABO-O and PGM 2-1. Steve's blood type, on the other hand, was ABO-AB and PGM 1. A test of the vaginal swab revealed the presence of seminal material, but failed to reveal *any* ABO blood type or PGM blood groupings. The police were assuming that, because they could not determine any blood type from the swab test, that the assailant must have been a non-secretor. But since Karen Phillips was a secretor, it is strange that the same swab test failed to detect the presence of her *own* blood type, which, of course, it should have done. This would indicate that these initial tests on the vaginal swab were unreliable and inconclusive. And it is even stranger that it was as a result of these tests that Steve was initially charged with rape.

Acting on the instructions of Assistant State's Attorney Colin Simpson, Tahir performed a second series of tests on December 9. One can't help wondering why the State felt these new tests were even necessary if they already believed the earlier tests were conclusive.

For a second time, the forensic analyst failed to detect *any* ABO blood type or to determine the PGM from the vaginal swab. It remains a mystery how, in the absence of conclusive scientific determination, the police and State's Attorneys convinced Judge Boscoe to include rape in the arrest warrant. At that point, the swab evidence excluded no one as a suspect; it included 100 percent of the male population—some 27,500 men in Oak Park alone.

After more tests of the swab in February (three months

after Steve's arrest), Tahir was finally able to detect ABO-O and PGM 2-1 and only those groupings. Again this would seem to indicate that the assailant was a non-secretor, but there is another possibility that the police did not think of. The same results could also indicate that the assailant was a secretor with the *same* blood groupings as the victim.* If the Oak Park police had inquired into the blood groupings of the Aurora rape suspect in December, they might have realized this other possibility. His blood was ABO-O and PGM 2-1— the same as Karen Phillips's! Although they were urged to do so, the police refused to investigate this suspect.

Since about 50 percent of the population has type O blood and 35 percent of this group, including the Aurora suspect, has PGM 2-1, this evidence, in itself, is not damaging. Since the assailant was either a non-secretor or had the same blood groupings as the victim, these results, of course, could not exclude Steve as a possible suspect either. But neither could they exclude 60 percent of the male population! Yet the police maintained that Steve Linscott could be linked to the rape of Karen Phillips on the basis of this evidence.

The police, in fact, seemed satisfied that Steve was their man. But there was evidence that might have excluded Steve as a suspect. For instance, Negroid head and body hairs were found on Karen Phillips's bedsheets; a Negroid pubic hair was recovered from the carpet where the body had lain; and Negroid hairs were found among the jimmy shavings outside Karen's door.

---

*It is also possible that too little semen was on the swab to gain any valid information. Nowhere in Tahir's report does he indicate any test to verify that a sufficient quantity of semen was present to ascertain ABO blood type. Again, this would mean that no male could be excluded.

Raising $45,000 for bond was a formidable task. John Montgomery and I wrote a letter that explained the situation and asked people to give money or make interest-free loans. The letter was mailed to nearly forty churches in the Chicago area, and a copy was given to each of Steve's supporters. The response was immediate. One church in a southwest suburb loaned $6,000 from a building fund. Still, it was not enough.

The delay drove Steve to his knees. One evening he prayed, *Dear God, please raise up one or two people to provide the funds.*

The following Sunday, January 4, a Christian woman in the community heard about the situation from Jim Chesney, the man who had owned Steve and Lois's first house in Chicago. She read the letter to the Circle Community Church in Oak Park during their Sunday evening meeting, and Gaius Berg, a young businessman, expressed interest and inquired how he could obtain more information. He was given the Montgomerys' number.

The next day, Gaius called John Montgomery and discussed the case. "Why don't you visit Steve tomorrow," John suggested. "It's visiting day."

At the jail, Gaius listened to Steve's story and was impressed. When he indicated that he and a friend could probably make a substantial contribution, Steve's heart pounded. But Steve felt torn between two desires: to be free, and also to do God's will.

He wanted to discuss his mixed emotions with Lois but his phone allotment that evening had been cut to fifteen minutes. The time went all too quickly and was almost up when Lois noticed the Montgomerys returning home. As they walked up the drive, she saw their smiling faces. John signaled to her to hold the phone.

"Hold on, Steve, Mr. Montgomery has something to say. It looks as if it might be important." At the other end someone tugged at Steve's elbow trying to get him off the phone. "Hold on, Steve! Don't let go." Lois could hardly contain herself. "Mr. Montgomery says that Gaius and his friend are willing to put up the whole amount!"

It was the answer to Steve's prayer.

Another court appearance was scheduled for Friday, January 9. Steve was awakened at 4:30 in the morning and told to get ready. After a quick breakfast, he waited until about 8:30 in the "bullpen" filled with other inmates. All were making court appearances that day. The room was filled with smoke and angry stares. One very muscular man looked Steve over and said, "Hey, man, I want you!" Steve knew what he meant: he wanted Steve as his "girl."

But the Lord removed Steve's fear. One of the aggressive man's friends came over to stare Steve down and put mental and, if necessary, physical pressure on him. Steve just stared back and said, "Man, everyone's got their own problems." Just that simple statement, spoken with the direction of the Holy Spirit, was sufficient to drive the man back to his seat.

Time and again, God protected Steve. He often used Vince, Steve's "celly." Vince, being street-wise, was able to interpret the signs and shield the naïve "white boy" from the schemes of some of the other inmates. Many of the prisoners told Steve that he was very, very lucky. But Steve knew better and thanked God for his providential care. He had not only been unharmed, but he had earned the respect of the men and guards.

Meanwhile, under the rules of discovery, Attorney O'Donnell filed motions for the release of all State files, documents, and evidence against Steve. This included "street files" and records of every interview conducted—everything. The State had no option but to comply.

There had been talk of requesting a reduction in bond,

but for some reason O'Donnell chose not to do so at the January 9 hearing. Gaius Berg and his partner, Jim Richards, sat through the hearing and afterward indicated their desire to put up the entire $45,000. But O'Donnell discouraged them.

"We are gamblers," they told the lawyer—they were stockbrokers and traded in "futures." They were willing to take a chance that Steve was innocent. "He's our brother and we want him out—today," they said. But O'Donnell and others urged them to wait until a bond reduction could be secured. Gaius and Jim wanted to consider that possibility and asked for time to think about it.

So Steve was not going to be released after all. As he was being led back through the underground tunnels at Cook County Jail toward his cell, he felt deeply disappointed. No dramatic answer to prayer had come. Tears filled his eyes. Silently, he told the Lord that he loved Him and was willing to accept His will. Accepting the disappointment as another test of his love, Steve recommitted himself to God.

By the time he reached his cell, "lock-up" was in force. The telephone on the wing had been shut off. Steve took a chance and asked the guard for five minutes on the phone. Reluctantly, the guard agreed. Steve called Lois but the line was busy. He waited a few minutes and tried again. This time he got through just as the guard signaled him to hang up.

"Have you heard the news?" Lois asked excitedly.

"What news?"

"Then you haven't heard! Good! I'll be the first to tell you." Lois paused for effect and said, "You're coming home! Gaius and Jim decided to put up the whole amount! They told the lawyer the matter was out of his hands and that they had decided they couldn't wait any longer."

At about 5:30 a senior officer came to the wing and

escorted Steve to the main receiving area. John Montgomery had delivered the check for $45,000, an amount that created quite a stir among the guards.

Lois was excited and smiling when she arrived at the jail.

"What's he in for?" one officer asked.

"Murder, rape, and aggravated assault," she replied with a perky smile and a shrug of the shoulders.

"And you want him back?"

"*Yes!*" she said.

The guards wanted to see this man who was worth $45,000.

"That's him!" Lois pointed excitedly.

Later, Katherine was waiting in the doorway of the Montgomerys' home. When she saw her father, she began to jump up and down. Steve ran toward her, picked her up, and hugged her. Their faces reflected the overwhelming joy they felt.

Steve was free.

Later, as they sat at the Montgomerys' dinner table, the reunited and extended family bowed their heads as John Montgomery gave thanks for the food and for all of God's mercies. Everyone held hands. Katherine laid one cheek on her father's hand and held it tightly. Steve could not help weeping at her expression of love. His little girl had experienced hurt, anger, frustration, tears, questions.

Now it was time for joy.

7

Tribulation
Produces Patience

By the time of Steve's release, his attorney, Arthur O'Donnell, had begun to receive copies of police files, transcripts of taped interviews, and forensic reports from the State. The State, however, said that they would not furnish the actual tapes of the interviews or the physical evidence. They alleged that the evidence was needed for further testing. Again, one wonders why further testing was necessary if the police had already told the press that the "physical evidence ... led them to believe that Linscott was the person they were seeking."

At the January 9 hearing O'Donnell had filed a motion to impound the tapes. He wanted them to be kept in the custody of the court clerk rather than in the possession of State's Attorney's office. Judge Anthony J. Boscoe agreed to rule on the motion at the next hearing.

Judge Boscoe, however, never had a chance. While

reviewing these materials, O'Donnell realized that not only had the judge signed the original arrest warrant, but he had also heard the tapes and had probably read the police files. O'Donnell feared that Judge Boscoe might be prejudiced. Therefore O'Donnell immediately filed a petition for a "substitution of judges." Judge Boscoe argued that he could be impartial and that his continuance would not, in itself, represent a denial of due process. Nevertheless, when O'Donnell continued to press for a substitution, Judge Boscoe excused himself from the case.

Judge Jack Welfeld was then assigned. But within an hour of being assigned, O'Donnell learned that Judge Welfeld too had listened to some of the taped interviews. O'Donnell once again filed for a substitution. Eventually, by agreement of both sides, Harry A. Schrier, a chief magistrate with no prior knowledge of the case, was assigned.

With each new day of freedom, Steve's forty-five-day incarceration seemed more like a dream. The experience had renewed his appreciation for his family and friends.

Several inmates had advised Steve to be careful once he was out of prison. They said, "The police might try to hook you up with another crime to have your bond revoked." Some of Steve's friends suggested that he find shelter with a church family instead of returning to the Austin Center.

Several families offered to share their homes with the Linscotts. One couple, whose two teenage daughters frequently baby-sat for Katherine and Paul, invited the Linscotts to stay. They knew Steve too well to believe the charges against him. Though Steve and Lois declined their offer, the invitation indicated the kind of trust that people had in Steve.

The Linscotts finally agreed to stay with the Montgomerys. It was the most convenient place since Lois and the children had already been their guests for nearly seven weeks. Also, the Montgomerys' house was in the Austin neighborhood just outside of Oak Park; this would help reduce the possibility of police harassment and observation.

Soon after moving in, several of the Linscotts' closest friends had gathered at the Montgomerys for an informal visit. The discussion inevitably focused upon the case.

"Why not investigate it ourselves?" someone asked.

"That's a good idea!" someone else responded.

So they decided to form an investigative committee whose goals were simple: find the killer and exonerate Steve. Jim Richards, a former assistant sheriff with the DuPage County Police Department, volunteered. He would serve as the main liaison. Attorney O'Donnell liked the idea and gave Jim a copy of the police reports. Jim made additional copies, eight in all, so that by the next meeting all the committee members were fully informed about the case.

Six days later the group met again. This time it was larger. I was present at this meeting, and so were Ron Baines, Gaius Berg, Jim Chesney, Steve and Lois, John Montgomery, Jim Richards, and Patti Sprinkle.

We discussed the police files and were alarmed at the apparent lack of a more thorough investigation. We found no evidence that the police had investigated any other leads.

Various tasks were then assigned: following up leads, interviewing the people named in the police files, searching for additional evidence, and doing legal research.

In the process of interviewing Helen Palella, a key State witness, Patti Sprinkle let slip that she had access to the police files. After that Helen was no longer cooperative, nor were her Temple associates, Karen's friends, and Jerry McDuffie.

A newspaper article in the January 28 edition of *Oak*

Leaves, headed "Case Not Built on Evidence—Murder Suspect's Friend Speaks Out," reported an interview with John Montgomery and helped put things in perspective for the public.

The article reported that, since their first meeting a year and a half earlier, Montgomery had gotten to know Steve well. As an elder at River Forest Bible Chapel, the church Steve and Lois attended, he taught the college-and-career class each Sunday and led a Bible study at his home on Wednesday evenings. Steve was a member of both groups. After recounting his credits in public television, the article said that he lived with his wife, his eighty-seven-year-old father-in-law, and his thirteen-year-old foster son. Three grown children lived away from home. Montgomery was fully committed to helping Steve; he not only helped post bond but housed him upon his release from jail.

Montgomery told *Oak Leaves* that he first heard of Steve's involvement with the police when Steve called to tell him he could not attend the Wednesday evening Bible study. That was the day of Steve's first interview with the police. Steve had not asked for his advice. If he had, Montgomery would have recommended immediate legal counsel.

Montgomery then discussed the evidence against Steve. The police claimed that the dream contained information that only the offender would know and that they only arrested Steve after finding physical evidence at the crime scene that linked him to the murder. Montgomery, on the other hand, said that the dream actually contained very few details. Montgomery said he knew this because he had read the transcripts of the police interviews and other police reports submitted to Steve's lawyer. The police, he said, had led Linscott to embellish his own dream and add details that were not in the dream itself. Montgomery added that the

99

police had played games with him, leading him on and making him believe he was helping them. Montgomery said he saw no details in the transcripts and reports that "only an offender would know." He doubted whether the dream had any value as evidence at all.

As he continued, Montgomery broke down the case into three parts: the crime itself (together with the evidence), the dream, and the speculations of the police. Montgomery stressed that Linscott believed he was helping the police solve the crime and offered only impressions and projections of the dream. Montgomery affirmed that Linscott did not know Phillips and that Steve did not even know for sure whether the dream victim was a woman. Steve thought the dream victim was black—Phillips was white.

Montgomery then told *Oak Leaves* that the physical evidence was shallow and circumstantial, that nothing in the police reports linked Steve with the crime. "The case is not built on evidence found at the scene of the crime, but on speculations of Steve's imagination beyond the scope of the dream," Montgomery told the newspaper. Once the police convinced themselves that Linscott was the culprit, they built their case on the dream assailant. "They thought they had the guy," Montgomery said.

Montgomery was concerned for three reasons: the case against Steve was built on speculation, not evidence; the case had been closed after Steve's arrest; and the real murderer was still at large. For these reasons Montgomery, along with Linscott's friends and area residents, urged Police Chief Wilbur Reichert to keep the case open.

Deputy Police Chief Harold Fitzsimmons alleged, in response, that the police "only listened as Linscott related his dream and asked for clarification on certain points."

In conclusion, Montgomery stated that Linscott's friends would put their faith in the criminal justice system and added that he would testify at the trial, if necessary.

The article created a furor. The prosecutors of the case were concerned about the dissemination of this information, and they brought a contempt charge against Steve's lawyer. The State felt that, through the press, the public was becoming the "trier of the facts." Although the prosecutors may have felt that it would hurt their case, the article (and the subsequent contempt charge) helped them in one way: it diverted attention away from the physical evidence.

Two weeks after Steve's release the Linscotts moved back to the Austin Center. It felt good to be home. The chaplains at the Center had explained that they needed Steve and Lois's ministry and that they wanted the Linscotts back. And in the midst of ever-mounting legal fees, the free rent of the Center seemed very attractive.

Steve made sure he was with people at all times so that the police would not be able to implicate him in any other crime. He was never alone. At one point, Steve and Lois believed that their telephone was tapped. The phone company, however, assured them that, after a phone check, they had found nothing. But in spite of the phone company's assurances, whenever friends called to discuss the case, Steve would caution them, "Be careful. Our phones may be tapped."

"Good!" some responded. "Apart from our defense strategy, we've got nothing to hide."

The February 19 hearing before Judge Schrier primarily concerned the State's petitions regarding the protection of their documents and Arthur J. O'Donnell's contempt-of-court charge. The State claimed violation of a Supreme Court Rule that reads: "Any materials furnished to any attorney pursuant to these rules shall remain in his exclusive custody and be used only for purposes of conducting his side of the case and shall be subject to such other terms and conditions as the Court may provide." When O'Donnell argued that the rule had never been tested in an Illinois Court, the State said that was irrelevant. The argument went back and forth until the Court finally imposed a protective order on both the prosecution and the defense. The contempt charge was put off until after the trial, and all parties with copies of the police files were ordered to return them to the Court. (To date, the contempt charge has not been removed.)

Toward the end of the hearing, O'Donnell again requested the release of information and evidence under the rules of discovery. O'Donnell's growing frustration was evident. Finally the State intervened to say they would allow him to peruse their files and obtain copies of any documents not already in his possession. O'Donnell was satisfied.

But it was not clear whether this information included the physical evidence itself. The issue would be debated during the trial.

Neither the defense nor the Court knew that the State would not have been able to produce one important piece of the physical evidence, even if they had been ordered to. Five days before the hearing, the State had dispatched Mohammad Tahir—with the evidence—to Scotland Yard in London, England. They later said that this was done because they felt the tests could not be properly undertaken in the United States.

In London, on the very day of the hearing, Tahir used the last bits of the vaginal swab in his tests, leaving none for testing by the defense. In other words, when the State first included this piece of physical evidence in its inventory of discovery materials furnished to the Court, the evidence no longer existed. Furthermore, the State did not reveal this fact when it was admitted into evidence at the trial a year and a half later.

The significance of this nonexistent evidence was hotly debated when it became known at the trial. Eighteen months later the Supreme Court overturned a decision in a case similar to Steve's. In that instance, it was ruled that the destruction of physical evidence violated the defendant's constitutional rights.

Why were the London tests needed? When the original tests of the vaginal swab proved nothing, Assistant State's Attorney Simpson ordered further tests. But Tahir was worried; much of the evidence had already been consumed in the previous testing, and he doubted that a sufficient sample remained to retest for ABO blood type and to test for GM (gamma markers). After deliberation the two men decided to conserve the vaginal swab for further tests at a later date and to test, in the meantime, the blood of the victim and the suspect for the gamma markers.

According to criminal lawyer Thomas D. Decker, "Gamma markers are genetic markers contained in human blood and other body fluids. They . . . attach themselves to immunoglobulin molecules. About twenty-five distinct gamma markers have been identified to date. Of the twenty-five possibilities, which are identified by numerals, each person has by heredity a discrete set of gamma markers which remain constant through time." Only three or four gamma markers are normally tested for forensic purposes.

After conducting the blood tests, Tahir discovered that Karen Phillips had gamma markers +1, +2, and +10. At this point, a vaginal swab test for those same markers would be redundant and wasteful of valuable evidence, because when the body fluids of a rape victim and her assailant are mixed, the presence of plus markers in the victim masks the presence of plus *or* minus markers for those numerals in the suspect. Since the victim in this case had *all* plus markers, no male in the world could be eliminated as a suspect based on this test. The conclusion would have been different had Phillips's blood revealed minus markers; then the presence of plus markers in the vaginal swab would indicate that those markers belonged to the assailant.

When Tahir tested Steve's blood for those numerals, he established the presence of gamma markers -1, -2, and $+10$. Although the test revealed nothing, it did, however, confirm that further testing of the vaginal swab for those same markers would be meaningless because the victim's plus markers would mask those of whoever murdered her.

Tahir ran the same test again in England and later testified that he believed the swab test for blood markers suggested the admixture of Phillips's and Linscott's fluids because the tests could not eliminate Steve as a suspect. Tahir was absolutely right—the results could be consistent with the mixture of fluids from *any* male in the world!

In London Tahir also did a blood-group test on the vaginal swab that proved to be more substantial. He finally detected the presence of ABO-O blood group. As has been already explained, Steve was a non-secretor with ABO-AB type blood. Had Tahir found any other type of blood, it would have eliminated Steve as a suspect. This was the *first* time since Steve's arrest that any scientific evidence even remotely suggested that he could *not* be eliminated as a suspect. But neither could 60 percent of the male population. The tests, in other words, showed that Steve Linscott was one of over two million males in the greater Chicago area who *could* have murdered Karen Phillips.

So what was the value of the London tests? Aware of the lack of incriminating evidence from previous tests, perhaps the State felt that having their specialist run further tests at the prestigious Scotland Yard would introduce a measure of credibility and awe at the trial. The London tests only narrowed the field of possible suspects to 60 percent and wasted the last pieces of swab evidence.

At a brief hearing before Judge Schrier on March 2, the State confirmed that they had given to O'Donnell a copy of Steve's handwritten statement of the dream and a photocopy of the composite sketch drawn by the police artist. The State recovered the eight copies of the police reports, transcripts of the taped interviews, and laboratory reports that had been disseminated to the investigative committee.

The Court also granted Steve permission to visit his parents in Maine before the next court date.

Upon his return to Chicago, Steve and O'Donnell agreed that a polygraph test should be taken. Steve had repeatedly requested this of the police, but for reasons of their own, they refused. Normally, the authorities are quick to order lie-detector tests and give considerable credence to them if they are disadvantageous to the defendant.

On April 8 Fred L. Hunter, of the Chicago firm of F. L. Hunter and Associates, administered the polygraph examination to Steve in his laboratory. At one point Mr. Hunter asked Steve to intentionally lie by answering no to the questions. "Is your name Steve Linscott? . . . Do you live at 316 North Austin Boulevard?" These warm-up tests indicated a keen sensitivity to untruth and a strong reaction to lying. When Steve was told to lie, the needle jumped. In response to the crucial questions administered in the five tests, there was barely a ripple on the graph. Here is Mr. Hunter's report:

On April 8, 1981, Steve P. Linscott, voluntarily submitted himself to a Polygraph examination in this laboratory. The purpose of this examination was to investigate his

involvement in the battery case of Karen Phillips on or about October 4, 1980. (Basically this laboratory was advised that the victim in this case had been struck on the head with a blunt object—probably a tire iron—and also had recently engaged in sexual intercourse.)

Prior to his examination, he signed an agreement to take the Polygraph examination and to allow the results and any relevant statements to be reported to Mr. Arthur J. O'Donnell. He also released all parties involved from any liability which may result from the examination. The executed release form is incorporated as part of our file in this case.

The following listed questions were asked of this subject during his Polygraph examination.

1. On or about October 4, 1980, did you hit Karen Phillips on the head with any object? Answer: No.

2. On or about October 4, did you hit Karen Phillips on the head with a tire iron? Answer: No.

3. Did you ever have sexual intercourse with Karen Phillips? Answer: No.

4. Were you ever inside Karen Phillips's apartment on North Austin Boulevard? Answer: No.

5. Between 12 midnight and 6:00 A.M. on Saturday, October 4, 1980, were you inside your apartment at 316 N. Austin Boulevard? Answer: Yes.

There were no significant emotional disturbances indicative of deception throughout his Polygraph records on the above listed questions.

Nearly a year and a half later, Jim Richards had an interview with Mr. Hunter to determine just how conclusive the polygraph examination was. "Did he just scrape through?" Jim asked, "or did he pass it with flying colors?"

"The results were unusually positive! In my opinion, there is no way he could have done it," Hunter responded.

Unfortunately, in Illinois, polygraph examinations are not admissible evidence. O'Donnell, therefore, was prohibited from making even the slightest allusion to its existence.

Estimates of the accuracy of polygraph examinations range from 70 to 86 percent. The Illinois Supreme Court, therefore, has consistently held that the results of such exams cannot be introduced as evidence. The Arizona Court, on the other hand, has found the test accurate enough to warrant its use as evidence as long as both the defendant and State's Attorney agree to its use. The Wisconsin Supreme Court found that when a polygraph examination is properly conducted and interpreted (that is the key), the results are sufficiently indicative of truth and falsehood. Other states agree. Though controversial, the tests are commonly used for business hiring and security clearances—for good reason.

In the spring of 1981 Steve was hoping for a summer trial. But as the days slipped by, a fall trial seemed more likely. But even this failed to materialize.

After an October 19 date was set, O'Donnell explained to Steve and Lois that an unforeseen emergency had arisen in another case that necessitated prompt Supreme Court action. He accordingly requested a continuance until November 19. This meant that the new year was the earliest the trial could begin. In reality, several more months would pass before the trial commenced.

In the meantime, Steve sought employment. Four weeks of searching led him to the Holiday Inn organization, where he was offered a temporary position as a reservationist in the Midwest Central Reservation Office in nearby Oakbrook. The job lasted five months. Twice, Steve was selected "Salesman of the Month" and received gold jewelry for his efforts. He proudly gave one award to Lois, the other to his mother. He also won a drawing for two days in a Holiday Inn in Wisconsin—a break he and Lois needed. The tedium of waiting for the trial was beginning to wear on them.

Mrs. Lynn Smid, Steve's floor supervisor, had this to say about him:

I found him very thorough and conscientious. I was always very impressed with his concern to get the best possible deals for his customers. He was very persistent and, at the same time, supportive of me. He never hesitated to suggest changes if he thought there was a chance of improvement. . . . He related well to people and had the ability to develop excellent rapport with guests. A local travel agency wrote him a complimentary letter praising him for his very personable and courteous manner.

When the job ended, Steve led Bible studies at Austin Center and worked for Servicemaster until around Thanksgiving—the first anniversary of Steve's arrest. A few days after Thanksgiving Steve returned to Emmaus as a full-time student, thanks to financial assistance from the GI Bill. At the same time he secured a position in the correspondence school as a part-time instructor, a position he held for six months until his trial.

Working in the penal division of the school, Steve helped grade courses from inmates in a five-state area, including Illinois. His involvement opened up opportunities for a counseling ministry. Theologically, the students' questions kept him on his toes and necessitated many hours of meticulous research. As Steve said, "I found that I was able to draw on my own brief experience in Cook County Jail and, as a result, was able to build a good rapport with my students. I understood their problems and fears, I knew their loneliness and identified with their frustrations. Was God wanting to use my own prison experiences for the benefit of those now incarcerated? Or was God using my present ministry to help prepare me for another term of imprisonment? God was certainly using me for the benefit of others, and I was conscious of growth in my life. But for what purpose? That was one question I was unable to answer."

The support the Linscotts received from the community never ceased to amaze them. It amazed their critics too. Sometimes Steve and Lois wondered if acquaintances really held them under suspicion but were just being courteous. But they could find no evidence of this. Instead, people were friendly, sympathetic, and genuinely interested in the case. No one appeared to steer away from Steve or show any alarm in his presence.

There were no negative reactions among the Emmaus staff and students to Steve's return. In fact, the administration welcomed him back; he had always been a positive influence on campus. Nancy Schaeffer Nelson, a fellow student, remarked, "We were so impressed with him. He was for real! And a great example to the student body. We didn't believe for one moment Steve could have done it."

It was good to be back in the classroom. Steve had missed the studies and realized that he needed its discipline. With the mission-field still primarily in view, Steve enrolled in courses on the Pastoral Epistles and Pastoral Theology. But his studies during the next two quarters served another purpose: they helped take his mind off his anxieties. By the end of that school year, despite all the interruptions, Steve had almost concluded his second year of Bible studies.

Occasionally the Linscotts would speculate about the possibility of a conviction. They knew that countless innocent people had been convicted, sentenced, and imprisoned.

The very thought of it happening to them was appalling. *Lord, you wouldn't do that to us, would you?* they prayed.

Sometimes Steve would ask his Christian friends, "Do you think God would allow me to go to prison for a crime I didn't commit?" The example of Joseph frequently came to mind. And the thought scared him.

All Steve and Lois could do was to trust their lawyer and hope in God.

Desperately Steve and Lois tried to shake off their anxieties, which were compounded by the compassion Steve felt for those prisoners to whom he ministered through the mail. Perhaps God wanted him to be with them, to help them further. *Lord, what are You preparing me for?* he prayed.

In many respects the months of waiting and anxiety were fruitful. Steve and Lois grew closer and experienced an intimacy far greater than anything they had previously known in their marriage. While some marriages fall apart for lesser reasons, Steve and Lois found that their marriage not only held together, but it grew stronger.

The brightest spot in these troubled months came in January 1982 with the birth of Victoria Christine. Vicki was their pride and joy, a symbol of hope for the future.

The new year brought with it an imminent setting of the trial date. The February 3 edition of *Oak Leaves* announced that jury selection would begin on March 15. Again, the *Oak Leaves* article was generally helpful to Steve. "He didn't do it," the paper quoted O'Donnell as saying. "He was helping the police. He had a dream. The young man offered his dream for whatever value it had and ends up getting charged with a very, very serious crime. He's got an impeccable background." O'Donnell mentioned the well-known use of psychics in criminal cases and stated that this would have to come up in the Linscott case. While he was not sure Steve was psychic, he referred to one premonition of Steve's that had come to pass. "The trial should be fascinating," O'Donnell said. Then he admitted to spending the past year gathering the witnesses and scientific evidence necessary to defend Steve. "The State's Attorney's office will have a difficult time substantiating the case," he concluded.

O'Donnell prepared a number of pre-trial motions and was anxious to hear Judge Schrier's rulings. But on the very day scheduled for the new preliminary hearing, Harry Schrier started hemorrhaging. He was rushed from his chambers, and the hearing was postponed indefinitely. After extensive medical tests and examinations, a malignant tumor was discovered, and Harry A. Schrier retired from the bench.

The search for a new judge began. While the lack of continuity was unfortunate, the Linscotts accepted the break as the overruling providence of God. The Fourth District Circuit Court appointed Judge Adam Stillo to preside over the trial—the fourth judge to be assigned to the case. As an Associate Judge, he had a reputation for competence and cautiousness. He was seeking public election to the status of "full Circuit Court judge" later that year. The main draw-back in his assignment to the case, and the reason Steve chose a jury rather than a bench trial, was his lack of experience in felony cases. The options at the Maywood Circuit Courthouse were, by this time, extremely limited. Stillo was one of the few remaining judges who did not have a prior identifiable interest in the case, although later, he was heard to say, "I've been assigned to that dreamer case."

The Court convened before Judge Stillo on Monday, April 19. The intent was to rule on four motions relating to evidence. Memorandums relating to these motions had been filed earlier by the defense counsel, and the State was thereby given the opportunity to prepare their rebuttals. The

State's case rested on certain pieces of evidence, and the intent of the defense motion was to have the Court declare each item inadmissible.

The first motion attempted to secure the Court's exclusion of the taped interviews that the police had made during Steve's questioning the week after the murder. The next motion objected to the introduction into evidence of the transcripts of those tape recordings; first on the grounds that the substance of the taped material should not be admissible; then on the basis that the transcripts themselves violated what is called the "best evidence rule." The third motion endeavored to exclude certain testimony as it related to hair samples on the basis that positive forensic identification by hair samples is scientifically impossible. The final motion sought to exclude the police artist's sketch on the grounds that Steve's description of the man was not substantive, but only the result of what he saw in a dream.

The motions were argued at length by the defense counsel and opposed by John E. Morrissey for the State. Each side cited relevant cases as the discussions went back and forth. Basically, O'Donnell argued that the tapes, the transcripts, and the sketch were all the result of either a dream or Steve's impression of that dream. The State contended that the dream was fabricated and in essence amounted to an admission of the murder.

Judge Stillo took the view that the onus of proof lay with the State and that the jurors could judge whether it was a dream or an admission of guilt. The value of hair samples was also left to the jury to decide. To the disappointment of Steve and all his supporters, Judge Stillo asked both sides to resolve what they could out-of-court, and he denied all four motions.

In the end, the State withdrew some of its objections, and the police artist's sketch was not admitted into evidence.

This avoided what would have become an extremely heated debate for a variety of reasons.

At issue was the fact that the sketch bore some resemblance to Steve. The police officers contended that he provided the artist with his own "ballpark" description. Steve argues that the artist was not drawing what he was telling him, that he never mentioned eyeglasses or sideburns, that the artist repeatedly gazed at him and continued drawing. On one side was the testimony of a young man battling for his life. On the other was the word of a young police officer with "no axe to grind." Who was telling the truth? To help resolve the issue, Steve was still willing to take a polygraph test—providing the police officer took one too.

Steve extended his polygraph challenge to every instance of significant dispute, so confident was he that he was telling the truth and had nothing to hide.

During the pre-trial motion hearing the State served notice that the taped interviews would assume significant importance in the trial. O'Donnell realized this and for that reason challenged the admissibility of the dream evidence on the grounds of relevancy. His search, aided by a legal computer system, failed to find a single case that dealt directly with the admissibility of dream evidence in the course of a trial. If it was simply a dream, as Steve and his lawyer argued, then this trial would become unique in American judicial history.

At the trial the burden of proving that Steve's dream was in fact a confession lay with the State, and the State, of course, had to prove its case beyond a reasonable doubt. In spite of this fact, not a single expert was called to testify regarding the dream evidence.

Although the defense felt confident that the prosecution could not prove their case beyond a reasonable doubt, one nagging thought persisted. O'Donnell was afraid that the dream evidence, with its possible link with the supernatural, might prejudice the jury against Steve.

The final item of business at the April 19 hearing was the setting of the trial date. May 24, 1982, was set for the selection of the jury.

8
Trial
by Jury

A roar of conversation rose from the crowd gathered in the halls of the Fourth District Circuit Court in Maywood. One by one, each person was led down the hallway, through Judge Stillo's courtroom, and into the jury room beyond. From this group of singles, marrieds, fathers, mothers, and grandparents too, a twelve-member jury and two alternates would be carefully selected. These people needed to be free of bias and to represent a cross-section of the community.

Judge Stillo reminded them to keep three things in mind: First, the innocence of the defendant should be presumed until all the evidence had been heard and argued. Second, the doctrine of "reasonable doubt" was always to be applied. Third, the burden of proving guilt rested with the State; the defendant is *not* required to prove his innocence.

Each prospective juror was interviewed by the judge

and the attorneys. Some were excused because they did not meet the jury profile in the minds of the attorneys. For instance, one person, a clinical psychologist, posed a threat to the prosecution's dream-as-confession argument. Several others were excused because they were related to policemen or lawyers. One man, who lived near the murder scene, was excused because he had read about the case in the newspapers. Another man admitted that he felt a trial carried the presumption of guilt. He was dismissed.

One woman had been mugged in Oak Park seven months earlier. Another woman was having problems closing on the sale of her home; she felt the legal hassles would distract her during the trial. Another woman was the wife of the pastor of a Missionary Baptist Church. A schoolteacher had difficulty accepting presumption of innocence. A young secretary was not sure she could sign a guilty verdict even if the State proved its case beyond reasonable doubt. A financial controller of a well-known insurance company had prosecuted and defended servicemen in military courts-martial. All were excused.

By late afternoon on the second day, forty-two people had been interviewed, and twenty-eight had been excused. This left twelve jurors and two alternates to try the facts of the Linscott case.

On Thursday, May 27, 1982, eighteen months after Steve's arrest, Judge Stillo opened the proceedings: "Ladies and gentlemen of the jury. You have been called to this courtroom in connection with the criminal case in which an indictment, consisting of four counts—three counts of murder and one count of rape—is rendered against the defendant, Mr. Steven Paul Linscott. He is seated at the defense table and is represented by his attorney, Mr. Arthur O'Donnell, who is assisted by Mr. Dennis Doherty.

"The State's Attorney of Cook County, Mr. Richard Daley, is represented by his assistants, Mr. Jay Magnuson and Mr. John Morrissey. My name is Adam Stillo. I am the judge of the Circuit Court and will preside over this trial."

The judge then proceeded to read the State's charges against Steve: "In December 1980 a grand jury indicted Steven Paul Linscott stating that on October 4, 1980, at and within the said County of Cook, he committed the offense of murder in that he intentionally and knowingly beat, strangled, and killed Karen Ann Phillips, with a tire iron in his hand without lawful justification.

"On the same date, October 4, 1980, Steven Paul Linscott committed the offense of murder in that he beat, strangled, and killed Karen Ann Phillips, with a tire iron in his hand, knowing that such beating and strangling made it a strong probability of death or great bodily harm to Karen Phillips, without lawful justification.

"Also, on October 4, 1980, Steven Paul Linscott committed the offense of murder in that while committing a forceable felony—to wit rape, he beat, strangled, and killed Karen Ann Phillips, with a tire iron in his hand, without lawful justification.

"Also on October 4, 1980, Steven Paul Linscott, a person of the age of twenty-four years and upwards, committed the offense of rape in that he had sexual intercourse with Karen Ann Phillips, a female, not the husband of the said Karen Ann Phillips, by force against her will."

Judge Stillo then ascertained that none of the prospective jurors knew any of the prosecuting or defense attorneys, Mr. Linscott, or any of the court officials, including himself. He then read the names of the prospective witnesses and invited any juror who had knowledge of any of them to say so. Finally, reading from his notes, the judge addressed the jurors: "At this time I shall touch upon certain boundaries,

117

fundamental principles of law, that apply to all criminal cases in order to assist you further in understanding and following the evidence and law of the case.

"Remarks at this time are not considered by you as instructions by the Court in this case. The indictments that I read earlier are not to be considered as evidence or presumption of guilt against the defendant. They are merely formal charges necessary to place the defendant upon trial.

"The defendant, under the law, is presumed to be innocent of all charges in the indictment. This presumption remains with the defendant through the trial . . . until you have been satisfied by the evidence in the case of the guilt of the defendant, beyond a reasonable doubt. The burden of proving the guilt of the defendant beyond a reasonable doubt is upon the State. The law does not require the defendant to prove his innocence."

The judge then charged the jury not to allow prejudice or sympathy to influence their verdict, but to decide the case on the law and the evidence. The instructions were routine and none of the points were emphasized or explained.

But it became obvious that the judge's words seemed only a formality to certain jurors. One juror claimed to have reached his decision after the first day—"I just know he's guilty," he said to one of the alternates. When informed that bond had been set at $450,000, another juror remarked, "A sure sign of his guilt." One juror exposed his colleagues to information extraneous to the trial, and another brought a newspaper clipping reporting aspects of the trial into the jury room. One juror was so deeply disturbed by the trial that he confidentially discussed it with his pastor, who met with him again and prayed with him as he agonized over his decision. He so badly wanted to do what was right that he overlooked the instructions of the Court not to discuss the case with anyone. Yet another juror admitted after the trial

that he knew Steve was a liar (and therefore guilty) because
of Steve's testimony that he didn't know Karen. This juror
assumed anyone would know his neighbors after a month,
even if they live in apartment houses.

At that time, none of these incidents was reported to
Judge Stillo. But much later, Bertha Schlienz, one of the
alternates, reported some of these misdemeanors to the
defense. During the trial, she impressed O'Donnell because
she listened intently, nodded from time to time, and as the
trial progressed, appeared sympathetic toward Steve. A
committed Christian, she was an active member of a large
Baptist church in one of Chicago's southern suburbs.

When Bertha was asked why she hadn't reported these
incidents of jury prejudice to the judge, she replied, "I didn't
know I could approach the judge."

Did the Court err in not adequately instructing the
jurors or in assuming they could comprehend the instructions read to them? The defense and the State could only
hope that the jury was free of bias.

9
Faith
on Trial

On Tuesday, June 1, 1982, Jay Magnuson, Senior Attorney in the Fourth District Circuit Court in Maywood, Illinois, began the State's prosecution of the case*: "We intend to give you a brief outline of this case—an outline of the evidence that we expect from the witness stand. We also want to tell you what we think the facts will prove. I would like to take opportunity at this time to apologize for any misstatements I make now, or later on in the trial during the closing arguments. If there is anything that I say now that differs from what you hear from the witness stand you are to disregard what I have said.

"We believe the evidence will show there was once a young lady named Karen Ann Phillips who was raised in North Carolina. Subsequent to completing a year or two at

*I (the author) have highlighted in italics several statements that would emerge as major points of controversy in the course of the trial.

Aurora College, she came to the Oak Park area, obtained an apartment on Austin Boulevard, and attended a nursing school in the city. The evidence will also show that she was found dead in her apartment on October 4, 1980.

"We believe the evidence will show that on October 3, 1980, Karen was at school, went to the hospital where she worked, and spent the day there. She left at approximately 4:30 that afternoon. She was next seen about 6:30 that evening at the Hindu Kriya Temple in Chicago. We expect the evidence to indicate that Karen Phillips was a religious person—that was part of her religion.

"We expect the evidence to show that Karen was at the Temple from approximately 6:30 in the evening on October 3 until 10:00, at which time she went home. We can show she went home because one of her girl friends, Helen Palella, spoke to her on the telephone at 10:30. These two girls made arrangements to meet the next morning to go shopping and then, I believe, on to a party after that.

"Helen Palella will tell you that Karen did not appear. She and another person began making inquiries. She went over to Karen's residence and inquired of the gentleman who lived next door whether or not he had seen any activity. At that point she and her friend called the police.

"We expect the police to testify that they responded, along with the Fire Department of Oak Park, to what they call a 'welfare check.'

"We expect the evidence to show that when these men entered the apartment they saw Karen Phillips lying face down in her living room, in a pool of blood, her mangled body lying there with her nightgown pulled up and wrapped around her throat.

"We expect the evidence to disclose that there were multiple wounds about her head, shoulders, neck, and legs; that she was on her face; that her legs were slightly spread apart; and that she was lying underneath her gown.

121

"We expect the evidence to show that the Oak Park police immediately began canvassing the area, going door to door making inquiries of various individuals. 'Did you see anything unusual? Did you hear anything unusual?' Among the people who were interviewed that Saturday afternoon on October 4 was Steve Linscott. He gave no information to the police at that time.

"For a period of three days the police were without a clue in this case ... until approximately 9:30 Monday evening. At that time Investigator Robert Scianna of the Oak Park Police Department received a telephone call from a man who stated he would like to pass on some information about the murder.

"Investigator Scianna immediately obtained the individuals's name and address. His name was Steven Linscott. He lived at 316 North Austin Boulevard, two doors away from where Karen's body was found. Karen had lived at that address for approximately one year and Steven Linscott had been in the area of 316 Austin Boulevard as a worker and then lived there until the fall of 1980.

"That telephone call to Investigator Scianna began a series of statements by Mr. Linscott which indicated his knowledge of certain facts of this crime. We would submit to you, Ladies and Gentlemen, knowledge of these facts could only be known by two people—Karen Ann Phillips ... and her killer.

"The evidence will show that during the telephone conversation Investigator Scianna was told that this information came to Mr. Linscott in a dream as he slept two doors away from Karen Phillips. Mr. Linscott described the murderer as a white male, blond, husky, in his twenties or thirties wearing a terry cloth *T-shirt with stripes,* possibly purple.

"Mr. Linscott further told Investigator Scianna that the

122

victim and the offender were comfortable together; that the offender beat the victim with a short heavy object, *possibly a tire iron;* that this happened in a living room setting; that the victim was on her hands and knees; that her face was down to the ground and that she seemed to be at peace. Some way into this conversation Investigator Scianna motioned to his partner, Investigator Grego, to pick up the phone. At the close of the conversation Mr. Linscott was asked to write down the facts for later pick-up.

"The evidence will show that Investigator Scianna, in the company of Sergeant Mendrick, did go to the Good News Mission, where Mr. Linscott was living and picked up a written statement. You will have opportunity to read that statement in conjunction with other statements made by the defendant. When the two officers picked up the handwritten statement there was further conversation in regard to the dream and Mr. Linscott demonstrated to the officers the manner of the beating.

"We expect the evidence to show that on October 8, two days after the original phone call, Mr. Linscott went to the Oak Park Police Station and had extensive conversations with Investigators Scianna and Grego. These conversations were partly tape-recorded. There are three tapes. Mr. Linscott again returned to the Oak Park Police Department on October 10 and had further conversations with the officers. Those conversations were also tape-recorded. Again, there are three tapes pertaining to those conversations. You will hear the tapes. There are five and a half to six hours [of] conversation. It is critically important that you listen to the similarities that correspond to the actual facts from the scene of the crime.

"You will hear Mr. Linscott describe the setting, where this took place and how Karen Ann Phillips was attacked. He will describe the victim, her background . . . and the motivation and thought process of the murderer. As the tapes are played you will hear the defendant approached by the police. The first approach is basically, "What have we got here?" Another approach is inquisitive, "Can you give us some more information; where are we going to find this guy?" You will hear them get friendly with Linscott and talk, probably for a whole tape, on religion. Finally, in the last tape you will hear the police officer put it on him, just cold right out, and accuse him of the crime.

"While they were making a composite on the third tape all you will hear is a "shirl" [sic]. I ask you to be patient and listen to those portions of the tapes, just like any other. It is critical that you listen to the details on those tape-recordings because through them Mr. Linscott reveals himself. *He reveals knowledge that could only be known by the murderer of Karen Ann Phillips;* knowledge that compares to the other facts which we will introduce at this trial.

"The defendant describes the murderer. *The description generally fits Mr. Linscott in most respects;* five foot five to five foot seven, square chested, blond hair, fair skin. He describes the lighting; you will hear from the officers and see from the photographs that there was a chandelier in the apartment, there was also a table lamp. Then there was a small table which will be referred to as an altar. It had religious pictures on it and three or four candles. This is important because at various stages of the rendition of the dream you will hear about the lighting conditions. Mr. Linscott says there was possibly a stereo in the room—the photographs show a stereo in the room. He describes a couch off to the side—Karen Ann's bed and mattress is over to the side. He said the murderer had a door to his back—you will see the doors in the apartment and regardless of where the murderer was standing, there is a door to his back. He describes the lighting conditions and says there is a dark area around—you will see around, and across, the ceiling big, thick dark wooden beams; there are dark wooden panels around certain walls in the apartment.

"He says this incident took place in one room. As serious and brutal as this attack was, he says it occurred in one place. From the photographs you will see that, regardless of how brutal the attack was there was no running into the kitchen, no running into the bathroom. It all took place right there in the middle of the living room floor.

"*Mr. Linscott initially described the weapon as possibly a tire iron, he described it to another individual as a tire iron. But, he basically abandons that description as the tape progresses.* He then refers to the weapon as some blunt object; he describes it as roundish at one end, not machine welded, dark, rough metal, tapering down but not to a point at the other end—the exact description of a tire iron. We expect the police to take the witness stand and testify that they scouted the neighborhood and that in the bushes outside Karen's apartment they found a tire iron. You will hear from the laboratory people that Karen Ann Phillips's hair and type O blood was on the tire iron.

"Mr. Linscott says he obtained this knowledge in a dream at approximately 1:00 in the morning and that the attack was quite late. We expect a witness will say that he lived in the apartment next to Karen's and that at approximately 1:00 in the morning he heard unusual sounds. He left his apartment, knocked on Karen's door, but no one responded. He returned to his apartment and heard further noises, but he will not be able to tell you anything regarding the words spoken. Mr. Linscott's time frame is exactly the time Karen Ann Phillips was killed.

"Mr. Linscott will tell you that in his dream there were no screams—the next door neighbor will tell you that as vicious as this attack was, there were no screams.

"In later renditions of the dream on the tapes, the defendant says she had nothing on, or very little. You will see the photographs of Karen Phillips as she lay there, face down with a gown completely pulled around her neck.

"Mr. Linscott had the feeling that the murderer was close by. There he is two doors down from where the murder took place.

"Listen closely to the portions of tape where he describes the attack. He describes the murderer swinging from above, then down to the waist and finally below his knees. Listen to him describe the victim as she goes down from the standing position, onto her hands and knees, her elbows, then onto her face. Listen to the Coroner's report regarding the rug burns on her forearms and elbows, rug burns and abrasions on the palms of her hands. You will hear that the frontal face abrasions were consistent with her face being on the carpet as the tire iron was landing on the back of her neck. These are facts which the man who would have been there would have known.

"Think again when you get to the point where Mr. Linscott describes the incredible passiveness of the victim. Then look at the crime scene photos. There is no struggle. There is no fight. Karen has virtually no defense wounds on her hands. There was no running from one room to the next throwing things at each other—just as Mr. Linscott says. Passiveness! Take that into account when you hear the people, who were with her that night at the Temple, tell of the peaceful nature of their religion. Then look at the photographs of Karen Ann Phillips; her fingers are together in a meditative position, indicative of the peacefulness and acceptance of her religion.

"*The beating itself, Mr. Linscott says, was seven times to the head,* then all about the body. There are approximately fifty-four wounds on Karen Phillips's body. There are nine marks on her head. One is a minor bruise, another is a minor abrasion. There are seven major lacerations, most of which fractured her skull, damaging her brain. Mr. Linscott describes the attacker as methodical, calculated, and calm.

"Ultimately, in the later renditions as Mr. Linscott talks, he talks and talks and talks and even ventured an opinion as to what the victim's background was. You hear that Karen Ann Phillips went to high school in North Carolina. She did *a year or two at Aurora College* then continued her education as a nursing assistant at Rush Presbyterian. Mr. Linscott describes the victim as not crude, somewhat intelligent, somewhat educated—high school and probably a little beyond. . . . It is a fair inference that he knew about the background of the victim before that so-called dream.

"Take into account these facts and statements, there are more on tape; they will show you that *the defendant has guilty knowledge of this crime.*

"But that is not where the case ends. The evidence will show that on October 10, between the second and third tape, Mr. Linscott voluntarily gave hair samples from his head and pubic region, blood, and saliva. Evidence will show that these items were compared with items taken from the apartment and Karen Phillips's body. You will hear how the police took what they call hair standards from her head and pubic region. We expect to show that two pubic hairs, dissimilar to Karen Phillips's matched the defendant's. The rug on which Karen was lying was ripped out, rolled out and shipped to the laboratory. From the rug another group of hairs was obtained—the head hairs of Steve Linscott.

"We expect the scientific evidence to show that there was seminal material in Karen's vagina. From the position of her body and clothing, and because of the beating, it looked as if Karen Phillips was raped. We expect the evidence will show that an analysis of Steve Linscott's saliva revealed him to be a non-secretor. The experts will explain from the witness stand that 85 percent of the public are secretors. All that means is that their blood type can be detected from their sweat, saliva, seminal material, or vaginal fluid. From this test many suspects are isolated, eliminated, or otherwise shown to be the semen donor. When the laboratory tested the vaginal swab they could not determine a blood type *because it came back consistent with a non-secretor*—15 percent of the population. Mr. Linscott could not be eliminated.

"There was nothing more we could do in the United States to eliminate Mr. Linscott. But there was one further test that could be done on the vaginal smear—a test that is not dependent upon an individual being a secretor or a non-secretor. Unfortunately, that test could not be performed here. The forensic scientist, Mohammad Tahir, was flown to Scotland Yard where he performed further tests on that smear which had been frozen in liquid nitrogen. He was looking for a gamma marker. He will testify that from blood tests from Karen Ann Phillips and Steve Linscott, and an admixture of their body fluids, he expected to get a reading of [sic] plus one, plus two. *When he finally did the test in Scotland Yard he came up with a reading consistent with a mixture of fluids from Karen Phillips and Steve Linscott.*

"We expect the evidence will show that Mr. Linscott will put up an alibi defense—that he was dreaming this exact occurrence simultaneously as it was being enacted two doors away.

"But this case goes further! Upon his arrest on November 25, he was told that he was arrested because his hairs matched. While he was being processed in Oak Park Police Station he had conversations with Officer Mendrick. During the course of those conversations *Mr. Linscott said, in essence, that the Devil gave him the dream when his armor*

*was down and that if they were his hairs in the apartment,
the Devil put them there. Mr. Linscott went even further in
those conversations and told the officer that when he woke
up the day following the so-called dream he examined his
subconscious.* That is not the only thing Mr. Linscott told
him. *He said that he examined his right arm to see if it was
sore, that anybody swinging a tire iron like that would have
a sore arm, but his was not sore.*

"The tapes and photographs tell it all. It is told by a
person who had to be there. Put the parts together your-
selves. Solve the crime!

"You are a cross-section, probably one of the best cross-
sections of society that a jury has ever been impaneled from.
We expect you to use your common sense, rationality, logic,
and your experience in life to decide this case. We will give
you the defendant's knowledge of the crime. We will give
you the scientific evidence. We will give you the facts. The
defendant will give you a dream."

Magnuson's opening argument was effective. He scored
heavily in the opening round and left an overall impression
in the minds of some jurors that was never erased by the
defense arguments.

O'Donnell had decided long before to stay away from
the dream, believing the defendant's record would speak for
itself. Magnuson had succeeded in making the crime fit the
dream. Upon closer examination, the "similarities" are, in
fact, strikingly dissimilar and actually consistent with Steve's
innocence.

As Steve sat there, Psalm 56:5 flashed into his mind: "All
day long they twist my words; they are always plotting to
harm me." Then he thought of Psalm 59:7: "See what they
spew from their mouths—they spew out swords from their
lips, and they say, 'Who can hear us?'"

Then it was O'Donnell's chance. In his opening argument he told the jury about Steve's background, including his academic interests, particularly psychology and philosophy, and various achievements. He told of Steve's varied work experience and excellent military record. He emphasized Steve's clearances for top-secret assignments and posting to the flagship of the American Seventh Fleet. He mentioned Steve's assignment to Guam and transfer to staff headquarters there. He alluded to his conversion and mentioned that he had been an announcer for a missionary radio station on the island. O'Donnell told about Steve's interest in Bible school, the summer activities in Maine, and Steve's duties at Austin Center of the Good News Mission.

Then he concentrated on the tragedy of Saturday, October 4. "Sometime in the middle of the afternoon several squad cars, an ambulance, and a number of people, including police officers, were in the area. Naturally, it attracted the attention of the residents in the area. About 4:00, police officers inquired of various neighbors if they had heard anything unusual the night before. Steve Linscott will tell you that he recalled a dream he had the night before. You will hear about the dream. I am not going to characterize it for you because I don't think it is my function to try to color, by my interpretation, the evidence that you will hear and read.

"Because of the nature of the tragedy I am sure everybody in the area spent time talking and thinking about the incident and ascertaining certain facts. Who was involved? Was it male or female? What were the circumstances?

"The next day Steve mentioned his dream to a resident staff member of the Center. He discussed the dream with his friend and asked if he thought he should call the police. The police have used dreams and psychic experiences in solving crimes. You will hear that admitted to in the tapes. Steve

130

talked to another fellow at the Center about the dream. You will be asked to determine whether he was resisting something or was actually skeptical of his own thoughts and the dream. I don't know whether he had a dream or thought he had a dream. I don't think it is important in this case.

"On Monday he talked to his wife about the dream after she had read the newspapers and told him that it was a girl who was involved and furnished him with other information. Finally, that evening he called the police and told them about his dream. You will see the original unabridged narration of the dream. The police came to the house, he gave them the document and had a conversation with them about it. They then left.

"The next day Steve was called by the police because the police officers wanted to talk to him about his dream. He appeared there Wednesday night. The police officers were very interested in his dream. They asked him to analyze it, dissect it, embroider on it, and to add to it while they had a three-way discussion about the crime. I am not going to characterize those tapes for you. You are going to hear them completely!

"They called him back to the police station on Friday night. 'Tell us about your dream again,' they said. About half way through the second tape Steve stopped the police officers and said, 'Wait a minute, you know, I have been thinking since I was in here last Wednesday that you fellows suspect me.' You will hear their response, 'Oh no!' At the very hour they were assuring Mr. Linscott that he was not a suspect in the case, unbeknown to him, police officers and Mr. Magnuson were searching—"

"Objection, Judge, that is not true," said State's Attorney Magnuson from the prosecutors' desk.

O'Donnell continued, "—were conducting a search at his home.

"Finally, they asked him if he could get into this person's head. What did he feel like? Where do you think he would go? How would you reach him if you had the opportunity to have contact with him? Steven participated and cooperated with them. Very near the end of the second tape he very innocently asked if he could talk to one of his counselors at school about how he would handle this person from his training as a minister. The police officers panicked! That will be obvious from the tape. They knew that once this unsophisticated rural young man, who had never been arrested for anything in his life (except for going through a stop sign), who had never been in a police station before, who was led by these police officers into believing that he was helping and cooperating with them; they knew that if he were to consult with older experienced persons somebody would advise him to get a lawyer.

"Then, they asked him if in order to exclude him as a suspect in this case, he minded if they took certain tests? No! He let them search the trunk of his car—they had already searched his home—and he voluntarily gave samples of what they wanted. They went to the hospital. The results of those samples were not immediately available. Nobody knew what the results would be until five or six weeks later . . . in fact not until November 19.

"They no sooner returned to the police station than they put it on him. You will hear the tape! 'We know you did it! Those tests are going to convict you! They are going to send you to the electric chair!' They proceeded to tell him everything—even his actual motive for murder. 'You were attracted to this girl. You wanted to have sex with her. She refused, and so you killed her!' That is what they said! Listen to those tapes yourself.

"The fact of the matter is that the police were convinced that he was guilty, based upon those tapes. They firmly and fervently believed those tests would confirm their belief. But, lo and behold, it did not turn out that way! They had irrevocably committed themselves to a course of action from which they could not withdraw or retreat.

"Approximately one of every five people on the face of the earth are non-secretors. Mr. Magnuson says 85 percent are secretors; the figures are somewhere between 15 and 20 percent. That means three of you sitting on the jury are probably non-secretors. The tests showed that Steven had AB blood type, Karen had type O blood. Okay, AB and O. Now, if Steven had been a secretor (if he had been four out of the five) and a vaginal swab came out ABO–AB that would be somewhat indicative of his guilt. Even then it only put him in a class of people. It does not positively prove him to be the person; it puts him within a class of people who could have had sexual intercourse with her.

"The police were convinced that the tests would reveal that. But it was not to be! His non-secretor status failed to positively, and scientifically, exclude him. That is not proof of guilt! There is nothing in those tests that established guilt.

"Mr. Magnuson says that the evidence will show that the hairs will match those of Steven Linscott. Listen very carefully to the man whom he is going to rely upon. Any responsible scientist knows that it is impossible to determine whether a particular hair comes from a particular head. It is really impossible from the test they submitted his hair to. You will hear the scientist say that he never uses the word 'identical.' For the past four or five years he hasn't even used the word 'similar.' All he really uses is the term 'consistent with.' What this really means is that 'it is not inconsistent with.'

"The fact of the matter is that the State has no evidence in this case, other than those tapes. In them the police cause the scenario structure. They recorded them! They interpret

133

the tapes to suit themselves. Let me show you how significant that is.

"On October 10, after they had taken him to the hospital and put it on him, he did not confess! Hear the tapes. He could not believe what the police were doing! Actions speak louder than words. They knew they had to release him. What does this mean? Simply, based upon what they had heard (in those tapes) they could not even hold him in custody. And if the tests did not add to it, and I am sure the evidence will show they did not, then they themselves were expressing nothing other than their own personal belief. Even they knew that that was not enough.

"When those test results came back seven or eight weeks after the incident, and they had not pursued their investigations, the police, then, had to make a decision, for they were in a dilemma. They are arguing that the tests did not exclude him. In reality, they did not add one scintilla of anything . . . except maybe 'consistent' hair samples. I ask you to listen very carefully to the testimony about the reliability of the identification of hair samples.

"There are no fingerprints! There is no physical evidence! Steve described the bloody scene. Where is the clothing? Where is anything? They searched his house. Is there anything there? No! They did not even bother to go back and check if he had an alibi. For a week they did not even go back to Karen Phillips's apartment building where five male persons lived. They talked to a couple of residents at the time, but they did not go back to thoroughly question any of the people who lived there. You will hear from the witnesses who lived in the premises.

"At the very beginning of this case I asked you to keep an open mind and to listen carefully to all the evidence. I am not going to tell you those portions of the tapes which are grossly dissimilar to the facts of the case. But I will tell you one thing. Steve thought the victim in this case was a black woman. Karen Phillips was white! I think it became patently clear from the opening statement that the State intends to seek conviction on the basis of those tapes. The scientific evidence cannot do it for them.

"Carefully consider all the evidence in this case. Consider the background of the defendant and the things that will be brought out on cross-examination of all the witnesses. I am confident that at the conclusion you will see the woefully inadequate proof which constitutes the State's case."

Despite strong signals that the State sought a conviction on the basis of the taped interviews, O'Donnell's strategy was to avoid, as much as possible, discussion of the dream. His reluctance to confront the dream became critical as the trial continued. One thing that really influenced the jurors was Steve's supposed intimate knowledge of the crime. "He knew too much," one juror said later.

After a recess for lunch, the Court reconvened for the afternoon session and for the commencement of testimony from witnesses. These examinations, cross-examinations, and the presentation of evidence would last many days.

Judith Voeller, Professor at St. Luke's Medical Center and Karen's instructor, testified to last seeing her at approximately 4:30 on the day of her death. Phyllis Nash testified to driving Karen home that day. Jean Gersten testified to being in Karen's astrology class the night she was killed. Margie Strall told the Court that she offered Karen a ride to her car parked a couple of blocks away but that she preferred to walk. Kenneth Wiese of the Oak Park Fire Department told how he entered the apartment and found the body. Police Officer Patrick Kelly testified to his examination of the victim, the apartment, and the physical evidence at the scene of the crime.

Helen Palella told of her friendship with Karen, of their involvement at the Kriya Temple, and explained the significance of the position of Karen's fingers. "Karen died doing an 'ommudra'," she said. "It is a centering of a person trying to find a peacefulness. It is often used when one is about to die. It is also a sign of forgiveness toward those who have caused harm." Mrs. Palella testified to calling Karen and speaking with her at 10:30 the night she died, and told of the arrangements to meet the next morning.

Mohammed Azadegan, Karen's next-door neighbor, told of the voices and pounding noises he had heard coming from Karen's apartment at 1:00 in the morning. He told of his knocking on her door.

Detective Robert Scianna recounted that at 9:30 on October 6, he was in the Oak Park Police Station with his partner, Ronald Grego, Supervisor Joseph Mendrick, and Helen Palella, when Steve called. He then attested to the details discussed in earlier chapters. He testified to the striking similarity between Steve and the description of the dream assailant given over the phone. He regarded as unusual the shirt Steve wore to the police station because, he claimed, it matched the description of the assailant's shirt. He testified to Steve mentioning a tire iron when he first called the station.

Under cross-examination O'Donnell elicited some interesting facts. Scianna's report dated *November 26*, the day after Steve's arrest, was the *first* report in which he mentioned Steve's phone call of October 6. It was also the first official report he had made concerning Steve. The report was written on yellow 8 ½ by 11 note paper, instead of the usual official, serially numbered complaint forms.

In Steve's dream, the assailant's T-shirt had two, possibly three, narrow horizontal lines across the chest. The shirt Steve wore to the police station had no stripes across the chest; it had a distinct collar, partially buttoned down the front, and was dissimilar in many ways to the T-shirt in the dream. Steve's narrative makes no reference to the victim being on her knees; it states the victim was lying down or crouching. Furthermore, the narrative says that the victim was black, though Steve was not sure. He saw a couch in the dream—in reality there was no couch in Karen's apartment, only a bed. The narrative described the weapon as a bludgeon. The police consistently claimed that Steve used the term "tire iron" when he called. The words "tire iron," however, were not once mentioned in the more than five hours of taped interviews.

Leslie Sanders, an ex-offender residing at the Good News Mission, testified that Steve had told him a "piece of metal" was used. He denied that Steve had ever used the term "tire iron" in explaining the crime to the residents of the Center. Unfortunately, only a week before the trial, Sanders had used the word "tire iron" in describing the incident to the prosecutor. (After his arrest, of course, Steve used the term countless times because he had been accused of murdering a young woman with one.) The State was able to take advantage of this inconsistency in Sanders' testimony. Sanders also testified that he had gone to sleep at 1:00 or possibly a little later on the night of October 3, not 9:00 or 10:00 as he had (supposedly) previously told the prosecutor.

Despite the fact that Sanders was a key alibi witness and a committed Christian, his poor showing made O'Donnell decide not to recall him as a witness.

The prosecution then called three police officers, all evidence technicians, to testify in regard to the collection and handling of evidence.

Dr. Edmund Donoghue told of his examination of the victim and autopsy report. He described the sixty-six wounds to the body and collection of further evidence. It was a gruesome report.

At this point, over O'Donnell objections, the taped interviews, parts of which were indistinct and distorted, were admitted into evidence. For the next five hours, the tapes were played to the jury, who noted the tones and inflections and silently formed their opinions.

It was the tapes that really made Bertha Schlienz, an alternate juror, change her mind about Steve's apparent guilt. For her, the prosecutor's opening arguments were convincing. O'Donnell had failed to minimize their force. But as she heard the taped interviews, Bertha saw through the police tactics. As the tapes continued, she silently cried out, *Steve, keep your big mouth shut! You're going to get yourself in trouble.*

It was now late Friday afternoon, and the Court recessed for the weekend.

On Monday morning Judge Stillo made an unusual announcement: "Counsel, we are going to be missing one juror, Ms. Nichols. Do you remember the nurse from the clinic? She is unable to perform."

"I remember the lady very well," O'Donnell said.

"She is unable to stay awake. She had to work last night—they could not find a replacement for her. I told her that I would send a car to pick her up, but she did not think she could stay awake. So, instead of belaboring the point, I excused her."

"Your Honor, I would like to object to your excusing that particular juror . . . and respectfully ask that I make a motion for a mistrial."

"I will have to deny that. I, in my discretion, felt that she would not make a good juror because she told me that she was unable to stay awake."

"We went to rather extensive 'voir dire' examination, both the Court and Counsels for both sides," said O'Donnell. "This witness indicated that she could serve as a juror. I must respectfully object to the Court excusing her and again respectfully move for a mistrial."

"I will have to deny that," Stillo repeated.

O'Donnell was frustrated. He had particularly wanted the nurse to serve because he was impressed with her from the outset. She was alert and of excellent character. Throughout the playing of the taped interviews he had observed her (as he did each juror) and it appeared to him that she had correctly and fairly sized up the police interrogation techniques. He wanted her on the jury panel more than any other juror. And now she had been dismissed.

O'Donnell believed that Judge Stillo should have at least adjourned sessions for a day or two, which frequently happens in the case of a juror's illness. But Stillo was not prepared to entertain any indictment against himself.

Detective Scianna was then recalled for further questioning by the defense. The following excerpts of his testimony contain some interesting points:

O'DONNELL: "Do you know whether any person, other than Steven Linscott, ever submitted saliva, hair, and blood samples in connection with the investigation of the death of Karen Ann Phillips?"

SCIANNA: "Mr. Linscott is the only one."

O'DONNELL: "During the week following this incident did you know there were also five male persons residing at 316 North Austin Boulevard [the Austin Center]?"

MAGNUSON: "Objection!"

JUDGE STILLO: "Let him answer if he knows."

SCIANNA: "I know there were other male subjects living in that building. The exact number is unknown to me."

O'DONNELL: "Did you ever go and interview them during that week?"

SCIANNA: "No, sir."

O'DONNELL: "Did you ever request any of them to give samples of blood, saliva, and hair for testing?"

139

SCIANNA: "No, sir."

O'DONNELL: "Wouldn't that have been a place to go in the investigation of this case?"

MAGNUSON: "Objection."

STILLO: "Objection sustained!"

O'DONNELL: "Do you know whether the Oak Park Police obtained fingerprints from any of the residents at 324-326 North Austin [Karen's apartment building]?"

SCIANNA: "Yes, sir, there were some fingerprints obtained."

O'DONNELL: "That was Mohammed, is that correct?"

SCIANNA: "He is one, sir. Yes!"

O'Donnell was unsuccessful in eliciting from Scianna, who was using all his professional expertise under cross-examination, information concerning whether other residents of the apartment building were ever fingerprinted. O'Donnell persisted.

O'DONNELL: "Did you take fingerprints from any other person who did not reside at 324-326?"

SCIANNA: "Yes, sir, I think there were fingerprints taken from other people."

O'DONNELL: "And who was that, if you recall?"

SCIANNA: "I am not sure, but I believe Mr. Templeton's fingerprints were taken."

O'DONNELL: "And he is the landlord! Is that correct?"

SCIANNA: "He is the landlord, correct."

O'DONNELL: "Did you also take the fingerprints of David Moritz [the television repairman who, earlier that week, had been given a key to and been in Karen's apartment]?"

SCIANNA: "I did not take them."

O'DONNELL: "I am not talking about you personally. When I speak of you, I am speaking collectively. Do you know whether or not the Oak Park Police took the fingerprints of David Moritz?"

Scianna: "Mr. O'Donnell, I can only answer for myself."

O'Donnell: "I am only asking you to answer if you know whether the Oak Park Police took them?"

Scianna: "I don't recall if they were taken or not, sir."

O'Donnell: "Did you take any fingerprints from Mr. Dominick Palella?"

Scianna: "No, sir, I did not."

O'Donnell: "Can you think of any other persons that you may have requested, or that the Oak Park Police may have taken, fingerprints of?"

Scianna: "Sir, I don't recall any other names."

O'Donnell: "Well, did you request the fingerprints of Jerry McDuffie from North Carolina?"

Scianna: "No, sir, I did not."

O'Donnell: "Did you contact anyone in North Carolina in connection with the investigation of this case?"

Scianna: "No, sir, I didn't contact anyone."

O'Donnell: "Do you know whether the Oak Park Police did?"

Scianna: "Yes, sir, they did."

O'Donnell: "Do you know whether or not they may have taken fingerprints from Mr. McDuffie?"

Scianna: "I don't believe that fingerprints were taken, sir."

O'Donnell: "Do you know whether the Oak Park Police ever caused or did in fact have samples of hair, blood, and saliva taken from Mr. McDuffie?"

Scianna: "I don't believe so."

O'Donnell: "But you did check on certain people's alibis for the evening of Friday the third, didn't you?"

Scianna: "That is correct, sir."

O'Donnell: "And one person whose alibi you, or the Oak Park Police, checked was David Moritz?"

Scianna: "Yes, sir."

O'DONNELL: "And you also checked the alibi of Mr. Templeton, the landlord?"

SCIANNA: "Yes, sir."

O'DONNELL: "Who else did you or the Oak Park Police check?"

SCIANNA: "Mr. McDuffie's alibi was checked, sir."

O'DONNELL: "Did you ever go to 316 Austin where Steven Linscott lived, and where you knew there were other male residents, to check out an alibi for him?"

SCIANNA: "His alibi was checked, sir."

O'DONNELL: "When?"

SCIANNA: "I believe it was on the tenth, sir."

O'DONNELL: "Who did you talk to, or who was contacted?"

SCIANNA: "His wife."

O'DONNELL: "Do you recall whether your reports indicated if anybody else was contacted?"

SCIANNA: "I don't recall that, sir."

O'DONNELL: "Now, you took fingerprint information from Steven, didn't you?"

SCIANNA: "Yes, sir."

O'DONNELL: "And the fingerprints were compared, weren't they?"

SCIANNA: "Yes, sir."

O'DONNELL: "And they eliminated him, as far as the fingerprint evidence was concerned, isn't that correct?"

SCIANNA: "Yes, sir."

O'DONNELL: "Then why wouldn't you check with some of the residents at the house as to his alibi, like you did with Moritz, Templeton, and McDuffie?"

Magnuson objected. The judge sustained the objection, but O'Donnell had scored his point! The police had not thoroughly tried to eliminate Steve or other possible suspects.

O'DONNELL: "You also checked on Mohammed's alibi and somebody in the Oak Park Police contacted his relatives, who were there earlier that evening, isn't that correct?"

SCIANNA: "I don't recall that, sir."

O'DONNELL: *"You don't recall that!"*

It was now clear the police had not carried out a detailed, thorough investigation.

Dr. Mark Stolorow, supervisor of the forensic serologists in the crime laboratories in Illinois, was the next witness called. O'Donnell objected to his introduction into the trial at this juncture on the basis that his expert testimony would be heard ahead of the forensic scientists who had conducted the various tests. The objection was overruled, and Stolorow told the jury about the procedures of forensic examination of physical evidence in his laboratories.

He explained: "Each laboratory is equipped with two kinds of microscopes. The *compound microscope* has more than one lens and is used for magnifying hairs from fifty to four hundred magnifications, the range used for hair comparisons. The other microscope is the *comparison microscope.* It allows the examiner to see in one field of view hairs that have been put on two separate microscopes and brought together by an optical bridge. It is thus possible, microscopically, to align two hairs, compare them, and draw conclusions. Scientific examination of hair shows whether it is of human or nonhuman origin. If human, certain racial characteristics can be determined. Examination may also determine whether hairs have been removed prematurely and whether the hair has been bleached or dyed. Other characteristics, such as pigmentation, thickness of cuticle, and diameter of the hair, can also be observed. Examined longitudinally, hair tends to be flat, oval, or somewhat rounded."

Dr. Stolorow testified that "after all the features have

143

been examined [about fourteen features can be microscopically observed] it may be concluded that two hairs from the
same head, when separated, can be matched. With the
variability among human hairs, most people have enough
differentiation that the vast majority of the population may
be eliminated as a potential source for a given unknown hair.
While a person may not be positively identified from a hair
source, it is possible within a degree of scientific certainty to
conclude that hair from a known source is 'consistent with'
hair from an unknown source.

"An examination will leave the examiner to conclude
that the unknown hair did not come from the standard, that it
is 'consistent with' *all* of the features of the unknown
standard, or that the examiner is unable to reach a conclusion."

In view of his earlier objection, O'Donnell refused to
cross-examine Mark Stolorow.

At best, forensic hair comparisons using the conventional comparison microscope are speculative. Not one feature is
compared objectively. Different examiners arrive at different
conclusions. Other, more objective test analyses used by
medical science are unfortunately not used for forensic
purposes. For this reason, opinions differ concerning the
value of forensic hair analysis. Prosecutors love the vague-
ness of microscopic hair comparisons.

Mohammad Tahir, the forensic analyst from the Maywood laboratory, then testified. He spoke extensively about
the blood and hair evidence. Although much of what he said
was highly technical, the substance of his testimony (already
described) will be reviewed here.

Tahir confirmed that 80 percent of the population are
secretors and that gamma markers can be detected in body
fluids regardless of whether a person is a secretor or non-
secretor. Having initially determined Karen's and Steve's

blood groupings as ABO-O, PGM 2-1 and ABO-AB, PGM 1, respectively, he tested the vaginal swab. He said that *no* ABO and PGM blood groupings were detected.

This would indicate that the test was inconclusive because it should have at least discovered Karen's blood groupings. But the prosecution concluded that the semen found in Karen's vagina was from a non-secretor and, therefore, linked Steve to the crime. Tahir did, in fact, state that the semen could have come from a secretor *or* non-secretor, but the prosecutors claimed that the test pointed to Steve.

Further tests on the vaginal swab in December again failed to reveal any PGM blood groups. There was still no scientific basis for suspecting Steve. Yet at that point he had been arrested because, among other reasons, the Oak Park police claimed his semen "matched" that found in Karen's body. At least, that is what officers Scianna and Grego told Lois when she visited the station after Steve's arrest.

Tahir noted that the vaginal swab test results were "consistent with" the admixture of the body fluids of Karen and Steve. This was all the prosecutors needed! That the result was also consistent with the admixture of Karen's body fluids with *any* male in the world was incidental and irrelevant.

Blood tests revealed Karen's and Steve's gamma markers as GM $+1$, $+2$, $+10$ and GM -1, -2, $+10$ respectively. But unable to conduct further tests in the United States, Tahir flew to Scotland Yard for purposes of additional testing. Although the British tests produced little that was new, the prosecutors profited from the mystique that surrounds the name of Scotland Yard.

In England, Tahir detected an ABO-O blood grouping in the vaginal swab *for the first time*. Only then it could be stated with a degree of scientific accuracy that Steve could not be eliminated from the "rape." But neither could 60 percent of the male population. But the police and the prosecution ignored this statistic. Nor did the State's own experts—Stolorow and Tahir—mention this fact.

In his cross-examination, O'Donnell attacked Tahir for reporting the discovery of semen in the vaginal swab without mentioning the lack of spermatozoa; O'Donnell was suggesting the possibility that the semen donor had had a vasectomy—which Steve had not. He elicited from Tahir the admission that neither he nor anyone else could say whether Karen Phillips had had sexual intercourse within twenty-four hours of her death.

It was during this cross-examination that O'Donnell discovered that the vaginal swab had been destroyed. Yet despite its nonexistence, and over O'Donnell's objection, Judge Stillo admitted the swab into evidence.

Regarding the hair evidence, Tahir testified that he had compared certain hairs found at the scene of the crime with Karen's hair and Steve's samples. He said that hairs taken from Karen's hands, the carpet, and from her body were "consistent with" Steve's head and pubic hair, even though some Caucasian hairs were found to be dissimilar to either Karen's or Steve's. But no attempt was made to compare these with her friends, acquaintances, or other possible suspects. The Negroid hairs that were found on the bedsheets, carpet, and outside the door were not compared with any other suspect's hair.

Tahir explained that "consistent with" meant there were no dissimilarities between the "unknown" hair at the crime scene and the hair of either the victim or the defendant. He claimed to have used a comparison microscope and testified to comparing approximately twelve characteristics. Later, under cross-examination, he reduced this figure to ten, and even later, he identified only eight characteristics compared.

The State's expert witness, Dr. Stolorow, told me later that only after finding *fourteen* similar characteristics could the conclusion "consistent with" be made. Even then, he said, positive identification is not possible. Though Tahir admitted that he could not identify Steve through the hair evidence, he also said that he observed no dissimilarities. His conclusion, therefore, was that the comparisons failed to exclude Steve. He ignored the fact that the hair failed to exclude countless others too.

On Tuesday morning, June 8, the jury, attorneys, and judge visited the scene of the crime. The jurors were shown inside the security door to Karen's apartment but were not permitted to enter the building itself. In spite of O'Donnell's protests, however, they were not permitted inside the Austin Center of the Good News Mission.

In the afternoon, twenty-seven exhibits were tediously admitted into evidence. Then Sergeant Mendrick, the State's last witness, appeared and described his visit to the Austin Center, in the company of Detective Scianna, to pick up the handwritten dream document. He testified to some of Steve's questions and statements while being processed at the police station after his arrest: "What would happen if someone came in and confessed to the murder of Karen Phillips; would I be released today?" Steve had asked.

To the question, "Do you believe some people can possibly have insights into the future or dream about the future?" Mendrick had responded, "Not in your case, Steve, because *hairs matching* yours were found in the murdered girl's apartment."

After Mendrick's testimony, the State rested its case.

O'Donnell seized the opportunity to file several motions. The first was for a directed verdict in regard to the charge of rape. O'Donnell argued that there was not one shred of evidence that indicated that Karen had sexual intercourse with the defendant—or anyone else, for that matter.* Predictably, the State disagreed. O'Donnell moved for a directed verdict in regard to the other charges. Another motion pressed for the dismissal of the indictment. The fourth motion, based on the destruction of the swab evidence, called for a declaration of a mistrial. The final motion requested the judge to instruct the jury to disregard any physical evidence and the results of the swab tests.

Judge Stillo denied every motion. It appeared to Steve as though he were the victim of a conspiracy, and he consoled himself with the thought that God would intervene and rescue him.

Lois Linscott was the first witness to appear in defense of her husband. Carefully, she told her story.

Chaplain Stroup made a brief appearance and was followed by Carlos Craveiro, who testified that on the night of the murder he was in the basement of the Austin Center working on a term paper for school. He was there from about 11:30 until 1:25 when he went to the 7-11 store for coffee. He returned about an hour later.

Privately, Carlos had told the defense, apart from a brief conversation with a plain-clothes policeman when he and Jim Saucerman had gone to the station on October 10 to look for Steve, he was never even interviewed by the police. More than a year later, two officers had come to the Center and shown him a picture of a young woman, presumably Karen, and asked him if he recognized her. He didn't. For some reason, the officers were never called to the trial to ascertain their reason for this visit. A week or two before the trial Carlos was visited again by the same two officers. The State had just learned that he was to appear as an alibi witness for the defendant.

---

*The evidence about seminal traces supported the State's theory that Phillips had intercourse. Tahir was unable, however, to estimate whether the intercourse had occurred within twenty-four hours of her death.

Five character witnesses followed in quick succession: David Reid (faculty member at Emmaus), Marjorie Chesney and Susan Murphy (residents of the house where the Linscotts first lived), and myself and John Montgomery (associated with the school and River Forest Bible Chapel) appeared on Steve's behalf.

The main witness called by the defense was an expert: Dr. Kenneth Siegesmund, an associate professor of anatomy at the Medical College in Milwaukee, Wisconsin. A recognized authority on histology (the anatomical study of microscopic structure of animal and plant tissues) and neurotomy (the surgical cutting or stretching of a nerve, usually to relieve pain), Dr. Siegesmund is also a specialist in forensic science, especially in the areas of micro and biological evidence, including hair and blood.

Dr. Siegesmund's testimony regarding the hair evidence was significant. He had tested five items, all hair. First of all, he used the conventional light microscope, which provides a stereoscopic view of the hair, and a more sophisticated high-powered light microscope. Using a longitudinal view of the hair, he examined some fifteen individual characteristics of the head hair samples found on the carpet, in Karen's right hand, and Steve's head hair. Based upon a reasonable degree of scientific certainty, he found differences and similarities, and concluded that there were not enough characteristics to establish whether or not the hairs matched.

Then, using an electron microscope, unlike the prosecution, Dr. Siegesmund performed further tests on the samples from the carpet and the suspect. He explained the electron microscopy technology: "It permits the examiner to view material up to one hundred thousand times magnification. Energy dispersive analysis, used in conjunction with this high technology microscopy, enables the user to perform multi-elemental analysis of whatever materials are being viewed." He observed the characteristics of the two hairs at magnifications up to ten thousand times, then photographed the two specimens at one thousand times magnification. Details were observed that were not apparent through conventional forensic microscopy. The differences were in the scale and density structures. The scale structure of Steve's hair was more dense, more serrated than the carpet hair. In comparison, his hair contained a high level of molecular white material. Steve's hair also contained more composition than the carpet hair, which also reflected a folding of the cuticle. The professor concluded that the two hairs did not appear to have the same source.

Dr. Siegesmund then explained his X-ray elemental micro-analysis of the same three head-hair samples. He observed that two of the hairs, the ones from the carpet and right hand, "appeared very similar in that the elemental profiles fit almost like a "hand in a glove." But the suspect's hair, he noted, showed major differences. These differences were portrayed graphically and exhibited to the Court. "The carpet and hand hairs had about ten times more calcium than the suspect's. The same hairs contained silicon, whereas this was totally absent in the suspect's hair. The carpet hair had a very, very high potassium level whereas the hand and suspect's hair had relatively low potassium levels." Based upon a reasonable degree of scientific certainty, the witness gave an opinion: "The hair sample removed from the carpet could not have come from the same source as the hair from the suspect."

The judge and the jury examined the exhibits. They seemed impressed.

In his cross-examination, the prosecutor "attacked" the professor's credibility and the unconventional methods, methods not used by the Federal Bureau of Investigations, Royal Canadian Mounted Police, Scotland Yard, or any forensic crime laboratory in the country. He also criticized Dr. Siegesmund's techniques and questioned how the professor would know whether the unknown hairs compared to the suspect's were in fact the actual hairs the State claimed "matched" Steve's hair. Apparently, all the hairs recovered from the carpet, for instance, had been placed in one slide labeled, "hairs from the carpet." Magnuson emphasized the odds of Siegesmund picking and testing the one carpet hair the forensic scientist found consistent with Steve's.

Magnuson also capitalized on the fact that the tests had been done hurriedly. Siegesmund had, in fact, rushed his examination, but the reason for this was not discussed. O'Donnell had originally ordered the analyses after the jury had been selected, but the prosecution had stubbornly refused to release the evidence before they had rested their case—the day before Siegesmund's testimony. The testing had to be performed and the testimony given within a twenty-four-hour period. A series of more comprehensive high-technology tests could have been carried out had there been more time. In the end, Magnuson succeeded in casting doubt on Siegesmund's testimony.

When his turn in the stand came, Steve was nervous. He had every reason to be. His credibility depended on a good performance. He knew that a cloud hung ominously above his head—a cloud darkened by all the accusations and gory details of the case. He was also nervous about his lack of preparation before taking the stand. The first and only time Steve heard the tape-recorded interviews was during the trial itself. It had been almost sixteen months since he had read the transcripts. Now, in the most critical hour of his life, he was expected to recall every statement and comment made more than a year and a half earlier.

Understandably, Steve lacked confidence on the stand. Nervousness and uncertainty showed throughout the entire

151

examination by the defense and prosecuting lawyers. He found the questions hard to answer because he couldn't remember the details. He fared badly. Steve knew it.

Anger, frustration, and panic began to build within Steve. He later shared his concerns with Lois who agreed that his performance was far from impressive. After sitting through the trial and bearing the humiliation without flinching, he had failed in his attempt to defend himself.

Mark Stolorow, supervisor of the Illinois forensic serologists, reappeared to rebut the testimony and tests of Dr. Kenneth Siegesmund. By minimizing the forensic value of electron microscopy and elemental analysis, Stolorow probably succeeded in negating in the minds of the jurors the professor's testimony.

In an endeavor to obtain an impeachment of Lois's testimony, Detective Patrick Kelly was recalled by the State. He testified that when he, in company with Detective Toll and Assistant State's Attorney Jay Magnuson, had visited Lois on the night of October 10, she had told him that she did not know for certain whether or not Steve got out of bed on the night of October 3. Kelly also alleged that Lois told him Steve had recounted an experience when, after taking LSD he left his body and looked down, and back, to view himself.

As an experiment in college, Steve had tried LSD once. But he had never had such an experience and had never told Lois that he had. Lois denies ever making such a statement to the police but admitted that she had told police that Steve once experimented with drugs in college.

With no further witnesses, the State and the defense rested their cases. Again O'Donnell filed a motion for a directed verdict. Judge Stillo denied it. O'Donnell then resubmitted the motions filed at the conclusion of the State's case in brief. Again, all were denied.

All that remained were the closing arguments, the

Court's instructions to the jurors, the deliberation of the jury, and the verdict. Anxiously, we waited for the finale.

In the closing arguments, Assistant Prosecutor John Morrissey spoke first. In his speech, he transformed Karen's bedroom into a living room of a small apartment. In the process, however, he made several statements that were not supported by expert testimony. For instance, he said that Steve "left eight to ten hairs of his in that apartment at 324 North Austin Boulevard" and "Ladies and Gentlemen . . . Karen was raped by a non-secretor; the defendant is a non-secretor." In due course these statements would assume significant proportions.

Before closing his arguments, Morrissey made an emotional appeal to the jury: "Linscott told you that the Devil put the hairs in the apartment of Karen Ann Phillips. Well, Ladies and Gentlemen, the Devil sits before you—right here in this courtroom. As sure as I'm standing before you now, he, without remorse, ended this lady's life by beating her brains out." It seemed a deliberate misquote of Sergeant Mendrick's testimony for the purpose of swaying the jury.

Then O'Donnell addressed the jury for the last time. He spoke passionately, personally, from the heart. He argued that Steve lacked the capacity, motive, and opportunity to perpetrate such a crime. Everything known about him was totally inconsistent with the act. He had absolutely no reason to kill. Had he done so, there is no way he could have concealed the crime from his wife and friends.

O'Donnell explained to the jury how impossible it would have been for Steve to get out of bed, dress, find a tire iron (not his own), perpetrate the crime, and return to bed without leaving a single shred of evidence that positively linked him to the crime. "You have to buy that scenario. It's preposterous!" he said.

O'Donnell attacked the prosecutor: "I think one of the

things that came out in this case that I feel seriously colors this entire prosecution is the degree to which an Assistant State's Attorney got himself involved in police work. He was emotionally involved in this case and lacked any degree of objectivity. When your ego is wrapped up in it, you do not think clearly. He lets him [Steve] go home, then calls his wife, and tells her that she's got a murderer on her hands."

Then O'Donnell addressed the issue of the vaginal swab evidence: "The most single, significant element of physical evidence in this case was the vaginal swab. You've heard the description of the tests. The significance of those tests is that they can potentially exonerate or exclude a person.

"On January 9 we filed a motion for a list of all the physical evidence. On February 19 the State answered and listed the vaginal swab and blood samples. That was the first official notice that we had that they had a vaginal swab.

"On that very day, Ladies and Gentlemen, Mohammad Tahir was in London totally consuming that vaginal swab in the testing process.

"Now, maybe the import of that doesn't strike you, so I'm going to give you an analogy. One of you ladies is driving your car on First Avenue. You have your purse open next to you on the seat. You don't come to a complete stop at the sign. A policeman pulls you to the side, comes up to your window, asks for your driver's license and tells you you didn't stop at the stop sign. While you're looking in your purse for the driver's license, he sees an open packet of Sweet 'N Low. He asks, 'What is that?'

"You pull it out and say, 'It's Sweet 'N Low. I only used half of it. Sometimes I go to coffee shops and restaurants that don't have it, so I keep it in my purse.'

"He sniffs it and puts his finger in it. 'It doesn't seem to me to be Sweet 'N Low.'

" 'Well, look at the wrapper. The little pink thing. . . .' So

154

he gives you a ticket. He's got your driver's license. He knows where you live. He knows your license plates.

"He says, 'You may be hearing from us.'

"A month later you get a letter to appear before the presiding judge of the Criminal Court of Cook County. You have been charged with possession of a controlled substance. You think, 'It's ridiculous!' You tell your friends, fellow employees, and your relatives, 'This is silly; that was Sweet 'N Low.' So you hire yourself a lawyer. You go to court.

"On the day you go to court, they hand you a form, a report from the Illinois Department of Law Enforcement, Division of Supportive Services. It reads, 'On such and such a date we examined the contents of that Sweet 'N Low, and found it to contain a controlled substance,' . . . cocaine, let's call it.

"By now you say, 'This is crazy!' Your lawyer is looking a little funny at you. 'Don't worry. We can have it analyzed and tested by five or ten different laboratories if you want.'

"The next time you go to court, the State's Attorney advises you, 'I'm sorry, but the substance was all consumed in the testing.'

"It isn't funny any more, is it? But he says, 'You don't have to worry about it. Our laboratory report is from a highly accredited laboratory with very competent people.'

"You say to him, 'I don't care who did the test. I know it was Sweet 'N Low, and I'm entitled to have a test done on that substance.' He says 'Sorry!'

"On the very day that they officially advised me of the existence of the vaginal swab, they had totally consumed it, making it physically and scientifically impossible to test it— tests that might have exonerated this boy."

O'Donnell moved onto the main evidence, defended Dr. Siegesmund, and accused the State of deception. He appealed to the testimony of the tapes, the State's testimony, and the tactics of the police. He emphasized the police use of psychics, but admitted that he didn't know whether or not Steve had a dream or thought he had a dream. That statement probably hurt Steve. His reluctance to defend the dream remains one of the significant omissions of his case.

O'Donnell's concluding remarks contained a pertinent comment: "Karen Phillips's death was a tragedy! Obviously, this girl was ambitious and attractive. Her life was snuffed out. Don't let sympathy discolor your reason. If there is one tragedy greater than her death, it would be the tragedy of convicting an innocent man."

Many of Steve's supporters concluded that O'Donnell had given a brilliant closing argument. Others felt dismay that he had not said more about the dream. It is perhaps unfortunate that the trial did not end at this point, but Jay Magnuson had the last word—at least for the time being.

During his closing argument, Magnuson paced around the courtroom floor. He was like an enraged, caged lion. He demeaned Dr. Siegesmund, O'Donnell, and the five character witnesses who testified in Steve's behalf: "He argues his client is incapable of this crime. He argues that he put four [there were five] people on there and they took the witness stand and said, 'I have known him for a year and he is a good person, honest, and chaste!' How many people do you think John Wayne Gacy [convicted murderer of more than thirty young men in the Chicago area] could have put before the jury? Character witnesses can be brought for anybody, by anybody."

Magnuson did his best to prove Steve's involvement, drawing attention again to the blood tests and hair evidence that were supposed to prove Steve's involvement. He argued opportunity—Karen lived one hundred feet away. He ridiculed the alibi testimonies and O'Donnell's construction of the probable scenario. The defendant alone was "omniscient," Magnuson insisted; he alone had all the answers.

Magnuson then resorted to self-justification on behalf of himself, the police, the examiners of the physical evidence, and his colleagues—just about everyone involved in the State's case.

The prosecutor touched on the swab evidence: "The important thing is the vaginal swab. There is the gamma marker coming back with the consistency combining Karen Ann Phillips and Steven Linscott. This was a test that either included Mr. Linscott in this massive possibility or excluded him. This test was done for his benefit and to his detriment— because it could have excluded him."

Magnuson then mentioned the dream and the taped interviews. He highlighted the similarities and ignored the dissimilarities. But these dissimilarities were not stressed— by either side. The imaginative, speculative minds of the prosecutors were never seriously challenged by Steve's counsel. Magnuson was explosive. But he scored points with the jury. When he was finished, many Linscott supporters were angry, frustrated, and bitter. Some just let the tears roll down their cheeks.

Midafternoon on Tuesday, June 15, the jury filed out of the room to deliberate and reach their verdict. The spectators were tense. Some went home. Most of Steve's friends, however, lingered near the courthouse, hoping for a quick decision—an acquittal on all counts.

While the jury deliberated, Steve and Lois calmly mingled with their friends in the hallway. Inwardly, however, they felt tight, uncomfortable, and anxious. At one point John Montgomery and I drew them aside and confronted them with the possibility of a conviction. "Be prepared for jail," we warned. We then prayed with them and committed them to God for his tender, loving care. Their faith in God and the judicial system was clearly on trial.

By 8:30 that evening, when the jury adjourned for the day, more than forty of Steve and Lois's friends remained outside the courtroom. Earlier they had conducted a prayer meeting that lasted over two hours. So great was the commitment to Steve that many people managed to rearrange their schedules to attend every session of the trial.

The next morning, after two more hours of deliberation, the jurors indicated to Judge Stillo that they had reached a decision. Quickly, everyone returned to the courtroom, which overflowed with Steve's supporters. Even then, a large group stood in the hallway to pray. The doors were closed. The jurors took their seats.

Judge Stillo turned in their direction. "All right, Ladies and Gentlemen of the jury! Have you reached your verdict?"

"Yes," the foreman replied.

"Will you please hand the verdicts to the deputy?" The deputy handed them to the judge who read them, pursed his lips, and passed them on to the court clerk. "Will the clerk read the verdicts?" he asked.

"We, the jury, find the defendant, Steven Paul Linscott, not guilty of the offense of rape."

Steve and Lois heaved a sigh of relief and relaxed. Many of their supporters breathed grateful prayers.

"We, the jury, find the defendant, Steven Paul Linscott, guilty of the offense of murder."

10
Aftermath

Everyone gasped. Then there was silence. Finally, O'Donnell said, "I request that the jury be polled, your honor."

As the names were called, each juror stood and affirmed the verdict. Most were solemn. Some showed signs of an emotional strain.

The Court ordered that bond be revoked and that Steve be returned to jail. O'Donnell filed a motion to rescind the order and to reinstate bond. It was denied.

Steve was handcuffed and whisked to a back room. Within moments, Lois was at his side; Judge Stillo had permitted a brief visit. The gravity of the situation had not yet struck Steve; "Lois," he said determinedly, "we're going to win!"

After a few more words were exchanged, Steve watched his wife disappear back into the courtroom. He prayed, *Lord,*

God of all comfort, comfort her now! The next instant he was led to the crowded "prison express" headed for Cook County Jail.

After being congratulated by the defense lawyers, the prosecutors marched triumphantly through the crowded courtroom to the hallway beyond. Before, they had always exited through the back doors of the courtroom. Many interpreted their act as a defiant "victory march" in the face of the Linscotts' supporters. It so enraged Lois, in fact, that she grabbed Magnuson's arm and spoke harshly to him on his way out.

The prosecutors jostled their way through the crowd. One supporter accompanied Magnuson down the hallway and said, "Don't for one moment think the matter is going to rest with the decision of this Court. We will fight this injustice, even if it means a shake-up of the judicial system—and this courthouse!"

Meanwhile, O'Donnell had decided on a plan. First, he would ask the Court to hold the bond money until such time as the Appellate Court of Illinois ruled on a motion to reinstate bail. Then he would file a motion for Steve to be released on bail, pending appeal. Finally, he would file further motions for a retrial to be considered at the post-trial hearing, which would precede the sentence hearing scheduled for July 21. In his motion, O'Donnell briefly described the charges, the earlier release on bail, and Steve's exemplary behavior during the period of bail. Cases in support of the motion were cited, and O'Donnell assured the Appellate Court that no risk of flight existed.

O'Donnell outlined the grounds for appeal: "The entire prosecution of the case was based," he said, "upon circumstantial evidence. Trial errors were raised to the level of constitutional proportions." O'Donnell maintained that the Court erred in denying the motion to suppress the tape-recorded interviews. He also believed that the Court committed reversible error in denying the motions to dismiss the indictment, to declare a mistrial, and to suppress testimony relating to the testing on the vaginal swab, which had been totally destroyed sixteen months earlier. He contended that the Court committed reversible error in permitting the prosecution to introduce over his objection, incompetent and irrelevant evidence, allegedly for the purpose of proving motive. The Court further erred, he claimed, in denying motions for direct verdicts, on both charges, made at the close of the State's case and at the close of all the evidence. After alluding to the need for a retrial, he concluded by drawing the Appellate Court's attention to the results of the polygraph examination in April 1981.

The State, of course, filed objections to the motions. In response, O'Donnell contended that the State's "evaluation of the evidence and certain matters were erroneous, incomplete, and misleading," and he argued a number of other points. "The written narrative of the dream was in many respects substantially dissimilar from the facts known to the police. The testimony relating to 'consistent with' hair findings was refuted by expert testimony which emphatically stated the hairs described were not those of the defendant. The State's representation that evidence of the semen found in the victim was also consistent, since it was determined that it belonged to a non-secretor—and it was proved the defendant was a non-secretor—is grossly misleading." Finally, he contended that the State's failure to mention the destruction of physical evidence was noteworthy. The fight was on.

The motion for bail looked good, and Steve pinned his hopes on an early release. He fasted, prayed, and believed his requests would be answered.

On July 13, nearly two weeks after motions had been

filed, Steve awoke from an afternoon nap. He fell to his knees in his cell and began to pray that bond would be granted. But he felt no peace or assurance, and intuitively, he knew bond would be denied. Within a couple of hours the news came.

He wept bitterly. He worried for Lois and the children, and slipped into despondency. *God has abandoned me! He no longer loves me or cares about me,* he thought. *Why would you leave me in this place?* He had been so sure God would again rescue him. He felt like the prophet Habakkuk who, when he saw injustice prevail, cried out to God saying, "How long, O Lord, must I call for help, but you do not listen." Steve knew God wasn't *dead.* But it occurred to him that God might possibly be *deaf.*

That night he frightened Lois by crying on the phone. He shared his despair. Denial of bail meant that he would be sent to a down-state penitentiary.

Lois tried to comfort him, but she too was feeling miserable. "People are praying," she stammered. Steve knew it, but fears and doubts continued to assail him.

That night he had an awful dream. He dreamed he was in hell and that the flames of the lake of fire engulfed him. He was in the midst of a terrible spiritual conflict.

The next morning, with little inclination to study Scripture or pray, Steve opened his Bible without enthusiasm. It fell open to Luke's account of the Lord's Prayer:

> Our Father in heaven,
> hallowed be your name,
> your kingdom come,
> your will be done,
>   on earth as it is in heaven.
> Give us today our daily bread.
> Forgive us our debts,

as we also have forgiven our debtors.
And lead us not into temptation,
but deliver us from the evil one.

He had often repeated that prayer when he was growing up, but it seemed somehow new to him now. As he read it, he pondered every word. Gradually he overcame his hostility, the feeling that God had betrayed him. He read the passage again as a prayer. He prayed it as his very own again and again, each time with more fervency. Slowly, his trust in God returned. God did love him. The Lord had never relaxed control of the situation.

Then Steve read Psalm 55:17, a verse that he would lean on for the next six months: "Evening, morning and noon, I cry out in distress, and he hears my voice."

Steve thought about Job and concluded that God had a purpose in allowing this imprisonment. "You win, Lord," Steve said as he committed himself, his life, his future, and his family into the hands of his heavenly Father. "Your will be done!" Steve had overcome despair, but the victory, as always, was God's alone.

Lois too was experiencing a spiritual struggle. She confessed to the Lord her hatred for the prosecutors, and she prayed for a forgiving spirit and a love that would include even her enemies. She knew what God wanted her to do: she wrote to Jay Magnuson to apologize for grabbing him and speaking to him harshly in the courtroom.

At that time of crisis, Lois was grateful for the many people who prayed with her and gave her their support, friendship, and love. Her phone was constantly busy as people called to discuss the case and find out how she and Steve were coping. At one point Lois had so many calls, in fact, that she became hoarse and lost her voice completely.

One Sunday afternoon she received an unusual call from North Carolina. The caller identified herself as a "spirit medium" and explained that she had just learned from Jerry McDuffie that an innocent man had been convicted for the murder of a woman named Karen Phillips.

The caller claimed that, at the time of the verdict, she had dreamed about a ritualistic murder and that the same dream recurred each night for about two weeks. In the dream she saw a group of four men and a woman enter the apartment of a young woman. This young woman was in the center of the group, while they danced around her. Music was playing. One man in the group threatened the woman with a knife. When she resisted, another man struck her on the back of the head with a metal object. She slumped to the floor and was brutally beaten to death.

When she heard about the actual murder, the medium went to her Ouija board. Before long, she claimed, someone named Karen identified herself and said she had been trying to communicate with her for some time. "She cried out that an injustice had been committed," the medium told Lois.

Friends wisely advised Lois not to be drawn into the occult to have her husband exonerated. She took their advice, but the call did cause her to wonder why the police had overlooked the Temple in its investigation.

During interviews with Lois, some reporters were particularly interested in the sensational "psychic" aspect of the case. Although Lois was always careful to be guarded in what she said, the "psychic" dimension found its way into print anyway. *The Globe,* for instance, ran an article with the headline: "Nightmare of Psychic who 'Saw' Murder."

Perhaps the most balanced article appeared in the *Wednesday Journal,* one of Oak Park's weekly newspapers, on June 30, 1982. The article, "Linscott's Wife Insists He's Not Guilty of Murder" by Eric Linden, reflects Lois's reaction at that time:

The wife of convicted murderer Steven Linscott, in an interview with *Wednesday Journal* last week, maintained her husband's innocence and also expressed surprise that the jury agreed with the prosecution's circumstantial case.

Lois Linscott spoke from her Oak Park home nine days after a 12-member jury convicted Steven Linscott of the October 3, 1980, murder of Karen Ann Phillips, who then lived in an apartment at 326 N. Austin Blvd. To gain the conviction, the prosecution, headed by assistant Cook County State's Attorneys John Morrissey and Jay Magnuson, centered their case on Steven Linscott's dream of a murder similar to Phillips's.

"I believe the jury made their decision based on a notion," Lois Linscott said. "The State's Attorneys said, 'It comes down to this: Did he dream it or did he do it?' And the jury's whole idea was that it's impossible to dream something [that a person hasn't actually experienced], so since they believed it's not possible to have a dream like this, they believed he's guilty—even though there's no evidence to support it.

"I just wish they could tell their side of the story, without interruption, and then let us tell our side of the story, without interruption."

Lois Linscott conceded that the prosecution showed a circumstantial case, but she quarreled with the specifics in it and expressed her impression that the State and the jury had less-than-open minds.

"We always thought you were innocent until proven guilty," she said. "But it seems if you come out and say something that might indicate you had something to do with it, and if you don't have anybody else to substantiate your story, then you're guilty ... until you're proven innocent.

"Steven voluntarily went to police soon after he read in the paper that Phillips had been beaten. He remembered his dream," she said, "and thought it might be of value to the investigation.

"The reason he talked so much was just that he really believed he was helping them, and they suggested that all his impressions would be of great value. The tapes he made are real evidence of his attitude. But during the trial their opinion was that he couldn't handle the guilt, so the only way he could get it off his chest was to confess it in the form of a dream.

"You know, Steve was never examined by any psychiatrist, so I was surprised the jury bought this, because most of it was just the State's Attorney's opinion. They didn't have anybody to substantiate that either."

Lois Linscott also maintained that the hair analysis was inconclusive ... as was her husband's description of the murder weapon ... as was his description of the shirt worn by his "dream assailant."

"I could have gotten up in court and lied and said I got up at the time of the murder. But I didn't look at the clock, so I just told the truth. I was up in the night with the baby for about 15 minutes and Steve was sleeping. So you know, they think a wife would lie for her husband, or something like that, but if I had any inkling that Steve could have got up in the night and done this, I wouldn't be saying these things.

"Then they tried to accuse Steve of being a real smooth liar, but in fact, Steve is not a good liar at all. I've seen him when he's made mistakes and done things wrong before and he doesn't have [the personality] to hide it. But the next morning [after Phillips's murder] Steve was just his old self.

"Another thing is: with the amount of blood they said was all over the apartment, you'd think he would have had blood all over somewhere on him . . . or you'd think he'd have had scratches on him . . . or you'd think he'd have been messed up just a little bit. But he wasn't any different than he normally is.

"Anyway it's not over by any means. There will be an appeal, and we're just hoping that the right guy who did it will be caught somehow, that the Appellate Court will rule we deserve another trial, or something. But as for this, it really comes down to what people want to believe. Is it possible to have a dream [about a real incident that isn't experienced firsthand] or possible to have psychic ability? It looks like they don't believe it's possible, then they decide he must be guilty. But like our attorney said, 'a dream is not enough for conviction.'"

Unknown to Lois, reporter Eric Linden also interviewed Jay Magnuson, who made some surprising admissions.

State's Attorney Magnuson last week called the prosecution's case "totally circumstantial." He said the prosecution "left it to the jury to presume a motive," and that there was no evidence that Linscott and Phillips had known each other. He said also there were no witnesses to the crime and that the hair analysis, blood tests, examination of seminal material, and other tests failed to prove Linscott was in Phillips's apartment.

"No, they don't show he's definitely the guy," Magnuson said. "But the thing about these tests is that any one of them could have eliminated the guy [from consideration as a suspect]. When you have the similarities in his dream along with that, we think it's a strong circumstantial case."

Although Steve had overcome his doubts, he continued to struggle. He knew that God was going to bring justice to this situation; in fact, public support for his cause was growing almost daily. But Steve continued to grope for meaning; he wanted to serve God even when he was not aware of the purpose for his suffering. So he decided to keep a journal as a way of keeping track of his spiritual health. The following entries show what he was feeling at that time:

JUNE 29: Lesson today is that we never learn valuable lessons cheaply.

JULY 10: Lois in tears today when I called. She found comfort in Isaiah 54:10–13 and was thankful for her study of that passage.

AUGUST 13: A difficult day in the sense that I can't see anything good happening. I just have to trust. Haven't spent any time in the Word today.

AUGUST 18: Another argument with Angelo (my cell-mate). I sinfully told him to "shut up" after becoming tired of hearing him. I later apologized.

AUGUST 20: Very "down" today. "Down" days leave me in such a state that all I can do is lie on my bed and moan, for the pain in my chest, throat, and stomach and the sorrow in my heart and mind are so great, they leave me weak.

AUGUST 21: Praying morning, evening and night for deliverance. The day-to-day struggle is tough but fasting made it easier today. Talked with a young backslidden believer. He was in tears over his case. Spoke with Lois three times today. At one point she was nearly asleep on her dinner plate. I was offended, but understand how hard it is for her.

AUGUST 24: Received a letter from Lois: "Honey, it's His perfect will that you be there today. Every day you are there and I am here alone is part of our special assignment from Him."

AUGUST 25: I know too that I will probably go to the penitentiary. I don't want to! I don't even want to think about it. But the Lord teaches me that He suffered and so paved the way for my suffering—for my present experience. It's unjust. This is what depresses me. I hate the very thought of it all.

AUGUST 31: Had a half hour visit with Lois. God is so gracious. She was kind of quiet today! I love her so much.

SEPTEMBER 1: Lord, I want Your will for my life more than life itself. Do all that is in Your heart to do to me, dear Lord. I want to accept Your will and rest in it. I love You, Lord! I trust in Your mercies to sustain and keep me.

SEPTEMBER 2: Heard from a man, from out of state, who was at a convention of 3,000 businessmen. Someone asked for specific prayer for us.

SEPTEMBER 11: I believe that in some sense our situation is connected to revival—I'm not sure how, but God will reveal it.

SEPTEMBER 17: Gave testimony of our faith in God in regard to our situation to Clarence, an older man, who is not a Christian. He has suffered hurt, severe depression, and breakdown as a result of his wife divorcing him. He expressed utter amazement that we are holding on to God with such genuine faith.

Ultimately, the months in Cook County Jail were profitable. Steve led several men to Christ during the evening Bible studies. His cell became a center of fellowship for six to eight believers who regularly gathered together for prayer. Steve ministered to that group and, in turn, was ministered to by them.

Marcus, one of the Christians, had a joy that was contagious. He would walk up to Steve and say, "Praise the

Lord, brother Steve!" It was hard not to laugh and rejoice when he was around. Marcus had been jailed for a trivial matter, and by mistake his bond had been set at $50,000. He was therefore assigned to Division Six. Steve often wondered whether Marcus was really an angel sent to encourage him.

And God encouraged Steve in other ways. One time, Steve learned that Steve Bradley, an old friend and missionary to Guam, was in the States and wanted Steve to call him at 9:00 P.M. *Impossible!* Steve thought, for he had already used his allotted phone time for that day. But Steve prayed. To his amazement he was granted a phone call at 8:30. He then traded this for an 8:45 time slot, and prayed again. While praying he was interrupted by an inmate who offered him his time at 9:00 and another friend's time at 9:15. *God is always doing little things like that,* he thought as he put the call through to his friend.

But in spite of their resignation, the hope of an appeal was still a great encouragement to Steve and Lois. Several friends (including myself) had already organized a campaign to overturn the conviction—a campaign to work within the legal system. To help our chances of success, Steve and Lois decided to find a new lawyer to handle the motions for a new trial and appeal. The decision was difficult because appeal lawyers are expensive and their fees astronomical.

But the Linscotts knew they needed a fresh start; there were too many things O'Donnell hadn't tried. For instance, his decision not to defend the dream had backfired. Only once did Steve hear the taped interviews—during the trial itself. Although he had read the transcripts sixteen months earlier, the details were no longer fresh in his mind. O'Donnell, it should be said in fairness, was operating on a shoe-string budget and had many other cases to look after.

The search for a new lawyer took several weeks. The

names of about ten top criminal lawyers were secured and their credentials checked. Criteria for selecting a new lawyer were developed. Then, one by one, the lawyers were interviewed by Lois, Jim Richards, and me. Each lawyer was asked to state how he would proceed in securing a new trial. All felt the chances of a new trial were good; one lawyer nearly guaranteed it.

None, however, seemed willing to grapple with the *facts* of the case. Legal technicalities seemed to interest them more. Lois, Jim, and I wanted Steve acquitted by letting the facts of the case speak for themselves. We practically despaired of finding the right lawyer until we came to Thomas D. Decker—the last name on the list.

Tom Decker's offices were on LaSalle Street in the heart of downtown Chicago. In his late forties, of medium height and build, he impressed us with his willingness to absorb the detailed facts of the case. He agreed to take it on.

Incredibly, God provided Decker's retainer fee through the generosity of a contributor. The heavy financial load was thus lifted from the Linscotts' shoulders, and they heaved a sigh of gratitude, resting in the knowledge that, from that point on, they would enjoy the finest defense.

The post-conviction hearing had been postponed several times—the first time to allow for the typing of the lengthy trial transcripts. Then, due to their vacation schedules, the prosecutors requested a continuance. The final postponement permitted the search for and retention of a new lawyer. The hearing was eventually scheduled for Monday, November 15, five months after the verdict.

With the help of Jim Richards, Decker began poring over nearly two thousand pages of trial transcripts and notes (plus numerous documents and files). Jim had studied the transcripts, particularly the technical sections related to the physical evidence, and became intrigued by what he read.

Decker and Jim decided to probe deeper. As a former deputy sheriff, Jim was used to investigations.

First, Jim flew his own private plane to Milwaukee, Wisconsin, to interview Dr. Kenneth Siegesmund, who had provided the expert testimony for the defense. Jim learned that there was much more Dr. Siegesmund could have said in Steve's favor. While experts are not allowed to rebut the rebuttals to their testimony, Dr. Siegesmund still believed he might have salvaged the case for Steve if he could have responded to Stolorow's statements. By the time Jim left Milwaukee, he had a much clearer understanding of the issues involved and decided that further research was warranted. He wanted to discover for himself the significance of gamma markers.

Jim visited Brian Wraxhall, a renowned forensic serologist with the Serological Research Institute in California. Wraxhall said, "I don't believe the State of Illinois could have done such a thing!" But he was convinced when he examined the transcripts for himself. Wraxhall's own testimony (in a sworn affidavit) was later used by Decker in his appeal. Wraxhall is recognized as an expert by the State of Illinois and had even testified for the State in previous cases.

Jim was unflagging in his efforts. He contacted B. D. Gaudette, the Canadian forensic scientist whose articles formed the basis of the prosecution's examinations. Jim concluded that the prosecutors had misinterpreted the research. Jim also contacted no less an authority on hair evidence than McCrone Laboratories, one of the leading hair-analysis labs in America—probably in the world.

In all cases, Jim heard the same answer: The physical evidence was not sufficient to convict Steve.

11
Motions
for a Retrial

Thomas Decker lost no time familiarizing himself with the case. Transcripts and motions were studied, and a summary of the case prepared. Consultations with O'Donnell, Jim Richards, Steve, Lois, me, and other members of the investigative committee provided invaluable information. Investigative notes and reports were carefully examined and cross-referenced. Methodically, Tom Decker sought answers to some ninety questions raised through his reading the files of the amateur detectives. There was no time to lose. November 15, the date set for the post-conviction hearing at which motions for a new trial would be heard, was only a few weeks away.

George R. Seibel, a criminal justice researcher, was hired to look into other suspects in the case. Seibel reached an interesting conclusion: A number of suspects had, surprisingly, never been investigated by police. One suspect, in particular, was very high on Seibel's list.

During the course of his investigation Seibel had an interesting encounter with the Oak Park police. He described the incident this way: "On October 29 [1982] a photo of a suspect was obtained as an investigative tool. The following day residents of the Oak Park area were questioned as to whether the suspect and Phillips had ever been observed together. During the course of one interview an Oak Park patrol officer walked into the store. . . .

"The ultimate result was that I had a gun pointed at me . . . prior to being given an opportunity to explain my purpose for being in the area. This prompted the patrol officer to radio the Oak Park police station, 'Send a detective! There is somebody nosing around on the Linscott case.'

"In a matter of minutes Detective Scianna responded to the call and rushed to the scene. Again, I explained my purpose for being in the area and inquired of the detective if he had any reason to wish the research discontinued. He was professional, seemingly unnerved, and replied that the canvass was a waste of time because Linscott is a non-secretor. After they took down my identification data, I was allowed to leave."

Not only did Scianna respond to the patrol officer's call, but so did several squad cars. It is strange that the police should be so sensitive to a private investigation. Obviously, Seibel had the police on the defensive.

On November 3, Decker filed his motion for a hearing to reconsider the evidence, a new trial, a dismissal, and an acquittal. A copy of the fifty-one-page document, which was a scathing attack on the State's handling of the case, was served to Prosecutor Magnuson. Attached to the motions and supporting arguments were three exhibits: Exhibit A contained the affidavit of Brian Wraxhall. Exhibit B was the supplemental crime-lab report submitted by Mohammad Tahir on March 2, 1981. Exhibit C was a forty-page sworn

174

statement by Bertha Schlienz, an alternate juror, describing the biases that she had observed among the jury.

In support of his motions, Decker cited eleven points that, in his opinion, merited the granting of a new trial. The presentation was restricted to matters raised or errors made during the trial. He was not permitted to transgress beyond the scope of the trial proceedings to introduce testimony or evidence not previously covered.

Decker began with the State's destruction of the vaginal swab evidence—evidence that was vital and potentially exculpatory. He argued that Steve's rights to due process were violated and that he was denied the opportunity— through further testing—to present evidence of his own that might have exonerated him.

At issue was the fact that after the indictment, Steve had filed a motion for discovery, including a request to inspect all physical evidence. On February 19, 1981, the State agreed to make such evidence available. But the vaginal swab evidence was no longer in existence—*that very day* it had been consumed in meaningless testing in London. Without serving notice to the defendant, and without his knowledge and without Court approval, the State had removed critical evidence from the country and destroyed it.

Decker was angry. He argued his point well; the State deprived Steve of the opportunity to conduct tests that could have excluded him as a suspect. He contended that Steve's right to due process was violated and that a new trial was required because the violation was purposeful—the State was on notice that Steve intended to inspect and test the swab—and because the tests that consumed the swab were meaningless. "They did not serve, and could not have served a legitimate State interest," Decker wrote. "The testing that destroyed the swab was capable only of confirming what the State already knew through its testing of Miss Phillips's whole blood; that her blood contained gamma markers +1, +2, and +10." Tahir tested the swab only for those gamma markers he knew Miss Phillips had—and *finding those gamma markers could neither implicate nor exonerate Steve or any other suspect*. Meaningful tests could have been conducted that could have disclosed gamma markers other than the ones possessed by the victim and defendant. Apparently, they were never considered.

The destruction of the physical evidence raises interesting questions. For instance: Do present forensic methods permit the collection of sufficient vaginal evidence to carry out the number of tests required to positively eliminate a suspect? The answer is no. Also, are the limited number of tests normally undertaken in forensic laboratories designed to eliminate or incriminate a suspect? Although elimination is the stated intent, the tests are too broad, too general. Often, incrimination seems to be the purpose. When a case rests on such a limited type of evidence, that evidence must be examined even more carefully. To do this the medical examiners need to collect more samples.

Tom Decker then maintained that false evidence was submitted to the jury when Tahir testified, and the prosecutors argued that the gamma marker tests were consistent with the theory that Steve had intercourse with Karen Phillips. He argued that the State's case rested wholly on three things—Steve's ambiguous statements about his dream; the speculative nature of Tahir's testimony that Steve's hairs were consistent with some which were found at the crime scene; and Tahir's testimony about blood testing. It was this final aspect of the State's case that Decker attacked in his second point.

Decker argued that the meaningless gamma marker tests carried out by the State were the only seemingly solid evidence that the defendant and the victim had intercourse.

But the evidence was flimsy. Decker pointed out that Tahir testified several times that the test results were meaningful because they were consistent with a mixture of the body fluids of Mr. Linscott and Miss Phillips, the same way he had described the similarities between hairs.

Mr. Tahir went beyond the use of the consistency standard. He was asked by a prosecutor what result he "would expect to get" after bodily fluids with the gamma markers of the defendant and Miss Phillips were combined and tested. His response was "GM plus one, plus two," that is, Phillips's markers. He also testified that this test result of "plus one, plus two" did not exclude the defendant as a possible seminal donor.

The prosecutors stressed and stretched this testimony in arguments to the jury. In his Opening Statement, a prosecutor stated that the fluids of the defendant and Miss Phillips actually were mixed together at the time Mr. Tahir performed his gamma marker test. (Of course, there was no such evidence. The purpose of the test was to determine whether such a mixture *had* occurred.) The argument also was made that, as expected, the test produced a "plus one, plus two" result which was "consistent with" a Linscott-Phillips mixture of fluids.

In their Closing Arguments the prosecutors repeatedly argued the significance of the gamma marker test. "If you combine Karen's vaginal fluid with Mr. Linscott's seminal fluid you would get the consistency reading that Mohammad Tahir got at Scotland Yard." The argument also was made that the GM test could have excluded Linscott as a possibility.

The gamma marker test established nothing about Steve—it neither inculpated him nor exculpated him as a

177

suspect. The test produced nothing about any person other than Karen Phillips. Because of the significance attached to this "evidence," Decker argued, the case falls within the rule that the presentation of false evidence requires a new trial. He used strong language as he continued:

In the Linscott case the prosecution knowingly used the truth falsely. In eliciting expert testimony about gamma markers found on the vaginal swab made after the victim's death, the expert and the prosecutors crafted an impression that the evidence pointed to the defendant. In fact, given the victim's positive gamma characteristics, the State witness's analysis was totally useless for inculpating *any* suspect, let alone identifying one.

To present the results of the gamma marker analysis as the State did, therefore, was purposely to mislead the jury as to its significance. Falsehood fully deserves its label when it rests only on the omission of information without which it will inevitably be misconstrued. When the State knowingly and falsely omits the crucially important foundation for its own evidence so as to mislead the jury as to the defendant's guilt, its case must fail. There was no direct lie, no plainly untrue statement, no perjury. The State encouraged the jury to believe what it knew to be untrue, namely that the gamma marker analysis evidenced the defendant's guilt. The State could succeed in its implicit mendacity only by keeping the defense from knowing what it knew. In the present case, State's expert destroyed the physical evidence in making his useless gamma marker test, eliminating the defendant's opportunity either to counter its results or to perform any other tests from which an exculpatory result might have been obtained.

After comparing the Linscott case with two other cases Decker concluded his remarks on this point:

Like that in *DeStefano* and *Murdock*, the prosecution's case here depended on a misrepresented consistency between the defendant's blood identifiers and the results of its useless and destructive test for gamma markers.

All three cases manifest not the prosecution's perjurious intent, but its unfortunate insensitivity to the fact that the government wins only when justice is done. As the Appellate Court noted in *DeStefano*, a prosecutor is the representative not of an ordinary party to a controversy, but a sovereignty whose obligation to govern impartially is as compelling as its obligation to govern at all, and whose interest, therefore, in a criminal prosecution is not that it shall win a case, but that justice shall be done.

Decker's third point focused on the prosecutor's arguments as to the meaning of Steve's status as a "non-secretor." He argued that when the examination of the vaginal swab failed to reveal the blood type of the seminal donor, two conclusions could have been drawn. The seminal donor was a secretor with type O blood (which includes close to half the population), or he was a non-secretor (20 percent of the population). As noted earlier, a third conclusion might have been the total inadequacy of the test, for it should have at least revealed Miss Phillips's blood type because she was a secretor. It did not even do that. Decker labored his point:

The negative finding as to the blood type of the donor therefore, had no probative value since a majority of male citizens could have committed the rape. Nonetheless, in his Opening Statement a prosecutor ignored the meaning of the "O" type blood possessed by the victim and argued that the negative laboratory finding pointed to (was "consistent with") a non-secretor such as the defendant—only 15 percent of the population.

The State's Closing Arguments were worse: "Karen was raped by a non-secretor, and the defendant is a non-secretor." An analogy to the hair "match" testimony also was drawn by the State: ". . . where is the link? The link is the semen matching the non-secretor. Mr. Linscott is a non-secretor."

The arguments thus made to the jury were—at best—deceptive. In part they were false. The arguments were improper and prejudicial and are governed by the legal considerations discussed in the preceding point.

Decker's next point was that the circumstantial evidence in this case was insufficient to sustain conviction. Since the physical evidence was hopelessly insufficient, what was left? The tape-recorded interviews! Steve's conviction was based upon the State's theory that the interviews were sufficient to permit the inference that Steve was the perpetrator of the crime; that he had not dreamed the details that were similar to the offense; that he had witnessed them while committing the crime; that his relation of the events constituted an admission of the violent acts. Of course, they offered no evidence to contradict Steve's testimony that these details came to him in dreams one night.

Decker skillfully argued that the evidence was insufficient. While conceding that it was common for jurors to draw inferences in the determination of guilt or innocence, he maintained that it was improper in this case—because there was a reasonable hypothesis of innocence. To reach a guilty verdict "the jury had to pile inference upon inference," he wrote. Decker argued:

As in physics, a logical chain can be no stronger than the weakest of its links. In a criminal case, guilt must be established beyond a reasonable doubt. Therefore, a chain of logical inferences can properly lead a jury to a verdict of guilty beyond a reasonable doubt. That is not true of the sequential inferences in the present case. Each is doubtful.

Inference #1: Defendant did not dream what he testified about.

Inference #2: Therefore, defendant must have lied when he testified that he had dreamed about Miss Phillips's injuries.

Inference #3: Therefore, defendant's information did not come from some other person. It was not told to him by, say, a neighbor or several neighbors. It was not unconsciously suggested to him by policemen. It came to him in no extrasensory fashion.

Inference #4: Therefore, defendant's information came to him wholly as a result of personal observations.

Inference #5: Therefore, defendant and no other person must actually have committed the crime. . . .

It is firmly established in the law of this State, and other jurisdictions, that multiple intervening inferences like those drawn by the jury in this case are untrustworthy and an invalid basis for conviction. As one Court explained:

"Courts . . . have always insisted that the life, liberty, and property of a citizen should not be taken away on possibilities, conjectures, or even, generally speaking, a bare probability. In criminal cases, they demand that when a conviction is to be based on a chain of inferences, *each and every link in that chain must exclude every other reasonable hypothesis. . . .*"

Decker's fifth point was the improper introduction into the jury room of a newspaper article about the trial and access to information regarding Steve's bail.

The Court had consistently warned the jurors to ignore extrajudicial information. They were told not to discuss the case with anyone or to read newspaper articles. But at least one article was passed among the jurors. After the trial an alternate juror reported that jurors had discussed Steve's high bond—a fact that was not disclosed in court—and the significance of the amount. The sentiment among the jurors was that the high bond was a clear indication of guilt.

Decker argued that these violations undermined Steve's rights to an impartial jury and to due process. He urged a new trial or at least a hearing—to which the jurors would be summoned—to adduce further evidence.

Where a defendant alleges a jury has been improperly influenced by prejudicial materials, such as newspaper reports, "the rule has developed that a trial judge has considerable discretion in determining whether such material prejudiced the defendant." In exercising that discretion, the Court must determine whether it reasonably appears that the jurors, or at least some of them, have been influenced or prejudiced to the extent that they cannot be fair and impartial. . . .

Decker then cited several related cases and continued:

These cases establish that the allegations of prejudice in the Linscott case satisfy the first step of the Court's analysis and require reversal of the defendant's conviction or, at the very least, a poll of the jury on the extent to which it was prejudiced by its knowledge of facts not properly before it. These jurors acquired highly inflammatory information con-

cerning defendant's bond which was not a matter before them but which created a sentiment to convict. Like the jurors in *Thomas*, at least one juror here argued from the newspaper articles and from facts outside the record in pressing for conviction. Clearly, the potential for prejudice is sufficient to warrant a poll of the jury.

Decker's next point concerned the hair evidence. He argued that Steve was further prejudiced by Magnuson's argument that the evidence showed that the hairs found in the victim's apartment were "identical" with the defendant's. Because of the widespread and often undeserved awe concerning forensic hair analysis, I will include Decker's entire argument:

In rebuttal closing arguments the prosecutor referred to Mr. Tahir's testimony that Mr. Linscott's hair was "consistent with" that found in the victim's apartment. The prosecutor continued:

"What does he mean by *consistent?* He means there is *nothing dissimilar.* I would suggest to you, Ladies and Gentlemen, if I said there were two American flags right there and they were both twelve by eight and that they had the same number of stars and they had the same number of stripes and had the same coloring you would sit there and say well there is nothing dissimilar about those two, *they are identical.* But not a scientist. A scientist will state that every aspect that I examined was *consistent.* And what does that mean. There was nothing different. *And to a layman it means identical as the two American flags."*

By advising the jury that the hairs in question were identical with each other, the prosecutor was saying that the hairs in the victim's apartment were the defendant's. The tactic was that considered in *People vs. Giangrande.* There a

183

basis for reversal was a prosecutor's question to the jury in closing argument, "Don't you find it a little suspicious that Michael Giangrande's head and arm hair would have ended up on the underside of the tape?" After an objection, the prosecutor amended her approach to say that "hair just like Michael Giangrande's was found on the tape."

The Court recognized that the evidence at the trial had been that arm and head hairs found with the victim's body parts were "microscopically identical" to the defendant's (which was Mr. Tahir's testimony in the instant case). But that did not mean the hairs actually were identical, that is, the defendant's. Even the prosecutor's correction was inadequate to correct the harm.

We note that the Court promptly corrected her misstatement. Nevertheless, the hair evidence produced at trial was a significant element of the State's proof, and the prosecutor's comment may have caused the jury to give undue weight to the hair evidence.

As in *Giangrande*, the hair evidence was critical to the prosecution of Mr. Linscott. In the Linscott case the prosecutor told the jurors that "consistent" (the conclusion of Mr. Tahir) meant "identical." The fact that the prosecutor did not say, "The hairs were Mr. Linscott's," is immaterial. The meaning of Mr. Tahir's testimony was overstated and the jury was told effectively, as in *Giangrande*, that no issues of fact remained.

The harm accomplished by the prosecutor's remarks is more evident when we focus on the type of scientific examination that gave rise to the remarks. Mr. Tahir used a comparison microscope in examining the hairs in this case. The technique is a venerable one. It has come under criticism, however, as too subjective to qualify as truly scientific.

Second, studies have shown an unacceptably high percentage of errors in the microscopic testing of hairs. These findings led the Law Enforcement Assistance Administration to sponsor a testing program in which between 235 and 240 crime laboratories participated. The LEAA Program results detailed widespread error in crime lab reports. By far the most frequent errors were in the analysis of hair. More than half the laboratories misanalyzed this evidence.

Thus, while we may conclude that hair examination by microscopic means is useful to forensic scientists, the technique is wholly undeserving of the superlative employed by the State here.

Controversy over the hair evidence continued to rage. Decker argued that Steve was further prejudiced by Magnuson's closing argument that the hair testimony was deserving of inordinate weight. Once again, the record speaks for itself:

Mr. Tahir testified that Mr. Linscott's hairs were consistent with the ones found in the victim's apartment. He explained that "consistent" meant that he was not able to find dissimilarities between the questioned and known hairs.

In his rebuttal closing argument—just after making the "identical" argument mentioned [in the previous point]— the prosecutor made reference to a Canadian forensic scientist and his conclusion about hair matches. In the context of the instant case, the prosecutor argued that the defense expert agreed with the Canadian authority that the likelihood of a hair match between two individuals was 1 in 4500, and as to pubic hairs, 1 in 800.

The argument thus magnified to an extraordinary degree the weight the jury was to place on the hair evidence. What was incorrect about the argument—and made it patently unfair—was that in testifying about the Canadian's findings, the defense expert made the point that the findings were based upon the completion of *forty* tests, not the much less exacting microscopic examinations performed by Mr. Tahir.

The injection into the case of this mathematical formula—wholly out of context and without foundational support—accorded to the hair evidence the same undue weight, and worked the same prejudice, as the prosecutor's statements in *People vs. Giangrande.*

Decker also argued that the expert hair testimony was too speculative for admission. He pointed out that the State's expert found about nine similarities between the known and the questioned hairs and that the examination involved *visual* comparison of the hairs with a comparison microscope. The defense expert, Dr. Siegesmund, on the other hand, testified that there are about forty such analyses that can be made microscopically.

The ordinary rule is that expert testimony is admissible despite limitations in technique of a particular test. Decker argued, however, that "a new trial should be granted when the testimony is suspect, is overemphasized by the government, is basically speculative, and is apt to be given undue weight by the jury." He continued:

The comparison microscope technique is well known in American jurisprudence. Nonetheless, its status in Illinois has yet to be determined in any authoritative sense, particularly under facts such as are present here. Thus, an early decision recognized that there was a difference of opinion with regard to the utility of such hair analysis but concluded that such a difference goes to the weight of the evidence, not its admissibility. . . .

Examinations of the sort done by Mr. Tahir are overly speculative. In the light of the limited examinations he made of the characteristics of the hair in question, the Court should rule that his testimony was inadmissible and order a new trial.

The question had been repeatedly asked, "How could a jury find Steve Linscott guilty . . . if he was innocent?" The answer is what Decker calls "a raw appeal to prejudice." He repeatedly emphasized this in his motions for a new trial. This time he alleged that Steve was prejudiced by the prosecutor's argument in rebuttal that the defense counsel had waited until trial to request access to the vaginal swab:

Defense counsel argued properly in closing argument that Mr. Tahir consumed the swab in testing in February of 1981, and that his action deprived the defense of the opportunity to run tests.

In his rebuttal closing argument the prosecutor responded as follows:

"Counsel argues about this vaginal swab, Ladies and Gentlemen. And he knows doggone well that he never requested that vaginal swab until the last alternate walked out of this jury door. And after the last alternate was picked that is when he requested that vaginal swab."

O'DONNELL: "Objection."

MAGNUSON: "It wasn't a year and a half ago. And he waited until the jury was picked, sworn, and told to come in here at eleven o'clock in the morning and asks that the stuff be shipped to Wisconsin. And then we have Mr. O'Donnell saying that it is the police, State's Attorney's Office, the Medical Examiner, the chemists across the street in the laboratory, all we want to do in this case is frame Mr. Linscott."

In fact, Mr. O'Donnell had not waited until the jury was sworn to request that the vaginal swab be produced. After the jurors had been selected, and *out of their presence,* he moved for production of a State *report* about testing on the swab. Nothing more on the subject was mentioned before opening arguments and the jury was not privy to the defense request.

The effect of the remarks by the Assistant State's Attorney was to demean defense counsel by, in effect, calling him both a liar and dilatory, and to deflect attention from the improper conduct.

Similarly, Mr. O'Donnell made no argument that the police, the State's Attorney's office, the Medical Examiner, or the chemist wanted only to "frame" Mr. Linscott, as the prosecutor claimed. This argument was nothing but a raw appeal to the prejudice. The Court should so classify it and take the only effective remedial action, which is to order a new trial.

Two further points remained. The first concerned the discharge of a juror without sufficient cause or consent of the defendant. The other alleged the testimony of Dr. Mark Stolorow was irrelevant and also prejudicial as it served to bolster the credibility of the State's expert witness.

Decker argued that the right of the continued service of a juror who had been selected by the defendant is basic and that it should not be undercut except for a compelling reason. While the discharge of a juror is a power committed to the discretion of the trial judge, an arbitrary exercise of the power may violate the defendant's protection against being placed twice in jeopardy. Decker claimed that the removal of Ms. Nichols was arbitrary and unnecessarily deprived Steve of his chosen panel; the proceedings, after all, could easily have been delayed a few hours.

188

O'Donnell had repeatedly objected to the introduction of Mark Stolorow, Coordinator of Serology for the Illinois Department of Law Enforcement, as a witness. His testimony was limited to general discussions, his own background and expertise, and a statement to the effect that the American Society of Crime Laboratory Directors regarded his laboratories as excellent ones. Decker commented:

The testimony was offered for the evident purposes of bolstering the credibility of the State's expert, Mr. Tahir, and of focusing additional attention on the scientific evidence in the case. We ask the Court to conclude that undue emphasis was again put on the hair and blood evidence, further depriving the defendant of a fair trial.

Steve and Lois were delighted with the work of their attorney and his two highly capable associates, Rich McLeese and Jim Huston. Their hopes for a retrial soared, and their expectations for the declaration of a mistrial were high. They became increasingly confident that Judge Stillo would realize the magnitude of the State's wrongful tactics. They prayed for an early release.

Even knowing that judges seldom reverse their decisions—which would be tantamount to self-indictment—did not dampen their spirits. Many people had written to Judge Stillo and provided testimonies regarding Steve's excellent character. The couple's faith in the justice system never wavered. They firmly believed the truth would prevail.

The trial, the public support for Steve, the growing publicity, and the impact of Decker's motions took their toll on Prosecutor Magnuson. Unofficial reports received by Steve and Lois indicated that he was not well. Apparently, his blood pressure was high, and there were indications of an ulcer. It was rumored that his doctor had advised him to give the case to another prosecutor. But Magnuson did not want to give up; he would pursue the case to the bitter end. Clearly unnerved, he lashed back in a strange manner, by filing a most unusual motion:

Now come the People of the State of Illinois by their Attorney, Richard M. Daley, State's Attorney of Cook County, through his Assistants Jay C. Magnuson and John E. Morrissey, to move that this Honorable Court order the following:

1. To bar the spectators from the hearing on post-trial motions and/or sentencing hearing, if applicable; or

2. In the alternative order that appropriate steps be taken to insure the integrity of said proceedings and the safety of those parties involved.

In support of said motion this movant informs this Court of the following:

1. That the defendant, Steven P. Linscott, was found guilty by a jury of the crime of murder on June 16, 1982.

2. That said case was prosecuted by Assistant State's Attorneys John E. Morrissey and Jay C. Magnuson.

3. That said trial was attended by large numbers of supporters of the defendant.

4. That immediately following the verdict many of these spectators verbally abused and threatened the two prosecuting attorneys in this case.

5. That while attempting to leave the courtroom the two prosecuting attorneys were grabbed, shoved, hit, and spat upon by many of these spectators.

6. That one spectator ... followed Assistant State's Attorney Magnuson down the hallway threatening to "get even," or "get his job," to "get him."

7. That while this spectator did the above he continually held said Assistant by the arm attempting to prevent him from leaving the area until a Deputy Sheriff appeared in the corridor.

8. That within days, supporters of the defendant made direct contact with the family of Karen Ann Phillips for the sole purpose of harassment.

9. That repeated and continuous anonymous phone calls have been made, since the verdict, to Assistant State's Attorney Magnuson threatening his job, his safety, and the safety of his family because of his involvement in this case.

Based on the above, it appears there is a clear effort to obstruct the orderly process of justice and to intimidate the prosecuting attorneys in their efforts in this case. Accordingly, we move this Court to hear any post-trial hearing in closed court or in the alternative set guidelines and restrictions on any spectators present to prevent any further contemptuous conduct and to insure the safety of those named individuals who have previously been threatened.

Decker then filed a further motion of his own.

The defendant Steven Paul Linscott, by his attorney, Thomas D. Decker, moves the Court to seal this motion and any orders that are entered in connection with it. The defendant further moves for the production of all physical evidence in this case for expert testing. In support of his motion, the defendant states as follows:

1. The request to seal this motion and the accompanying orders is made to avoid publicity and defamation.

2. The undersigned attorney has been advised by Brian Wraxhall, a well-known serologist, that the State's expert in this case did not perform certain tests for blood which could well be germane even at this point.

3. The defendant also requests the opportunity to test the hair samples in this case for two reasons. One, the State's expert identified as similar to the defendant's hair, a hair found in the dome light of his car. The undersigned attorney is informed and believes that this hair actually came from the head of the defendant's daughter. Doubt is thus cast upon the conclusions drawn by the expert and we believe that further testing is in order.

4. The second reason for the testing of hair is that the defendant intends to test the negroid hairs found in the victim's apartment. We have attached hereto a report concerning a black man which the undersigned attorney believes to be true and accurate. The report recites facts that provide some reason to believe that this man may have been involved in this case. We intend to compare the hairs found in the victim's apartment with the hairs that we believe to be the suspect's.

The courtroom was packed for the post-conviction hearing, as Judge Stillo took the bench. As public outrage grew, groups had gathered to pray for justice at the hearing. More than ever—across America and Canada—people hoped Adam Stillo, still basking in the glow of his recent election to full Circuit Court judge status, would reflect legal competence and moral courage in his decision.

Briefly, Decker reviewed his motions and supporting arguments. Judge Stillo seemed to listen attentively and sympathetically.

Then Jay Magnuson, looking agitated and ill, addressed the judge. Instead of rebutting the cases and arguments cited by the defense, he concentrated on justifying his actions and remarks. It was self-preservation. To Steve's supporters it appeared that Decker had his opponent on the ropes and that the prosecutor was fighting for survival. Magnuson was not himself; he looked dazed and bewildered.

Decker responded briefly and in his own quiet way appealed for the granting of the motions.

Every eye was fixed on Judge Stillo.

He hesitated momentarily. Then he said, "I deny the motions." He did, however, make one concession. To Magnuson's consternation he permitted the release of the hair evidence for purposes of further analysis and comparison. But a week later, he withdrew that permission.

Again, Magnuson had won.

There was to be no new trial. The evidence in support of a retrial appeared so convincing that this shock far exceeded the shock of the original verdict. The blow was crushing; Steve was sure that a new trial would be granted. Now, release and reunion with family and friends was out of the question. Now, all that remained was the final sentence hearing at which the judge would decide how many years Steve should have to spend in prison.

As Lois walked from the courtroom, stunned, too weak and broken to put on a brave façade, she wept.

As the couple left the building—to go their separate ways—they felt utterly forlorn. God had forsaken them, failed them! He had denied not only their own prayer requests but those of hundreds across the land. The cry of the prophet Isaiah was on their hearts: "Oh, that you would rend the heavens and come down, that the mountains would tremble before you!" Like Elijah they had looked for the gale, the earthquake, and the fire. Instead of the mountains being smashed, it was they who had been broken. One question burned in their hearts: Why, God?

12
Forty Years
in the Wilderness

A day or two before the sentence hearing, an article appeared in the "INC" gossip column in the *Chicago Tribune*. The syndicated article told of the extraordinary security precautions in effect at the sentence hearing of Steve Linscott. They were designed to protect Prosecutors Jay Magnuson and John Morrissey, who had said that, since Steve's conviction, they had received telephone threats from his supporters. The article also referred to the Prosecutors' allegations of having been jostled and spat upon while leaving the courtroom in Maywood. The threats were anonymous. Magnuson was reported telling of one recent caller who had said, "Are you the person who prosecuted Steve Linscott? We are going to get you." In his eleven years as a Prosecutor, including cases against street-gang leaders, Magnuson was quoted as saying, "I've never experienced anything like this."

FORTY YEARS IN THE WILDERNESS

Security was indeed tight on Tuesday, November 23, 1982. Extra care was exercised by security personnel at the entrance to the Circuit Court Building, and additional officers were stationed outside Judge Stillo's courtroom. Each spectator was subjected to a security check.

But the supporters who gathered that morning were not the type who would try to take the law into their own hands. They simply believed in justice. Certainly, many would leave no stone unturned in an attempt to ensure that wrongs were righted. Many knew that this effort could result in an investigation of the way the police, State's Attorneys, and the judge had handled the case. But there was no vindictiveness. Only appropriate legal action would be considered. This was all Steve's supporters had in mind.

Criminal law requires a special hearing to impose a sentence. A variety of reports are submitted, and arguments concerning sentencing alternatives are heard. The defendant is afforded the opportunity to make a statement in his own behalf. All sentences are imposed by the judge and are based on his independent assessment of the elements of the hearing.

The law states that for murder, imprisonment should be from twenty to forty years. If the Court finds that the murder was accompanied by extremely brutal or heinous behavior—indicative of wanton cruelty—it may sentence the defendant to a term of natural life imprisonment or death. Or the judge can impose an extended term of forty to eighty years. In view of Steve's record and the many written appeals on his behalf, Steve's supporters hoped the judge would be lenient.

The State began by recounting the features of the case. Magnuson asked for an extended prison sentence; Karen Phillips's life, he said, had been snuffed out at twenty-four years of age. With modern technology, life expectancy for a woman could be, say, eighty-five years. Karen, therefore, had been brutally denied perhaps sixty years of her anticipated life span.

After Magnuson had finished, Decker quickly reviewed the main points. Decker had planned to have three character witnesses testify on Steve's behalf, but rather than have them appear in person, Judge Stillo asked Decker to state the substance of their testimony.

Fay Smart, widow of one of the three founders of Emmaus Bible College, had known Steve since his arrival in the Chicago area three years earlier. She had ample opportunity to observe him in church, school, and social situations, and had entertained him and his family in her home on many occasions. She was more than convinced of his integrity, chastity, and morality.

Julie Mostert, a tall, slender, beautiful young woman, is a registered nurse and had worked with Steve on a missionary project while she was a student at Emmaus. She was single at the time and had the highest regard for Steve. Earlier that year, she had been willing to interrupt her summer vacation in Canada and fly, at her own expense, to Chicago to be a character witness at the trial.

Lynn Smid was Steve's supervisor at the Holiday Inn Reservation Office, and had observed him closely for five months. While not a professing Christian, Lynn had no hesitation in testifying to Steve's excellent character.

In view of Steve's record, Decker appealed for leniency and asked that Steve not be consigned to a maximum-security penitentiary.

Then Lois was given the opportunity to address the Court. She was dressed in black slacks and a white long-sleeved dress blouse, with frills around the cuffs and neck. Her cheeks looked flushed. She had needed extra make-up that morning, because she wasn't feeling well; a slight fever and a persistent cough had been bothering her for the past week. The strain was intense. Only those who knew Lois knew how devastated she was when the new trial was denied. Only those who had wept and prayed with her knew how hard she struggled with anger and bitterness. But in her turmoil, God again proved His love.

Lois spoke softly, but clearly. Her delicate hands hardly trembled as they held the notes of the speech she had carefully and prayerfully prepared. Though her voice often wavered, she was able to control her emotions throughout her address. Her eyes were moist with tears. She said, "Steve Linscott is both my husband and best friend. I've known him for about eight years and the last five and a half years we have been married. Not once during these years have I ever seen behavior on his part that is consistent with his committing this horrendous crime.

"In his relationships with other people Steve has been very trusting of them. He simply takes folks at their word and tries to help them when he can.

"I have never observed in Steve personal prejudice toward anyone for any reason . . . including racial or religious differences.

"Steve is very open and honest with others, though not aggressively outgoing. He's never been one to 'cover up' his feelings. If there were conflicts between us it was very like him to initiate the process of resolving them. During conflicts, which were no more frequent than most married couples, he never physically or verbally threatened me. We have always been able to work things out by sitting down, talking, making compromises, and praying together.

"Steve has always been truthful and honest with me. He's never hidden anything from me. When he's made mistakes he's been quick to face his faults, admit them, apologize when needed . . . and continue on constructively.

"As long as I've known him, Steve has always been a

gentle, responsible, and caring person. One of the first things that impressed me about Steve was his affection and care for his six brothers and sisters, one of whom has a rare blood disease which has resulted in her being mentally retarded. The first time I met him he was voluntarily baby-sitting this sister for his parents so they could have an evening out. His love, tenderness, and sense of responsibility was very apparent.

"During our courtship and marriage Steve has always been sensible and responsible. He's always handled money in a responsible way and a first priority has been to pay our bills. He seldom uses our only credit card. And yet in spite of his New England thriftiness, he has deliberately splurged on special gifts for me . . . at times when I least expected them, just to remind me of his love.

"Steve, himself, is a hard and diligent worker and has never put me in a position where I was forced to work outside of the home in order to make ends meet.

"Steve has always been very tender and affectionate as a husband, lover, and father. We've enjoyed a very normal and growing sexual relationship together, both before and after the occurrence of the crime . . . and he has *never* given me reason to doubt his faithfulness to me. He's not a flirt, but has always had healthy friendships with women.

"Steve has always encouraged me to participate in activities outside of the home which I feel are enriching to me as an individual. In turn, he has welcomed these opportunities to spend quality time with the children.

"As a father, Steve has consistently shown deep love and care for our three children. He eagerly participated in each of their births and very willingly and capably took over the cooking and household chores while I recuperated from the deliveries. From diaper changing . . . to reading them stories . . . to romping and playing freely with them, Steve has done a superb job of fathering. When disciplinary measures were taken, he always precipitated them with adequate warning . . . and then followed the disciplinary action with lots of physical and verbal affection. I think two words that would best sum up Steve as a father would be *'affectionate'* and *'kind.'*

"Steve has consistently treated me as his equal and truly respects me and also my opinion about a given matter. He has never gone ahead and made a major decision without obtaining my input.

"The decision to move into the Good News Mission, Austin Center, was our decision. Of course, as students trying to save money, we were glad for the opportunity to live in a rent-free apartment. But we were also excited about the prospect of helping provide a Christian homelike environment for ex-convicts who were sincere about starting life again—so to speak—but this time with God's help.

"Steve is a person of personal initiative. He has always been a positive thinker and hasn't been afraid of trying to do something he's never done before. For instance, during the period of time immediately following his release on bond he was unable to find work right away. I began working full-time in nursing and he took care of the children. At the *same* time he managed to do a major job of remodeling the main kitchen in the Austin Center—something he had never had experience with before! It took him a while to do it because he had to fit the project around the children's needs, but all the same, he did a great job!

"Steve's faith in God is genuine. He's not an actor—and never has been! On the contrary, he's a sincere and devoted Christian."

All this time, Lois had faced Judge Stillo—she had been talking to him exclusively. As she concluded her remarks, she asked permission to address her husband. She turned in

Steve's direction. Steve turned too and looked directly at her. Their eyes met.

"Steve, my message to you is found in the Word of God: Isaiah 54:10, 11, 13, and 14 [NASB]:

> For the mountains may be removed and the hills
>   may shake,
> But My lovingkindness will not be removed from
>   you.
> And My covenant of peace will not be shaken,
> Says the Lord who has compassion on you.
> O afflicted one, storm-tossed and not comforted;
> Behold, I will set your stones in antimony
> And your foundations I will lay in sapphires. . . .
> And all your sons will be taught of the Lord,
> And the well-being of your sons will be great.
> In righteousness you will be established.
> You will be far from oppression, for you will not
>   fear
> And from terror, for it will not come near you."

It was now Steve's turn to speak. His face was drawn, and he looked nervous. His voice quivered. He found it hard to control his emotions; several times he wept. There was much he wanted to say and little time to say it.

Steve began by referring his Christian friends to the fourth chapter of Paul's second letter to the Corinthians, a reference to let them know where he was in his experience. Then he continued:

"The people of God are to be commended for their wisdom and perseverance, and for not bowing to the thoughts of Job's friends to Job. I know that in the end God will justify me and will reward your labors for us.

"I was raised to respect the authorities of this land, and I do yet. Our naïveté of the hard and ruthless realities contained in our society created this situation.

"Many have referred me to another young man who also had a dream of a particular event. I'm not referring to Abraham Lincoln or others in history who have recorded dreams of a prophetic or psychic nature. This other young man, like myself, also told his dream with a clear conscience to those whom he normally would have trusted—his own brothers.

"I'm referring to the story of Joseph in the Bible. When the brothers saw Joseph approaching, they said, 'The dreamer cometh, let's put an end to him.' The bias from the beginning is obvious.

"He, like me, was threatened, deceived, placed into detention, and sent into all the degradations of slavery.

"My record speaks loudly, I believe. I was raised in a military family. My father retired as a Chief Petty Officer. We have always lived under the umbrella of Naval facilities. I went two years to college, and then five years in the Navy. My Navy evaluations from my superiors—four times a year—were all excellent. I served with the admiral's staff for two and a half of those five years, and was recommended to that position because of being made 'honorman' of my company in boot camp.

"That's part of my military service. My civilian life is just as consistent as those five years in the Navy. I don't want to parade my laurels. I just want to point out the fact that, despite my consistent lifestyle—which is supported by all these witnesses—I am, all of a sudden, accused of murder. This is totally inconsistent with all that is known of me.

"My desire and goal while studying Bible under the missions program at Emmaus was to ever be an asset to society—home or foreign. I only wanted, and still want, the very best for people around me.

201

"Dreams are as much a part of the biblical record as faith and salvation. The first two chapters of the New Testament contain the record of five separate dreams. Numbers of people, reporters and others, have asked me why I would speak of a dream in the first place. Perhaps most people would not—being practical, calculating people. But not all people think exactly alike. Some segments of society would not think it untoward at all. Of those that may hold to the validity of dreams, only a few would be public-spirited enough to consider reporting them to the police, or informing them of such. I wouldn't have, without the additional props of a policeman's visit and the encouragement of friends. I hope that helps to explain to some reporters and others who have asked my reasons for doing so.

"If I had been at any time erratic or out of character, my good and dear wife would have noted it. My wife is a practical, just, and good person. We both love the truth more than life itself."

At this point Steve broke down. After a few moments he continued.

"I realize that this is a function of the State today. I'm not attempting to rehash parts of the case. I have opinions on the evidence and other parts of the case, but it is not for that purpose that we are here today.

"Many of the good people present today would have greatly preferred to have seen an entirely different outcome. We haven't given up hope.

"I will not attempt to belabor the sufferings that we have all undergone. It has been a severe testing—for many." Summoning as much strength as he could, Steve raised his voice and continued, "My wife and I and my children and friends stand together today and say with the saints of old, 'My God is able to deliver me.'

"Joseph's final state was not as God first allowed it to be.

"We affirm our belief in and trust of the Lord in this matter. We continually look for His help and aid. We trust in the living God. I fully realize that even though many want to bring up many things about the past two years, this is not the appropriate time to do so. I respect the authority and power of this Court. I simply cast myself upon the mercy of the Court and ask that the many items we have presented for this moment be considered."

For several days before the hearing Steve had studied the crucifixion and sufferings of Jesus. Many details came into focus as he contemplated his own fate. Seeing how Christ handled each situation was a challenge to him.

Every eye was focused on Adam Stillo as he summed up the hearing. Lifting them off his desk and holding them in his hand, he admitted to receiving a lot of letters and said he was taking them into account. He noted Steve's life before and after the tragic killing of Karen Phillips. He had listened to the testimonies of character witnesses. He had heard the pleas of the State for an extended term. He was ready to impose the sentence.

"I hereby sentence Steven Linscott to forty years in prison."

To those in the audience it was as if a bomb had exploded. Steve's heart was stayed on the Lord and was calm.

Decker immediately asked for consignment to a medium or minimum-security penitentiary, but Judge Stillo was unable to intervene and denied the request. He did, however, advise that application for special consideration be made to the Prisoner Review Board. To assist the defense's deliberations, the judge offered to hand over his thick file of letters received from the friends of Steve and Lois. Turning to Steve, he wished him good luck in the years ahead.

In the end the judge seemed strangely moved, as if he wanted to help Steve but realized it was too late.

Judge Stillo had admitted into the trial physical evidence that was, and will continue to be, controversial, evidence that did not exist at the time of the trial. Even if it had, it would have had little or no real value, but the defense was not allowed to prove that. The judge denied every motion filed by the defense. He accepted a verdict of "guilty of murder." He had read and denied the motions and arguments for a new trial.

Now that it was all over, he was wishing Steve Linscott "good luck," and washing his hands of the whole affair.

13
God
Meant It for Good

One night around 10:30, four tired men pored over a Rand McNally road atlas looking for Centralia, Illinois. All they knew was that it was about three hundred miles downstate from Chicago. Finally, these four men, all elders of the River Forest Bible Chapel, located it on the map. Centralia, a rural town, was to be the Linscotts' home pending the outcome of the appeal. Lois Linscott had described it to them as "a neat little town of about 16,000 people." How she and Steve became residents of Centralia is another remarkable story.

After sentencing, Steve returned to Cook County Jail to await his assignment to a maximum-security penitentiary. His first stop was to be Joliet, Illinois—forty miles southwest of Chicago—but overcrowding and a flood delayed the move. Steve didn't mind; he feared Joliet.

Because a prisoner is locked up all day at Joliet, the

prison has few acts of brutality compared with other maximum-security facilities. Nevertheless, most of its inmates had committed violent crimes. Steve shrank at the prospect of forty years' association with these felons. "I'm glad people across the country have committed me to God and to his tender loving care," Steve said to his wife.

After two weeks of delays, Steve was taken in chains to Joliet with a group of twenty other prisoners, all of whom had sentences ranging from thirty years to life. Steve was handcuffed to an eighteen-year-old youth—the leader of the Chicago Amphitheatre gang rape, who had a hundred-and-twenty-year sentence.

Steve's first "celly" had recently become a born-again Christian and had returned to Illinois to turn himself in to the authorities. Through the ministry of the Good News Mission at the DuPage County Jail, his faith had grown quickly. On his way from DuPage he prayed that God would assign him to a cell with a Christian who would help him grow. He had another motive too—his own personal safety and survival. His prayers were answered in Steve for the ten days before he was moved to another prison.

Joliet is a processing point from which prisoners are assigned to other penitentiaries to serve out their time. While there, inmates will see a psychologist and receive a complete physical examination. Though Steve was afraid, he was probably too deeply hurt to consciously feel the fear. Providentially, he found fellowship with a prisoner whose Bible courses he had corrected while working at Emmaus. Thus the prisoner helped Steve realize that, like in Navy boot camp, one *could* survive.

Steve's next cellmate was a notorious criminal, the leader of one of Chicago's most dangerous gangs and highly respected by many street gangsters. At his command men were hurt—everyone carried out his orders. Not for one moment could Steve afford to let his inner tremblings be seen. It was imperative that he appear tough and fearless.

Bravely, Steve witnessed to this "celly" and gave the most powerful testimony of his life. He felt like an earthen vessel containing a priceless treasure—the gospel. "I felt like the apostle Paul witnessing to Agrippa," Steve told me one day. "The man was hard, but he showed real interest and said that he might 'try the Lord.'"

Meanwhile, Decker had applied to the Prisoner Review Board to have Steve reassigned to a medium-security prison. The chances were good. Steve's record was exemplary, and the many letters written to Judge Stillo on Steve's behalf proved helpful.

Steve fully expected to be consigned to Menard, Statesville, or Pontiac penitentiaries. Compared with these places, Joliet was a resort.

Surprisingly the authorities assigned him to the Centralia Correctional Institute, a medium-security prison surrounded by high double barbed wire fences. It was the newest and most modern facility in the state. Once again, God had controlled the situation. Normally, a person convicted of such a crime would not be so favored.

Upon arrival at Centralia, five days before Christmas 1982, Steve decided to be wary about whom to trust, which was difficult for someone with his open, honest, trusting demeanor. Serving time was not going to be easy—he never expected it to be.

In August 1982, two and a half months after Steve's conviction, Lois and the children moved in with the Sprinkles. Bob Sprinkle was the pastor of Circle Church in Oak Park. His wife Patti, a member of the Linscott investigative committee, had worked tirelessly on the case. Their friendship and love were invaluable.

After Steve's move, Lois visited Centralia to "spy" out

the land, locate an apartment, and secure a job. With her were Bob and Judy Ramey. Bob was one of the Emmaus faculty members who had taken a real interest in the case, and Judy was a counselor at the Wheaton Christian Counseling Center.

The trip was successful. In one day they found a lovely two-bedroom apartment, arranged a job interview for Lois, and located a baby-sitter. Then they visited Steve. For the first time in over six months he and Lois could throw their arms around each other and embrace.

Few women remain committed to their incarcerated husbands because prison adds such a tremendous strain to a marriage. Many inmates are largely forsaken by their families. But Lois Linscott was different. She had taken Steve for better or for worse, and she knew theirs was a special marriage. And she knew her husband was innocent.

Steve told Lois about his first interview with the prison chaplain at Centralia. The encounter had not been pleasant. After sharing with the chaplain his life and testimony, Steve was told, "I can't stand anyone who comes to prison and claims to be perfect!"

"I'm not perfect. But I *am* innocent!" Steve retorted.

The meeting with the chaplain had left him feeling depressed. Christmas did nothing to help either. Steve felt no joy or gratitude—just the pain of an aching heart. He had claimed so many victory verses of Scripture only to feel defeated and disappointed.

Night after night he struggled with God. *Where have I erred concerning my knowledge of God and the relationship of prayer to the Christian life?* he asked himself. *God just wants to disappoint me!*

Steve was placed in a section with two wings joined by a large recreation room in the middle. He was one of twenty-five men sharing one wing. Although each man had his own room and key, movement was restricted—more so, in some ways, than in a maximum-security facility. Unless summoned by an authority, no one was permitted to leave his housing unit. The main advantage of a medium-security facility is the added safety. Centralia had the further advantage of being modern and clean.

Steve was the only born-again believer in his wing. Starting a Bible study proved difficult because all "religious activity" had to be approved by the chaplain's office, and Steve's evangelical approach did not mesh with the liberal theology of the prison chaplains.

Since the Sunday services at prison left him unfulfilled, he wrote to his outside friends urging them to pray for a spiritual renewal in the prison.

Steve quickly settled into a routine. He awoke at 6:30 A.M. and spent the next thirty minutes in informal prayer. When the guards opened the doors at 7:00 A.M., Steve dressed, prayed again—only longer this time—and read his Bible. Only then did he eat breakfast and prepare for work. For a starting salary of $19 a month, he worked seven hours a day as a clerk for the captain in charge of inmate assignments and daily movements.

Realizing the need for physical fitness, Steve regularly exercised in the gym; weight-lifting, in particular, helped him work out his frustrations. He felt better, slept more soundly at night, and relished the physical development of his upper body.

It also gave him an added sense of security.

For more than a year Steve lived opposite a man nicknamed "Strawberry." Professionally, he was a "sneak thief," that is, he sneaked into apartments while the occupants showered or slept or were away, and stole whatever he could find.

The two men often talked about God. Strawberry asked

many questions and wanted to know all the benefits of becoming a Christian. (He particularly had the financial benefits in mind for he had noticed that Steve had been sent a stereo from one of his friends.) Strawberry was searching. Over and over he asked what faith is and how to know if you have it. How did Steve know God was real and would do things he claimed He would? For over a year Strawberry scrutinized Steve's life, looked for inconsistencies, asked the same questions again and again. And always, it seemed, he disagreed with Steve's answers.

In January 1984, as the two prisoners talked as they had done numerous times before, something happened. Steve explained, "I was able to define faith and the gospel in a convincing way—as only happens when the Holy Spirit is determined to have it done. After I described the faithfulness of God, my daily experiences with Christ—which were so real to me—and the eternal life that only God can give, Strawberry listened more intently than at any other time. He seemed ready. So I pulled out the 'Four Spiritual Laws' and led him to faith in Christ. I played it kind of cool with him after he prayed because I wanted to be sure that he wasn't just mouthing the words. The next day he commented that he wasn't sure he had experienced anything. But I noticed a change in him—his attitudes and behavior were different. There seemed to be a real carefulness not to sin. Soon afterward he was transferred to the honor dorm, making it impossible to follow him up."

More than a year later Steve was also promoted to the honor dorm and found himself with Strawberry. Spiritually, Strawberry was at a standstill. Without Christian fellowship he was still struggling with his hurts and doubts. But he was glad to see Steve.

Before and during the trial, the press generally reflected a bias against Steve. His guilt was largely assumed. Fortunately, after his conviction and sentencing, the tide turned.

At the end of 1982 Randy Frame, an assistant news editor with *Christianity Today*, looked into the Linscott story. Randy pored over the transcripts of the taped interviews and the trial, and he read the motions and supporting arguments for a new trial. He conducted time-consuming interviews with the lawyers and those involved in the case. He even called the Oak Park Police Department, but no one there was willing to discuss the case. Prosecutor Jay Magnuson denied him an interview, but Assistant State's Attorney John Morrissey permitted a brief discussion. Randy also visited Steve in Joliet—just before his transfer to Centralia.

Randy was shocked by what he discovered. Committed to the principles of fair and honest reporting, he maintained his objectivity. His article "The Strange Case of Steven Linscott" appeared in the February 4, 1983, issue of *Christianity Today*. It started a chain reaction whose effects were felt across the country and around the world. The magazine, with 180,000 subscribers, is read by pastors, leaders, and teachers of the evangelical church world-wide. The response was immediate. Pastors shared the tragic story with their congregations; letters of encouragement, enquiries, and offers of help poured in from around the country; Christians everywhere were alarmed by the injustice.

Ken Christensen of Collinsville, Illinois, read his copy of *Christianity Today* the same morning it arrived. He was concerned by the article and contacted me for more information. By coincidence, Ken's father was undergoing eye surgery in Centralia the following day, and Ken had already planned on being there. He decided to call Lois. He also alerted Dr. E. L. Goss, interim pastor of the First Baptist Church in Centralia, and his cousin, Susan Johnson, and her husband Royce, both of whom were ophthalmologists and members of Dr. Goss's Church.

God was working! Dr. Goss (who happened to be from Steve's own state of Maine) and the Johnsons were sympathetic and became close allies and friends. Dr. Goss visited Lois and Steve, and made some preliminary enquiries of his own. "We must act," he told the deacons of First Baptist, "and involve the church." These Christians extended open arms to the Linscotts, adopted them into their family, and made them "watchcare" members of the church.

Dr. Goss ("E.L." as he is affectionately known) spent many hours with Steve, studied all the transcripts, reports, and literature on the case, and invited me to address the growing number of interested Christians in the city. In a remarkably short time, Dr. Goss had familiarized himself with just about every aspect of the case.

A number of people in his church formed the Linscott Concern Committee. This group included, among others, a bank vice-president, an insurance supervisor, an ophthalmologist, an engineer, a business manager, and a schoolteacher. Like others before them, this committee studied all the materials relative to the case, met with Jim Richards when he was in town one day, and arrived at its own conclusion: Steve Linscott is being held at the Centralia Correctional Center on a forty-year sentence for a crime he did not commit.

On April 18, 1983, Ray Kimmell, chairman of the Linscott Concern Committee, wrote a letter to some four hundred American Baptist churches in Illinois and neighboring states, and enclosed a reprint copy of the *Christianity Today* article. Ray wrote, "Many of you will be skeptical of Steve's innocence, but let me assure you that we have spent hours studying the trial transcripts and the evidence the State submitted. We have studied the police tapes and other trial documents. We have also had the availability of speaking with those who have been with this matter from the beginning and who are mentioned in the article. We have no doubt of Steve's innocence and trust you will come to the same conclusion."

Dr. Goss prepared a "fact sheet about the innocence of Steve Linscott" and wrote an accompanying letter of his own. The letter began:

At about this date in the glorious spring of 1945, I came with the United States Army [as a chaplain] to a beautiful little town and church in southern Bavaria. The people were so kind and loving in that church and community. That afternoon, I stood among 500 emaciated dead bodies in a concentration camp four miles away. "Why, oh, why did you let such actions go on?" was my question, when I returned to the people in the village. "It wasn't our business; it was a law! What could we do?" To this day, I have never been able to accept that foolish answer.

Today—this very day—one of the finest young men I have ever known is in prison—four miles from where I write. It is beyond belief that I should take this lying down. I must protest with every breath in my body! I hope you feel this way, too!

Dr. Goss wrote a longer memorandum addressed to the citizens of Steve's home state, Maine. In this three-page letter he said, "I have studied Steven Linscott personally— in long, private conversations; spent extensive periods of time with his family; studied his Maine background and Navy record; read the entire transcripts of the trial and viewed the actions of the police, the prosecutor, and the defense attorney. Gradually, I obtained the complete picture and understood it fully."

E.L. became deeply involved in the case. He wrote to Congresswoman Olympia J. Snowe in the United States House of Representatives and Governors James R. Thompson and Joseph E. Brennan. As he ended his interim pastorate in July 1983, after five months on the case, he wrote a personal letter to prosecutor Jay Magnuson. One paragraph, in particular, is worth noting:

We would suppose that if you people feel as secure as intelligent human beings in your position, as we do as intelligent human beings in ours, that you will be prepared to stand and contend. We mean this as happening in the court of public opinion . . . and in every other place. On the other hand if I were in your place, before this goes any further, I would wonder if I had not, like the "Blindman of Hindustan," obtained a wrong picture of the elephant and needed to objectively review my whole position. If I were you, I would find a skilled and dispassionate friend, or colleague, who would study the whole matter over again with me item by item. Such a friend could show you all kinds of slips that might have been made. To err is still a human characteristic—for me and you.

The letter capped months of involvement, concern, and prayer that led to an ever-widening circle of Linscott supporters. The desire to free Steve intensified. The number of letters to the Illinois governor increased as people felt compelled to urge a rectification of this travesty.

Steve wept when Dr. Goss's interim pastorate in Centralia ended, but Steve is convinced God sent E.L. to help him. No one will ever be able to measure his tenacity as he championed Steve's cause. Seldom a day passed without his writing a letter or making a call or a visit. Steve and Lois and their children grew to love him. Often, as soon as Lois arrived at church, E.L. would take little Vicki in his arms. Vicki loved his bear hugs and would cuddle up to him.

For five months E.L. Goss was there when Steve and Lois needed him most. Sometimes he visited Steve just to cry with him—to feel his hurt and his pains. Even his Maine accent cheered Steve and Lois. Dr. Goss was an answer to the Linscotts' prayers.

Even now, when he thinks of Dr. Goss, Steve thinks of Matthew 25:31–46 in which Jesus teaches that one's attitude to him is evident by one's treatment of his brethren: "I was in prison and you came to visit me," Jesus says. Both the righteous and unrighteous respond, "Lord, when did we see you . . . in prison and go to visit you?" And Jesus replied, "I tell you the truth, whatever you did for one of the least of these brothers of mine, you did it to me."

As the days, weeks, and months passed, Steve waited for God to intervene. But nothing happened. Yet as he plodded along in the routines of prison life, he knew many were working for his release.

The brightest spot in Steve's life was Lois's weekly visit with the children. Lois never missed her four-hour appointments; many times the guards graciously extended the visits an hour or so.

Steve did his best to minister to his wife during visits and when he telephoned her in the evenings. He tried to be strong. He wanted to calm Lois's fears and frustrations, and he was careful not to let his incarceration impede his leadership in their relationship.

During Lois's visits, the guards watched every move. The rules stipulate that couples are only allowed to kiss and embrace at the beginning and end of the visit, though they are allowed to hold hands in between. Katherine, Paul, and

Vicki, however, would get as close as they could to their father, sit on his knee, hug and kiss him all the time—the rules said nothing about children.

The guards were friendly and let the children approach them for pencils to write with and sometimes just to chat. It would be hard for them not to be impressed by the closeness, love, and commitment of the Linscott family.

But the children felt the hurt of separation. Katherine had just turned four when Steve was first incarcerated. Five months had passed before she was allowed to see her daddy again. Even then the visit was brief—just a few minutes before the start of the sentence hearing. On that occasion there was no privacy, no physical contact. Paul was nearly three at the time and asked Lois, "Are we going to jail with Daddy now?" How she wished they could!

As time wore on, Katherine became more vocal. "It's so sad to leave Daddy here," she would say. When Steve called home, Katherine often picked up the phone and chatted with him before handing the receiver to Lois. "When are you coming home?" was the one question she asked most frequently. She was sure Steve would be released before her fifth birthday and prayed to this effect with typical childlike faith. When that did not happen, she was hurt. Her sixth birthday passed. And her seventh. Lois found it hard to explain the continued delays to a child who believed God answered her prayers.

Little Paul's affection for Steve grew steadily. "He's *my* daddy!" he would exclaim proudly. He regularly insisted, "Daddy is my *best* buddy." But many nights before falling asleep he broke down and cried. He needed his father.

Each summer the prison organized a picnic in the yard for families to join the inmates for activities and relaxation. After the picnic in June 1984 Paul, sobbing, went up to a guard and said, "I want my daddy to come home *today!* Can he come home?" The tears were streaming down his cheeks.

The guard could only stammer, "Someday he will, Paul. Someday!"

By January 1984 Vicki, two years old, instinctively knew when it was time for their weekly visit with Steve. On visiting day she would pat Lois on the knee and exclaim excitedly, "Daddy, daddy!" She knew.

God was surrounding the children with His goodness and mercy.

After three months in Centralia, Steve resigned his clerical job and enrolled in courses sponsored by Kaskaskia College. The continuing education program was another distinct advantage of the Centralia institution. Evening courses in sociology, biology, English, astronomy, and math completed the sixteen hours needed for his associate of arts degree in general education.

In June 1983 he became religion editor for the in-house newspaper, *The Forum*. With an inmate population of almost 1,000 and a staff of 250, the paper had a wide circulation. Steve relished the chance to share the gospel. Within three months he became assistant editor, and six months later he assumed the editorship of *The Forum*.

As an assistant editor, Steve worked with editor Mike Hanrahan to put together an award-winning paper. Three issues of the newspaper were selected from this period for submission to the department of journalism at Southern Illinois University on the occasion of the nationwide Annual Penal Press Awards Journalism Contest.

Steve's commitment to excellence was rewarded. In December 1983 *The Forum* won top honors. The judges were amazed. They did not believe such quality could be achieved on a simple A. B. Dick mimeograph machine. Proudly, the A. B. Dick Company reported the story in their own in-house magazine.

But the successes didn't stop there. Steve won an

honorable mention in the best-column category for three of his "God's Word" columns. After Steve became editor of *The Forum* in 1984, the paper won four more awards—the highest number in its history. Steve also won top honors for a story entitled "The Rapture."

As the months passed, Steve fought discouragement and despair, always convinced the Lord had a plan for his life. When disillusionment overcame him, he would turn to Philippians 3:10—"I want to know Christ and the power of his resurrection and the fellowship of sharing in his sufferings." The truth of that Scripture was burned into his heart and mind by the Holy Spirit.

Through his incarceration Steve was able to understand Christ's sufferings in a new way. He discovered that the answer to suffering is God himself. But his problems were far from over. Although Steve believed vengeance belongs to God, he still found it hard to eliminate the bitterness he felt toward the system and those who had wronged him.

Steve found that God is loving and gracious. God gave him leeway to express his feelings, fears, and frustrations, his opinions, doubts, and anger. Like Job, he wished at times that he could ascend into heaven, challenge God face to face and say, "Oh, God, what do you think you are doing?" But Steve knew that God already understood.

Steve's social life was limited. Inmates tended to keep to themselves. Although he had little in common with his neighbors, Steve tried hard to build rapport—with few successes. Prisoners are distrustful—anyone could be an informer. Because any sign of weakness is misinterpreted, inmates become hard, tough, suspicious, and hypersensitive.

One day at mealtime, for example, a small bean accidentally dropped off Steve's plate, bounced off his knee, then fell onto another prisoner's shoe, before finally landing on the floor.

"Hey, man, that hit my shoe!" the man said angrily.

"Yeah, but it hit *my knee* first!" Steve responded.

The man glared at Steve for a moment and shrugged.

This seemingly insignificant incident revealed several things: Steve's eyes showed that he was not afraid, that he was not weak. His comment showed that he did not apologize unnecessarily; that it was an accident. Inmates have drawn knives over such little things.

A similar experience occurred in Joliet the year before. A large group of men was waiting to be led into the yard, when an officer suddenly called for everyone to pair up and stand in a straight line. One large bearded inmate resolutely stood to one side while the officer continued to shout his orders. Steve reached out, touched the man on his arm, and quietly said, "Straight line."

The man turned, glared at Steve, and shouted, "Don't you ever touch me—don't touch me!" His eyes were filled with hate and panic. He looked as if he were going to punch Steve, but he only said, "Keep your hands off me!" Steve tried not to show fear, for he immediately realized that it was not his job to interfere. It was a valuable lesson!

Steve needed constant wisdom and courage. This was evident one day in the prison yard at Centralia. A friend of his called him over to the tractor he was driving and asked him to carry some gloves into the prison unit. Steve agreed. But as he walked away, he noticed a staff member's name stenciled on the gloves and instinctively realized that he was participating in a theft. He tried to return the gloves to his friend on the tractor who refused to accept them back. Finally, Steve handed them to another staff member.

It was not long before the entire unit knew of the incident, and Steve received much flak for refusing to help in the theft. The inmate who had tried to trick him bombarded Steve with verbal abuse.

But Steve's honesty and wisdom also earned him the respect of many of the men who lived around him. They knew he was a Christian. They knew what he stood for and eventually nicknamed him "preacher."

Time and again, God granted Steve the supernatural wisdom for which he prayed. Once Steve was about to publish the story of a nasty incident in the prison. The story was written, typed, and ready for press when, fortunately, he discovered the incident had been fabricated. He pulled the story despite strong resistance from his fellow inmates.

"God is so complicated," Steve said one day, "that to try and understand the big picture is impossible." He discovered that God really delights in helping people mature. "The best fruits come from the best tilled soil; the finest characters are always forged in a furnace."

The spiritual support of Christians in the town of Centralia for Lois and the children overwhelmed Steve. They ministered financially too. For instance, one day Lois took her Mazda to the garage to have a brake repair done. The estimate was $220, but Lois kept the information to herself. Somehow, one of the deacons found out and insisted that the church pay the cost from special funds.

Scripture helped Lois too. "The last thing I want is sympathy," she said to friends. "Psalm 56:8 has been a real encouragement to me, 'List your tears on my scroll.' As I have cried to the Lord, I believe he has done just that. *He* knows, *he* cares, *he* understands."

Scripture showed Lois that to heal her own hurts and frustrations she needed to reach out to others—Sandy and Mary Lou, for instance. Both lived in Chicago and occasionally traveled to Centralia to visit their husbands in prison. Lois opened her home to them, talked with them, and helped them any way she could. Her burden was to minister to *all* the wives and families of inmates of the prison as the Lord guided her.

One way she did this was to help Charles Colson's Prison Fellowship gain a foothold in the area. Stirring interest among local Christians to become active in prison work, especially visitations, was difficult. Apathy was widespread. Few wanted to become involved with inmates of penal institutions, fearing possible repercussions and the cost in time, energy, and money. Yet every other Friday, a small group—representing some six churches in the area—began to meet at the First Baptist Church to pray and plan. Lois was thankful for their commitment.

One day Lois asked God for someone, preferably the wife of an inmate, with whom to work. God led her to Cindy. At the time Cindy had one child and was pregnant with her second. In spite of her rough upbringing, she had professed faith in Christ as a teenager, though her faith had soon cooled. Lois helped Cindy relocate in Centralia, where she too could be near her husband. Lois found her new friend hard and unresponsive at first, but slowly, Cindy softened and started attending church with Lois.

Many families opened their lives to Lois and the children. The teenagers in these families seemed to delight in baby-sitting the children. The older people loved Katherine, Paul, and Vicki as much as their own grandchildren.

Both Steve and Lois knew that God was protecting their marriage. After each visit, Lois felt the renewed pain of separation. But that was a healthy sign, she concluded. Her love for Steve remained deep. Although the separation from her husband made her fearful, with her wide circle of friends—male and female—she developed and enjoyed good social relationships. God sustained the sanctity of their marriage because they both wanted it that way. And they worked hard to keep it pure.

Publicity of the Linscott case began to snowball. *Eternity* magazine featured an article about the case, and at about the same time, *Interest* magazine carried a reprint of the *Christianity Today* article and included an extensive interview with Lois. The following excerpts from that interview show what Lois was feeling at that time:

Q: *What about you personally, Lois? What do you find hardest about the ordeal you have been through in the last two and a half years?*

A: Probably the hardest is the unfairness. I miss him. I miss him when the kids go to bed and it's quiet. I guess I would miss him, too, if he was guilty . . . or if he was dead. If he was guilty, I would think at least justice has been done. But the hardest thing is that it's just not fair. But we know from the Bible that things are not always fair in life.

Q: *How do you deal with anger? Do you find yourself angry or resentful?*

A: I try not to be angry because it takes so much energy out of you. Anger doesn't get you anywhere unless you can channel that energy into something productive.

Q: *How do you win the victory over resentment toward the police and the prosecutors? Can you forgive them? Can you understand how they might see it? What do you find in your heart?*

A: If I am not walking with the Lord I get very bitter and angry. There were times when I was ready to go into that Oak Park police station and really tell them off. Only the Lord kept me from doing it. Such anger would come up in my heart when I drove by there. But when I am walking with the Lord I don't have that anger. I just feel sorry for them. I know they are human beings who need the Lord, and then I can see it from their side that they are probably doing the best job they can.

I spoke harshly to the prosecutor after the verdict. I kept excusing myself saying I had every right to do that. But finally I had to call him and apologize. After that I felt a lot better.

Q: *Is there a temptation to be angry with the Lord? To wonder why He let this happen to you instead of to someone else?*

A: There wasn't much anger when Steve was arrested . . . or even at the verdict. That was more of a shock. I was so shocked I couldn't feel anything. But when we really worked hard getting another lawyer and getting our case together for a new trial—and then the judge denied the motion for a new trial—that's when I really felt the anger.

The judge read the case . . . and the case was excellent! I really felt he knew Steve was innocent and that it shouldn't have turned out like this. So I was very angry at God then, for a couple of weeks. Everything in me wanted to throw in the towel. I was tired of praying to God. Prior to the motions for a new trial, I'd get up at five in the morning and pray and have Bible study and pray again. Probably there were ulterior motives. You know, trying to get on God's good side. But I was really angry at Him when the motions for a retrial were denied.

Q: *What helped you through that?*

A: Remembering the response of Peter to the Lord when He asked His disciples, "Will you also go away?" A lot of folks had left Him. Peter said, "Well, where else shall we go? There's no alternative. You're the best choice we've got" [John 6:66–69].

That's the only thing I could think of—I don't have any

alternatives. The alternative was anger and bitterness . . . and the desire for revenge. I knew I couldn't cope with that and would probably go crazy.

The Lord rewarded me for just hanging on and not lashing out against Him with my mouth. I wanted to! I wanted to tell folks this is not fair—why is God doing this—and curse Him with my mouth. I knew that would be wrong, even though everything in me wanted to.

That week the Lord did two miracles in my life that proved to me that He loved me.

Q: *Can you tell us those miracles?*

A: I was in nursing school in 1976. I had a roommate—a real sweet girl—and we were good friends. I tried to witness to her. We parted company when school was over and lost track of each other. Well, this particular week she called me.

It wasn't easy for her. Remembering I might be marrying a Linscott, she started calling all the Linscotts listed for Ellsworth, Maine. There must be a hundred of them. When she got the right one they would only tell her we were in the Chicago area, because they didn't know who she was. She called information, and fortunately there aren't too many Linscotts out here.

Anyway, when she finally got me she said, "Lois, I have had such a compulsion to call you." She told me she had accepted the Lord a couple of years ago, partly through my witness. She said her husband had had an alcohol problem, that he had come to the Lord . . . and now they were serving Him together!

It was a real encouragement! . . . and it happened right during this week of the hardest spiritual struggle I have ever had.

Q: *And the other miracle?*

A: It was a very small thing! But to me a miracle nonetheless. A couple of weeks earlier I had been given a real nice pair of black slacks. I hung them in the closet thinking I needed a white blouse to go with them. Then I just forgot about it.

Well, that week when I was having all the trouble someone gave me this box. Inside was a white, dressy blouse . . . and a note from a lady I knew. It said, "Lois, I bought this blouse a couple of days ago for myself. I was going to wear it to a function coming up, but the Lord told me to give it to you."

That was amazing to me. It wasn't the blouse, but the fact that the Lord was working . . . and showing me that He was.

I guess the Lord would have gotten me through that hard time without the miracles. But they were real acts of love.

As a result of this positive media coverage, letters began to arrive from all over the world. Prayer groups were formed to pray specifically for Steve. Faculty members of Christian colleges and schools prayed for him and challenged their students to do the same.

In April of 1983 Harvey Rogers, a former missionary to Colombia, drove all the way from Rochester, New York, to visit the Linscotts. He left Lois with a carload of food parcels donated by Christians in New York. Harvey had written to dozens of churches in the Rochester area to appeal for prayer and financial support for Steve and Lois. In one of his letters, he wrote, "Christians in Rochester continue to be outraged by all that has befallen the Linscotts. I guess we should call it 'righteous anger.' I have never seen such united prayer for any one person, or situation, like I have for Steve. Maybe this will be used by God for spiritual renewal in our prayer meetings across the country."

From the Research School of Chemistry in the Australian University in Canberra came an enquiry concerning the blood evidence. The author was one of many scientists who had become concerned at the inconclusive blood tests used in Australia's much publicized Chamberlain case and stated that too many prosecutors make the crime fit the suspect instead of finding the suspect to match the crime.

In July 1983 the Centralia radio station WILY interviewed Lois, Jim Richards, and me on its "Hotline" program, which many local residents and inmates listen to. In response to one question, Jim explained how the physical evidence used against Steve was insufficient, and he was so convincing that some listeners thought he was Steve's lawyer.

One police officer called in and said, "If what you are saying is true, then this guy must have had a bum lawyer." After hearing the program, a prison official told Steve, "It makes you wonder how many others in prison are innocent!"

Dr. A. Douglas Davis, an associate professor of physics at Eastern Illinois University, was one of the many new people to become involved after Steve was moved to Centralia. Doug drove to Centralia, studied the materials, and began scientific research of his own. His conclusion: There was not one shred of evidence linking Steve to the crime. He shared his findings with many of his influential friends, including politicians. He wrote to Governor Thompson: "Tragedies are a part of life. A physician prescribes the wrong medicine and a child is crippled for life. An aircraft engine mechanic overlooks one bolt and two hundred people perish. A power plant operator refuses to believe his instrumentation and the result is 'Three Mile Island' . . . or worse. Perhaps Steve Linscott must be counted as one of the inevitable tragedies of life . . . like a crippled child . . . or a downed aircraft . . . or a nuclear accident. But there is a difference. This tragedy can be ended."

One Saturday in the fall of 1983 Doug gathered some friends and colleagues together and prepared an informational package on the case. A set was mailed to every newspaper, radio, and television station in Illinois that had a readership or listenership in excess of 50,000 people. It was this mailing that in November 1983 brought the Linscotts before the metropolitan Chicago audience.

NBC's Channel 5 in Chicago picked up the story. On two consecutive evenings they broadcast special reports on their 10:00 P.M. news program. The broadcast was preceded by a full-page advertisement in the daily *Chicago Tribune*. The reporters did extensive research and interviewed many people related to the case. Since Jay Magnuson refused to be interviewed, John Morrissey represented the prosecution.

Although the report was objective and presented both sides of the case, it contributed to the growing public sympathy for Steve. The ratings indicated that over a half million people watched the news those two nights. The broadcasts were timely too; they were aired just weeks before the oral arguments were heard before the Appellate Court.

In Milwaukee, WVCY (Wisconsin Voice of Christian Youth) had decided to produce its own television documentary about the case—the first major project undertaken by this young station. This hour-long documentary featured Steve and Lois, Dr. E. L. Goss, Dr. Royce Johnson (an ophthalmologist on the Linscott Concern Committee), Jim Richards, and me. This time, both prosecutors refused to participate.

Excerpts from the taped interviews were heard with a simulation of the events by local paid actors. Vic Eliason, the station manager, narrated. It was a compelling production. It was shown twice in the Milwaukee area in December 1983, and it started another wave of letters to the Linscotts. WVCY then offered the documentary to every Christian television station in America, hoping to bring even more people into contact with the strange case of Steve Linscott. As Dr. Goss explained to the prosecutor, "There are now tens of thousands of people who understand Linscott's innocence. Even more know of the unfairness of the trial. We expect that soon the tens of thousands will become tens of millions. This means the story of actions of the police and the prosecution will be an open book."

It is important to note that none of this publicity was initiated by the Linscotts. The fact that this independent media coverage seemed to climax in December 1983 was providential because the oral arguments were heard in Appellate Court on December 21.

As Steve prepared for the hearing, he thought back to the summer of 1980 when he had led a Bible study on the life of Joseph. In his own quiet times in prison, Steve made a list of at least twenty-one similarities between his own situation and Joseph's—the accusations, the arrest, the persecution, the untrue charges, the incarceration. Joseph had experienced them all. And like Joseph, Steve knew that God had preserved and prospered him even in prison. As Steve thought about his accusers and the Appellate Court hearing, he could honestly speak the words that Joseph had spoken to his brothers many centuries before: "You intended to harm me, but God intended it for good" (Genesis 50:20).

14

Appeal
Unto Caesar

Derek Bok, president of Harvard University and former dean at the Harvard Law School, has been an outspoken critic of the inequities in our judicial system. The April 22, 1983, *Boston Globe* reported these statements he made to the Harvard Board of Overseers:

The blunt, inexcusable fact is that this nation, which prides itself in efficiency and justice, has developed a legal system that is the most expensive in the world, yet cannot manage to protect the rights of most of its citizens. Our competitive society arouses in lawyers great temptations to shoulder aside one's competitors, to cut corners, to ignore the interest of others in the struggle to succeed.

There is far too much law for those who can afford it and far too little for those who cannot. Most people find their legal rights severely compromised by the cost of legal services, the baffling complications of existing rules and procedures, and the long frustrating delays involved in bringing proceedings to a conclusion. The legal system looks grossly inequitable and inefficient.... Despite the staggering expense of the legal system, the lack of access for the poor and middle class is "embarrassing to behold."

Decker elaborated: "Indigent persons often obtain significantly better representation than others (the poor and middle classes), particularly in serious cases. In Cook County, Illinois, for example, murder cases assigned to the Public Defender's Office are handled by a select group of volunteers. Their results are significantly better than those obtained by retained counsel. This is not to say that indigents receive the same quality of representation as wealthy people—any more than the housing, education, and opportunities of indigents measure up to the wealthy's. The wealthy and indigent are both well represented; the poor and middle classes—probably 95 percent of the population—are helpless in the face of official onslaughts such as we have seen in the Linscott case."

By the time the appellate judges heard Steve's oral arguments, the cost of the appeal had risen to over $90,000—and that was not the final cost.* The expense would have been prohibitive without the financial backing of contributors—especially Jim Richards. Without this support the retention of a defense counsel of the caliber of Thomas Decker and his capable associates would have been impossible. His skills, thoroughness, and commitment to the case were needed because the State, on the defensive, resorted to every legal device in the book.

---

*It should be noted that Decker did not profit from the case—he graciously kept his costs to a minimum. Included in the figure are the costs of research, professional investigations, and tests.

The media interest, the flood of mail, and the growing financial backing for Steve surprised even his most ardent supporters.

After months of investigation and preparation, Decker finally completed his first appellate brief and filed it on June 9, 1983—almost a year after the conviction. The brief covered six points, all of which had been included in the earlier motions for a new trial and presented at the post-trial hearing. But the facts of the case remained. Decker began by strenuously arguing that Steve Linscott was entitled to reversal and a new trial—because during their arguments to the jury prosecutors misrepresented the evidence and prejudiced his cause. He maintained that Steve's cause was prejudiced when the prosecutors drew unsupported conclusions from the blood and hair evidence.

The prosecutor told the jury that "Karen was raped by a non-secretor," and that the defendant's pubic hairs were found in the victim's crotch. Because his conclusions were not based on the evidence in the case, they were improper, prejudicial and cause for a new trial. . . .

Based on his tests, the State's expert, Mohammad Tahir, accurately reported his conclusions to the Oak Park Police: "Seminal material located on the vaginal swab *could have* originated from the suspect." Mr. Tahir's live testimony at the trial affirmed his written conclusion: "The defendant's blood was consistent with the blood and semen testing." Material on the vaginal swab "could have come from a secretor or non-secretor," Mr. Tahir testified.

Prosecutor Magnuson, however, wanted more conclusive evidence. So he made it up. Though Mr. Tahir had testified that either a secretor or a non-secretor could have left the semen on the test swab, Mr. Magnuson stated: "Karen was raped by a non-secretor . . . and the defendant is

a non-secretor. The link is the semen matching the non-secretor. Mr. Linscott is a non-secretor. It came from a non-secretor. Mr. Linscott is a non-secretor. . . ."

Suppose an expert had testified that a crime was committed either by a right-handed person or by an ambidextrous person. And suppose the defendant was proven to be ambidextrous. Plainly, the hypothetical prosecutor would misstate the evidence and prejudice the defendant's cause if he told the jury the crime had been committed by an ambidextrous person—a small fraction of the population. The prosecutors in the present case created the same prejudice when they told the jury the victim had been raped by a non-secretor, like Mr. Linscott.

Mr. Magnuson's factual-seeming, repeated statements that a non-secretor had raped Miss Phillips were unsupported by Mr. Tahir's studies. . . .

Magnuson's exaggeration of testimony about hair comparisons stands on all fours with the prejudicial misconduct for which the Illinois Appellate Court reversed *People vs. Giangrande.* There, as here, the State's witness testified that certain hair fragments "could have originated from defendant. . . ." But the prosecutor in *Giangrande,* like Mr. Magnuson here, was not content for the jury to know only that the hairs might have come from the suspect. Therefore, in what the Court held was a substantially prejudicial exaggeration of the evidence, she asked the jury in closing if it was not "a little suspicious that the defendant's head and arm hair would have ended up with the victim's body."

If it was prejudicial for the *Giangrande* prosecutor to identify the evidentiary hairs as those of the suspect, then it was prejudicial in this case as well. Here both prosecutors did it, one of them repeatedly:

MORRISSEY: "[Defendant] left eight to ten hairs of *his* in [the victim's] apartment."

MAGNUSON: "His pubic hairs in her crotch. *His* hairs are found in the most private part of the woman's body.

"What does [Mr. Tahir] mean by consistent? He means there is nothing dissimilar.

"I would suggest to you, Ladies and Gentlemen, if I said there were two American flags right there and they were both twelve by eight and they had the same number of stars and they had the same number of stripes and had the same coloring, would you sit there and say well, there is nothing dissimilar about those two; they are identical.

"But not a scientist. A scientist will state that in every aspect that I examined they were consistent. And what does he mean? There was nothing different. And to a layman it means identical, as the two American flags."

But Mr. Tahir's testimony did not mean that. Hair comparisons are too subjective, too inexact for that. If Mr. Tahir had meant the hairs were identical like two United States flags, he could have said so. But he was more precise! He testified to the limits of his craft when he said the hairs at the crime scene were "consistent" with defendant's, meaning the two had "no dissimilarities." On cross-examination, the expert persistently refused to call the hairs "similar." They were "consistent." No more! In this whole record, only the prosecutors concluded that the evidentiary hairs were Mr. Linscott's. For that misconduct, a new trial is warranted here, just as it was for Mr. Giangrande. . . .

Then Decker touched on the dream before returning to it in detail.

Although the State had presented no scientific evidence to refute Mr. Linscott's account of his dream, Mr. Magnuson in summing up implied that such dreams were impossible. He invited the jury so to conclude by using their own "common sense."

We submit that it was the State's obligation to offer proof that coincidences between dreams and actual events do not occur. Such proof was not offered, the Court may conclude, because there is no scientific support for such a theory.

Moreover, dream telepathy, the process of thought transference from one mind to another through dreams, is a phenomenon whose existence has been proven experimentally. The most common themes of the spontaneous telepathic dreams experienced in everyday life are death and distress. Telepathic dreams are more likely to be in color, detailed, vivid, and [more] confusing to the dreamer than are ordinary dreams. People most likely to dream telepathically are those who tend to remember their dreams and who are open to the possibility of ESP.

Decker continued his attack. He contended that, in violation of Steve's right under the fourteenth amendment to due process of law, Steve's guilt fell short of proof beyond a reasonable doubt. He argued that similarities between Steve's dream and the victim's surroundings were inconclusive, speculative, and wholly consistent with Steve's innocence; that blood evidence against Steve was consistent with the guilt of 60 percent, or perhaps all, of the men in the world; that the hair evidence was consistent with the guilt of any member of a class of unknown size whose hair was similar to Steve's.

Then Decker addressed the improper introduction in to the jury room of a newspaper article about the trial. He argued that a juror's access to information about Steve's bail prejudiced the jury's deliberations and denied Steve the right to an impartial jury and to due process. He went on to argue that Steve was entitled to dismissal of the case because Judge Stillo erred in discharging a juror without sufficient cause and without Steve's consent; that the State's unnecessary and willful destruction of evidence in a useless scientific test deprived Steve of his due process right to challenge scientific evidence against him.

Finally, Decker argued that the testimony that Steve's hair was "consistent" with hairs found at the scene of the crime was so speculative, subjective, and unreliable that its admission over Steve's objection was error that substantially prejudiced his cause and required reversal. He argued that the evidence that two human hairs were "consistent" invited the jury to speculate about Steve's guilt; that identification by comparing two human hairs is so unreliable that the risk of misleading the jury substantially outweighs its value as evidence; that because the blood evidence was so meaningless Judge Stillo erred in allowing its admission. "It no more pointed to Linscott than it did to the 'man in the moon,'" Decker wrote.

This left the hair as the *only* physical evidence against Steve, and Decker proceeded to explain the fallibility of hair tests. While hair evidence is a useful tool in adding to the weight of substantial evidence collected, it is nevertheless unreliable as a forensic tool. Forensic reliance on the conventional comparison microscope needs reappraisal. The method is too limited, too subjective, too speculative, especially when more objective techniques are available. Medical science frequently uses elemental analysis of hair to determine chemical levels such as those tested by the defense expert, Dr. Siegesmund. Electron microscopy is used successfully in a number of scientific fields.

It is unfortunate, and in Steve's case tragic, that forensic science does not use testing techniques used by the medical profession, particularly in instances where the total physical evidence lies in subjective microscopic hair comparisons. Having admitted the evidence, Judge Stillo could easily have instructed the jury concerning its probative value. Not to have done so seems unfair.

Hair evidence can be a valuable forensic tool when it is not compelled to stand on its own. Suppose a woman is raped in the back stairwell of an apartment building. She describes the assailant to the police as six foot tall, about 200 pounds, with black wavy hair, recently cut, and approximately thirty-five years of age. Also, he is deeply tanned, wears a thin moustache, and has a front tooth missing and a scar on his right cheek. He is also wearing a ring on his right hand.

A police artist is called. From the sketch, the police think they know who the assailant is. From a picture album the woman immediately identifies him. She picks him out again at an identification line-up. The man is arrested. Witnesses saw him in the vicinity of the crime—around the time of the rape—wearing the same navy blue Windbreaker described by the victim. The print of his tennis shoe also matched the prints on the floor of the dusty stairwell. Forensic blood and hair tests fail to eliminate him.

In this hypothetical case, hair and blood evidence is useful when added to the cumulative weight of evidence. But on their own, they are inconclusive. Forensic testing techniques are not sufficiently accurate to enable the analyst to affirm positive identification.

In Steve's case, this physical evidence, when made to stand on its own, fell far short of even being circumstantial.

By law, the State has thirty days to respond to an appeal brief. In this case, the State failed to meet its July 9 deadline. Another three weeks elapsed before they even filed for an extension. Over Decker's objection the Appellate Court advanced the new date to October 7. Even then the State failed to comply. It was almost November before Michael Shabat and Kevin Sweeney, assisted by David Cuomo, filed their "brief argument for the plaintiff-appellee" on behalf of Richard M. Daley, State's Attorney for Cook County.

In presenting their viewpoints, the State's lawyers lifted the defendant's statements out of context and studiously avoided explaining the circumstances and conversations that prompted the remarks. For instance:

Now that the dream itself was completely explained, the defendant launched into a lengthy analysis of the killer's psychological profile. In response to Scianna's question as to whether the killer felt remorse for murdering the woman, the defendant said, "There's no way I—he can get rid of this feeling of guilt." Defendant further claimed that, because the killer's conscience bothered him, he would probably "give himself away" by "dropping a trace." Defendant then warned the investigators that they had to be careful when they finally apprehended the murderer because he would "go into a shell" if he perceived he was about to be arrested even though the defendant believed he would welcome getting caught. Finally, the defendant told the investigators that the killer was a family man with a wife and children who would probably be found in the area.

The brief does not explain that these responses were invited by leading questions asked by the police investigators. Steve did not "launch into" any analysis; he was asked to speculate on his dream.

In one instance, eager to match the twenty-four-inch-long tire iron, they turned Steve's description of the dream weapon into "a long metal object." On another occasion—

when Steve said that the weapon in the dream was shorter, like the pendulum of a grandfather clock—the police then claimed that the actual murder weapon was only fourteen inches long.

With reference to the conclusion of the second police interview, the lawyers stated, "It was now about 3:00 in the morning. Before returning home, however, the defendant lingered around in the police lobby for at least twenty minutes." The implication was (they seemed to be hinting) that Steve was still trying to pluck up the courage to confess. In reality, he was talking to Chaplain Stroup who had been patiently waiting in the lobby area for several hours.

Misquoting Sergeant Mendrick's own testimony, the lawyers stated, "Defendant then inquired what would happen if someone walked into the police station and voluntarily confessed to the murder of Karen Ann Phillips." This, of course, is only part of what Mendrick had said. According to the police sergeant, Steve went on to ask, "Would I be released today?" An entirely different construction was conveyed to the Appellate Court. In eighty-one pages of the State's response, the defense felt that there were many inaccuracies.

The State argued that Steve waived his right to review Magnuson's alleged improper closing argument for two reasons. First, he failed to object to the argument in court; and second, the argument was proper because it was based on the evidence and was invited by the defense counsel's improper argument.

The State of Illinois then went on to argue that Steve was proven guilty of murder beyond a reasonable doubt—because his incriminating statement, coupled with the physical evidence that linked him to the crime, clearly demonstrated that he was the person who had beaten Karen Phillips to death by repeatedly striking her in the head with a metal tire iron. The State further argued that Steve's claim that he was deprived of his right to a fair and impartial jury because certain jurors allegedly read newspaper articles about the case was utterly without merit.

The lawyers contended that the trial court exercised discretion in a sound manner when it excused a juror from service because she was so physically exhausted that she could not have properly performed her duties as a juror. They held that Steve's claim that the State intentionally destroyed the vaginal swab evidence—knowing that the defendant had requested to inspect it—was meritless. They argued that Mr. Tahir's testimony—that the unknown hairs and pubic hairs found at the crime scene were consistent with Steve's hairs—was properly admitted into evidence because it was relevant to the issue of whether Steve was the person who murdered the victim, and was based on generally accepted scientific principles.

The State's lawyers attempted to explain away the defense's arguments. They asserted that the admission of the physical evidence and the prosecutors' supposedly improper remarks were not in the least prejudicial to Steve. The State cleverly weaved the seemingly guilty statements of the defendant into a pattern that, when taken out of context, might give the reader a feeling that Steve was guilty, as the jury had judged.

They argued: "It has long been the law in the State of Illinois that a reviewing court will not overturn a jury's determination of guilt unless its judgment is found to rest on such doubtful, improbable, unsatisfactory or insufficient evidence that reasonable doubt as to defendant's guilt remains." The lawyers contended that "the evidence introduced in the instant case proved defendant guilty of murder . . . beyond every conceivable doubt." They did their best to defend the trial prosecutors and judge. On several occasions they maintained that the defendant had waived his right to appeal. Repeatedly, they argued the defendant's arguments were meritless. In each instance they cited authorities. Tenaciously, they argued that improper prosecutorial errors were harmless and caused the defendant no prejudicial harm.

Having filed for an expedited hearing and for permission to exceed his allotted number of pages—primarily for the purpose of including the Gaudette (the Canadian authority) articles quoted repeatedly by both plaintiff and defendant—Decker took his time in preparing his final brief. He frequently sought advice from the Linscotts, Jim Richards, and me. This willingness to seek comment and advice from those who had supported Steve and Lois was characteristic of Decker. He was committed to seeing that justice was done.

In his rebuttal, Decker countered each of the State's charges. He maintained that the evidence did not support, nor did the defense counsel invite the prosecutors' closing arguments. He argued that no evidence supported the prosecutors' assertion that the victim was raped by a nonsecretor and that Steve's hairs were found at the crime scene. He denied that the prosecutors' abusive and prejudicial assertions in closing arguments were harmless—they resulted in a guilty verdict. He contended that the entirely circumstantial nature of the evidence was insufficient to convict Steve. He addressed the improper actions of certain jury members, the destruction of the vaginal swab evidence, and the speculative, subjective, and unreliable hair evidence. Then he moved on to the dream.

Decker attacked the dream evidence with all his might. His response to the State's "dream confession" theory was crucial—it was the first time any defense of the dream had been attempted:

The State asserts that Mr. Linscott's dream account so "conclusively established" his guilt that no review of the prosecutors' abusive arguments should be made under the plain error doctrine.

In fact, any significant similarities between Mr. Linscott's dream and the actual crime depend either on misstatements of his own words or on circular attempts to cut the real crime to the dream's pattern. Strong evidence suggests that Miss Phillips was murdered by an acquaintance, but not that Mr. Linscott ever met her.

Mr. Linscott consistently talked about the dream-figure, not himself. In tape-recorded interviews, the police pressed him to try to imagine what the murderer was feeling and what he would do. The police encouraged him with reminders of a person who had dreamed about Chicago's DC-10 crash, told him that he had given them "invaluable information," and reminded him that he had studied psychology in college. The police urged him to imagine himself in the killer's place. Perhaps naïvely, he joined the police officers in speculating about the killer's feelings and future behavior.

But despite all the police officers' ploys, the defendant never said anything that could be construed as a "confession." Not when the police officers pretended compassion ... and not when, at the end of the October 10 interview, they turned accusatory.

Decker argued that the State had so overstretched its arguments that he believed they were simply grasping at straws. He pointed out the State's contention that even if Steve never expressly confessed, he nevertheless "gave unambiguous signals" that he was indeed the killer. He attacked the State's "indirect confession" theory, which pointed to purported similarities between the dream-killer described by Steve and Steve himself. Decker argued that the theory has at least two major flaws:

The first is that many of the purported similarities between the killer in the defendant's dream and Steve Linscott himself are nothing more than the product of the State's imagination. For example, the State makes much of the fact that the defendant described the killer in his dream as being between five feet five inches and five feet seven inches tall. And how tall is the defendant himself? Six feet! The difference in height is substantial, and unmistakable. It is one between a professional quarterback and the tackle who blocks for him.

Other purported "similarities" between the dream-killer described by the defendant and the defendant himself are likewise more fanciful than real. For example, the State emphasizes the fact that the defendant described the dream-killer as having a "husky build." Yet an examination of the State's own photographs of the defendant reveals that the defendant himself, a slender man of less than average weight, had no "husky build."

Further, the State emphasizes the fact that the defendant described the dream-killer as having worn a "terry-cloth short-sleeve shirt with two or three narrow horizontal lines across the chest," and suggests that the defendant himself wore a similar shirt to the first police interview. Yet the shirt worn by Mr. Linscott was not a "terry-cloth shirt." It had terry-cloth material only on the sleeves. The shirt he wore did not have two or three stripes across the chest; . . . it had one stripe across the sleeves and none across the chest.

The State's claim that the dream scene was close to Mr. Linscott's home is simply outlandish. He told the police he had no idea during the dream of the locale of the beating. Since hearing of Miss Phillips's murder, though, he had been aware it was "close by."

Other striking dissimilarities between the dream-killer described by the defendant and the defendant himself are simply ignored by the State. For example, Mr. Linscott wears glasses. Did the dream-killer wear glasses? No! He also described the relationship between the killer and the dream-victim as, seemingly, a long and trusting one. Given the recency of Mr. Linscott's residence in the neighborhood, such a relationship with Miss Phillips could not have formed.

The second major flaw with the State's indirect confession theory is that the resemblance between a dreamer and his dream-figure are to be expected. That dream-figures often possess a combination of the dreamer's physical attributes and those drawn from acquaintances has been recognized for as long as dreams have been seriously studied.

It is so plain that the defendant never "confessed"— directly or indirectly—that the State, in an attempt to bolster its position, resorts to misrepresenting the record. The State argues as follows: "When he was finally arrested, defendant immediately asked Sergeant Mendrick what the police would do with a person who voluntarily confessed to the crime, thus demonstrating that he still wanted to confess but that his fear of police motive prevented him from doing so." According to the State's version, Mr. Linscott asked what would happen to the person who confessed. But Sergeant Mendrick recited a question about what would happen to Mr. Linscott if someone else confessed. Mendrick testified: "He had asked me what would happen if someone came in and confessed to the murder of Karen Phillips, would he be released today." Mr. Linscott hardly would have asked whether the true murderer would be released. His interest was in obtaining his own release if the murderer came forward. Thus, there simply was no confession . . . not even an unconscious one.

The State misrepresents Sergeant Mendrick's testimony in several other respects as well. For example: "Defendant openly admitted to Sergeant Mendrick that his 'dream' was so vivid and lifelike that he actually suspected himself of having committed the murder." But, as an examination of Sergeant Mendrick's testimony reveals, Mr. Linscott made no such admission. The Sergeant had asked him the following question: "Since this dream was so vivid, is it possible you thought you were dreaming but were actually in the girl's—murdered girl's apartment, something like an LSD trip where the mind is watching the body?" And how did Mr. Linscott answer? Negatively!

Further, the State contends, "Defendant volunteered to Mendrick that he would explain in court just how his hairs were found on the crime scene." But what Mr. Linscott said was, "If his hairs were found in the murdered girl's apartment, the Devil had put them there," the sergeant testified.

The State claims Mr. Linscott showed "intimate familiarity" with unpublicized details of the crime in both his narratives and his answers to police questions. But there was no "intimate familiarity." Further, if it is suggesting that there had been no news stories regarding the crime before the defendant told the police about his dream on October 6, 1980, then the State is simply wrong. The defendant and his wife both testified that they had discussed such a news story earlier that day.

Because the State has made an issue of publicity, the defendant asks the Court to take judicial notice that the story in question, which appeared in the October 6, 1980, *Chicago Tribune*, reported the victim's age (24), occupation (nurse's assistant), cause of death (bludgeoning), and living situation (she lived alone). One hint that Mr. Linscott's dream account owed a literary debt to the *Tribune* story lies in his choice of the word "bludgeoned" for his own handwritten narrative. An uncommon word, evidently it first appeared in the *Tribune* article.

Mr. Linscott's accounts of his dream are characterized by those qualities that are generally associated with dreams. For example, the scene was indistinct and incomplete. Among other things, he never got a direct look at the dream-victim, and he did not see how the dream-killer had entered the room or left it. Such incompleteness of detail is characteristic of dreams.

Another common characteristic of dreams is that they are largely, if not exclusively, visual experiences. This was true of Mr. Linscott's. There was no sound whatsoever in the dream: neither when the dream-figures were talking, nor during the beating.

A third common characteristic of dreams is the tendency of an especially disturbing dream to cause the dreamer to awaken. That happened here. Twice! Further, it is common for such a dream to then continue after the dreamer has returned to sleep. That also happened with Mr. Linscott's dream. Finally, dreams involving violent encounters, like Mr. Linscott's, are common.

The State, however, contends that Mr. Linscott's dream account constitutes "overwhelming" evidence of guilt because the account contained a "precise" picture of the victim's apartment and the manner of her death. An examination of the defendant's dream account reveals, however, that there was no such correspondence between it and the facts of the real life crime.

Mr. Linscott's dream was set in (1) a living room in an apartment that was at least as large as the apartment in which he and his family lived (which had two bedrooms, a living room, a kitchen, and a bathroom); with (2) a couch; and (3) a light that was below the dream-killer's head. The room in which the real life crime took place, by contrast, was (1) the single large room of an efficiency apartment; with (2) a bed that dominated the room, occupying a third of it; and (3) an overhead light fixture.

One of the most striking features of the room, emphasized by the State, was a table with religious articles and pictures on it. Yet Mr. Linscott, upon being asked by the police whether there were any religious articles in the room in his dream, indicated that there were none!

The State makes much of the fact that there was a stereo in the real-life victim's apartment and also one in the room in Mr. Linscott's dream. But what Mr. Linscott actually said about a stereo came in response to police questions pressing him for additional details. He said: "And when you asked me earlier it seems that I was thinking too there was some impression [sic] that it was a living room, because possibly I thought . . . that there might have been a stereo or something like that around. Not that I see that in the dream at all, but there was just that I had the impression that it was a living room, and possibly it is."

Other items in the apartment which do not accord with Mr. Linscott's dream scene are a very large steamer trunk, a large number of books, a hanging plant . . . and the remarkable lack of chairs. There's not only no couch (there was one in the dream), there's nothing but a wooden folding chair and the bed to sit on.

The victim of the real life crime was white. The victim in Mr. Linscott's dream, however, was not white . . . but black.

The victim in Mr. Linscott's dream accepted the beating passively, without resisting. The State contends the real-life victim also did not resist. The State's reasoning, however, is circular. It uses features of Mr. Linscott's dream to prove the facts of the real-life crime. No independent evidence supports the conclusion that Miss Phillips did not resist the attack. Indeed, the blood and hairs, stuck on her hands, suggest that she did in fact try to defend herself.

The State bolsters its nonresistance argument by pointing to the victim's finger-positions, said to make it "obvious" she accepted the beating passively. Miss Phillips's fingers were apparently found in a position known as an "ommudra" which in her religion might mean she knew death was imminent and wanted to "find a centering." But a search for final peace is not inconsistent with previous resistance, so that a mental leap from the finger-positions to nonresistance is at best speculative.

The condition of Miss Phillips's room certainly suggests a struggle occurred. Exhibits show a television set tipped over, a lamp was found on the floor, and various belongings were scattered about the carpet.

Secondly, there is no evidence that the killer—evidently an acquaintance and perhaps a sharer of her religious beliefs—did not place her fingers in the ommudra. Such tampering would be consistent with the killer's apparent rearrangement of Miss Phillips's nightgown after she had fallen to the floor. There is also some question as to whether the ommudra really means what Helen Palella testified it to mean. If Palella is correct, and if Karen put her fingers in that position, to whom was she trying to convey the message?

The killer? If so, the implication is clear. He understood the significance of the sign and was probably linked to the Temple.

According to the State, the murder occurred at approximately 1:00 A.M., about the same time as the murder in Mr. Linscott's dream. Once again, however, the State reaches its conclusions only by misrepresenting what Mr. Linscott actually said. Mr. Linscott never said that the murder in his dream took place at 1:00 A.M. He said that the dream itself took place, he thought, sometime between 1:00 A.M. and 3:00 A.M.

During the closing argument at trial, the State claimed that the manner in which the dream-victim and the real-life victim were killed was similar, for the dream-victim was "not shot or strangled or died in another manner, but was beaten." The State apparently relied on the defendant's tape-recorded answer when he was asked whether, in his dream, there had been "just the beating with the object." He answered affirmatively. In its brief, the State again, emphasizes this purported death-by-beating similarity. Indeed, the State's heading for its second argument refers to the victim having been "BEATEN ... TO DEATH." Once again, however, the State arrives at its conclusion only by misrepresenting the facts.

According to the medical examiner, there were *two* causes for the real-life victim's death—beating ... and strangulation. Furthermore, in contrast to the dream-victim, the real-life victim was stabbed as well as beaten, once behind her left ear and twice on her right side.

Decker continued to expose the State's biased and distorted representation of the facts and centered on the additional details elicited from Steve by the police in the course of their questioning:

For a large part of the October 8, 1980, interview, the police sought to obtain additional "similarities" by questioning the defendant. Mr. Linscott tried to answer each of the officers' questions, though he often prefaced his responses by saying that he wasn't sure, or didn't know whether he was actually remembering the dream . . . or just guessing.

The State contends that Mr. Linscott's answers to the police officers' questions contained details that he could have known . . . only if he had committed the murder himself. In fact, however, the answers did not contain any such incriminating details.

In his narratives, Mr. Linscott said nothing about the victim's educational background. But during the October 8 interview, one of the police officers asked him whether he had formed an impression of Miss Phillips's educational background. He tried to answer: "No, I didn't, but I thought that she was not a crude person, but just kind of maybe somewhat educated, somewhat intelligent—at least high school . . . and beyond a little bit." The State contends his answer disclosed what only the murderer knew. There are, however, several significant flaws with the State's theory.

Obviously, Mr. Linscott's answer was vague enough to be just a guess. And it was wrong! Miss Phillips held a Bachelor of Science degree and had started training to be a nurse shortly before her death. She thus had gone "a little bit" beyond *college,* not high school. Lastly, Mr. Linscott's answer could have been based on the *Chicago Tribune's* description of her as a "nurse's assistant."

The State asserts that Mr. Linscott described the dream victim as having "strong religious beliefs." Once again, however, the State arrives at its conclusion only by misrepresenting what Mr. Linscott said, which was: "You asked on the phone, you know, could she—did you see any religious articles or anything like that, and I said no. And the only thing that I might catch that she might be a religious person is that she seemed to have a lot of peace, you know, she didn't seem to have an awful lot of turmoil."

The State asserts that Mr. Linscott knew the murder weapon was a tire iron. The State may be correct about the weapon, although a lamp found on the floor of the apartment was stained with a reddish substance in which several hairs were stuck. (The victim was also strangled.) But the State is wrong that Mr. Linscott described the weapon as a tire iron. The State quotes selectively from the defendant's description of the bludgeon used in his dream. What the State omits is that Mr. Linscott summarized his description by calling the weapon "some sort of weight or counterbalance like a clock, grandfather clock." Later, he said it was "quite thick, and possibly heavy," and was eight or nine inches long. The tire iron was about twenty-five inches long, like most. For whatever reason, the State seeks to reduce it to fourteen inches. Thus, the dream weapon did not look to the defendant like a tire iron, an object with which he would have been familiar because of his ability to do some of his own auto repairs.

Detective Scianna, who conducted the October 8 interview, testified at the trial that in his original phone call to the police, the defendant had described the weapon as "possibly a tire iron," but said later the same evening that he wasn't sure what the weapon was. The officer may have erred in his recollection, for the defendant contradicted it at the trial.

In using most of the interview on October 8 and part of the interview on October 10 to find, and record, similarities between the murder and Mr. Linscott's dream, police never once asked about his alleged statement that the dream murderer had used a tire iron. They could easily have done so, just as they had returned to earlier questions about Miss Phillips's religious interests. Police could have reminded the defendant of what Detective Scianna thought he had said two days before, and then asked him whether he still thought the weapon was not a tire iron but rather "some sort of weight or counterbalance like a clock, grandfather clock." But the police, inexplicably, failed to do so.

Mr. Linscott first told the police officers that he didn't know how many blows the dream killer had struck. Then the defendant tried to guess: "I really don't know. But I know it was several, seven sort of area [sic] or something like that." He repeated he "couldn't see her at all," but speculated that "possibly" while the beating first focused on the dream-victim's head, it was then "spread . . . around . . . rather than . . . on her shoulders and head. . . ." At another point, he speculated that "maybe" the victim was struck once or twice in the head.

In its brief, as at trial, the State pursues the number-magic in an attempt to reduce the sixty-six wounds counted by the medical examiner, to the smaller number Mr. Linscott described. The State arbitrarily focused on head wounds. Even so, there were nine of those, not seven, and a total of thirty-two wounds above the shoulders.

Since Decker had been restricted to thirty pages of brief, he had no option but to present his concluding remarks at this point:

Steven Linscott contacted the police regarding his dream after police officers, canvassing the neighborhood, had told him and his wife, "if you think of anything, no matter how silly it might seem to you, let us know, because we don't have any leads." Before calling the police, Mr. Linscott mentioned his dream to his wife and a friend, both of whom thought that it might be helpful to the police, and encouraged him to report it. Wanting, perhaps naïvely, to be a good citizen, he did.

It is evident from the police officers' tape-recorded interviews with Mr. Linscott that they decided very early on—perhaps before the first interview even began—that he was "their man." Consequently, they structured their questioning to build a case against him.

The State contends that Mr. Linscott's account of his dream constituted a "confession," and that he displayed an "intimate familiarity" with the facts of the real-life crime. But there was no such "confession," and no "intimate familiarity" with unpublished facts. Mr. Linscott's dream account was anything but "overwhelming" evidence of guilt and thus may not serve to support the conviction. For the same reasons, the many prejudicial errors which infected his trial cannot be dismissed as "harmless."

In laying a foundation for the appeal in the post-conviction hearing and in the two appeal briefs, Decker and his associates, Rich McLeese and Jim Huston, had performed brilliantly. Steve and Lois, and others who had worked intimately on the case, were satisfied. Two things remained: the oral arguments and the judges' decision.

The courtroom was packed for the oral arguments on December 21, 1983, more than a year after notice of appeal had been filed. Present were reporters from the *Chicago Tribune* and NBC's Channel 5 television station. It was by far the most positive hearing to date. In a memorandum to the "friends of Steve Linscott," Decker described the hearing this way:

Oral arguments were addressed to Justices of the Appellate Court today. We took about thirty-five minutes, the State perhaps twenty-five.

252

The case was assigned to one of five "panels" of judges who hear appeals in Chicago-area cases. Each panel consists of four Justices, who rotate on cases so that only three are assigned to each case.

As it turned out, our Judges—White, McNamara, and Rizzi—are well-regarded in terms of ability and fairness. By a happy coincidence, these Justices are also the authors of a 1981 decision, *People vs. Giangrande,* which is perhaps the most important authority on which we rely for the proposition that the State may not argue to a jury that hairs shown to be "consistent" with an accused's actually are his. Such an argument produced a reversal in the *Giangrande* case.

We were also able to take the position that the prosecution's violation of the *Giangrande* rule was a deliberate one (deliberately prejudicial arguments will produce reversals more easily than inadvertent ones) because in a February 1982 hearing before Judge Stillo, a prosecutor told the Judge about the *Giangrande* case.

Questions asked by Justice Rizzi and Justice White suggested at least that they will take a hard look at the sufficiency of evidence at the trial.

Assistant State's Attorney David Cuomo opened his oral argument by announcing that Mr. Linscott had "confessed" through his dream account, and that his confession was corroborated by "physical evidence." Launching into similarities between Mr. Linscott's dream account and the killing itself, Mr. Cuomo was repeatedly interrupted by Justice Rizzi's demands that he recount the physical evidence.

To Mr. Cuomo's mention of hair and blood evidence, Justice Rizzi pressed, "Did anyone testify that was the defendant's hair? Did anyone testify it was the defendant's blood?"

"No," Mr. Cuomo replied, accurately. He explained that by "physical evidence" he had meant physical similarities between the real crime and Mr. Linscott's dream account.

To Mr. Cuomo's statement that Mr. Linscott fit the physical description of the dream-killer, Justice Rizzi observed that the personal characteristics "would apply to a heck of a lot of people. They're not all guilty."

Arguing the evidence showed Miss Phillips had not resisted her killer (as in Steve's dream), Mr. Cuomo stated that her body bore no defensive wounds. Justice White asked, "What is a defensive wound?" To Mr. Cuomo's reply, Justice Rizzi observed, perhaps sarcastically, "That's proof beyond a reasonable doubt that she didn't resist?"

When Mr. Cuomo asserted the prosecution at the trial had identified hairs found at the scene only as the killer's hairs, not as Mr. Linscott's, Justice Rizzi argued with him: "But you also said the defendant was the killer." Mr. Cuomo answered by asking the Justices to read the prosecutors' assertions in context. In rebuttal, I read from the trial transcript three pages in which prosecutors had identified the hairs as Mr. Linscott's.

In my time I tried to sketch each of the major arguments made in the two written briefs we previously filed. I pointed to the dreamy quality of Mr. Linscott's account, the dissimilarities between it and the murder scene, the fact that Mr. Linscott had initially gone to the police like a good citizen responding to an officer's plea even for seemingly "silly" leads, the elusiveness of blood and hair evidence allegedly linking Mr. Linscott to the scene, and to the fact that prosecutors had knowingly stepped over the line these very Justices had drawn in *Giangrande*. The Justices asked few questions, none in argumentative tone.

I analogized that the expert testimony about gamma markers was like an expert, having found water but no alcohol in a drink he had tested, asserting that his results were "consistent" with a solution of Scotch and water.

While the oral arguments went very well for our side, it would be presumptuous to assume the Justices agreed with all, or even some, of our arguments. It appeared they did, but that appearance has been deceptive before. Sometimes Justices ask the harder questions of the side they agree with as a way of refining the points they will use in writing their opinion. It's possible that's what they were doing in pressing Mr. Cuomo as they did. Still, we came away with positive feelings. All we can do now is wait and pray.

15

The
Long Haul Ahead

Appellate Courts have been known to take up to two years, even three, to reach a decision. The nature and number of appeals and the amount of reading and study involved are significant factors in determining delays. But "emergency" cases have been decided within a month. "There is no 'average' time period," the court clerk said. While a year might be a reasonable time to wait for a decision, the delays seem like an eternity for those involved—especially the innocent.

If the judges needed a reminder that the Linscott case was before them, Decker had a good excuse. It came in the form of another Illinois Appellate Court decision dated May 18, 1984, which addressed some of the same issues in Steve's case. Within two weeks Decker filed a "motion for leave to supplement his briefs with additional authority, affidavit, and draft order."

It was timely, as was a fairly recent Supreme Court ruling that addressed the destruction of crucial physical evidence under circumstances very similar to Steve's—the particular situation was almost identical. On this single point the Supreme Court granted the defendant a new trial and ruled that his constitutional rights had been violated—something that Arthur O'Donnell had tried to get across to Judge Stillo without success.

The months passed slowly. The summer of 1984 came and went. To Steve and Lois, it seemed as if the Court had forgotten them—as if even God had forgotten them. The first anniversary of the oral arguments offered no sign of relief from the tedium. The year ended without the slightest acknowledgment of the case by the appellate judges.

The new year began with a request for a pardon from Illinois Governor James Thompson. The procedure calls for a petition to be filed with the Prisoner Review Board, allowing it to make recommendations to the governor. The petition was filed March 1, 1985.

Decker began the petition by saying, "Steven Linscott should be granted a pardon for the most fundamental of all reasons: He is innocent!"

Hundreds of letters were written to Governor Thompson and to the Prisoner Review Board on Steve's behalf. The testimony from all who knew Steve was remarkably consistent. Decker selected thirteen of these letters as important exhibits in the petition for pardon.

Since no expert testimony relating to the dream evidence was presented at the original trial, the law prohibits the inclusion of that testimony in any subsequent hearing or appeal. But this evidence can be contained in a pardon petition. Realizing the consequences for Steve, Decker had, some eighteen months earlier, asked Dr. Bernard Rubin to analyze the dreams and submit an expert opinion. Dr. Rubin, as a recognized authority in the state of Illinois, has appeared as an expert witness in a number of cases and has submitted reports to the Illinois Parole and Pardon Board, the Illinois Federal District Court, and the United States Department of Justice. Therefore, Decker grabbed the opportunity to bring Dr. Rubin's opinion to the attention of the Prisoner Review Board—even though the appellate judges could not be made aware of its existence.

Dr. Bernard Rubin affirmed these points:

First, that the only witness to a dream is the dreamer. Therefore it is important to examine a reported dream to determine whether it has qualities of a dream. The dreams reported by Mr. Linscott have the qualities one usually associates with dreams. They are vivid, but with vague details; dreamlike, that is, isolated from the systems of consciousness; single-minded, that is, no other content and thematic coherence, but lacking in imagination. Therefore, the dreams were likely dreamed.

Second, that the interpretation of both dreams by anxiety is typical of nightmares. It is also common to wake from such a dream, and when returning to sleep resume the dream story interrupted by wakening. This supports the notion that they were dreams and of the anxiety type.

Third, that dreams of violence occur frequently in the dream-life of humans, without resulting in acts of violence. In fact, dreams of endangerment, and dreams of falling are the most common forms of nightmares, which begin in childhood and continue throughout much of adult life. Such anxiety dreams are reported by more than one-half of all persons reporting dreams. Therefore, it is likely that the nightmares of violence woke Mr. Linscott on two occasions in the same night, helping him to remember their theme.

The hearing before the Prisoner Review Board was heard April 2, 1985. After presenting his materials, Decker made an innovative move. He introduced Jim Richards and let him speak in Steve's behalf. Skillfully, passionately, Jim outlined the main facts of the case.

Then Lois spoke. She departed from her carefully prepared speech and spoke movingly in support of her husband. The board listened and allowed them more than their allotted twenty minutes. Their hopes were rising as the suspense continued.

On Friday, August 2, Decker received communication from the Appellate Court that a decision had been reached and would be released the following Wednesday, August 7. Late Tuesday afternoon Decker's office was notified by the court clerk that release of the decision had been canceled— with no explanation.

The Appellate Court decision, filed August 7, 1985, was released on Wednesday, August 14—more than one year and seven months after the oral arguments were heard. Justice Rizzi delivered the opinion:

Defendant, Steven Paul Linscott, was found guilty of murder in a jury trial, and he was sentenced to forty years in prison. He contends that as a matter of law, the State did not prove him guilty beyond a reasonable doubt. We agree, and we reverse the judgment of conviction.

It was a split decision, however. Justice White concurred with the decision, Justice McNamara dissented. The majority opinion ruled, however, and that was all that mattered. The Linscotts were ecstatic!

Justice Rizzi's opinion took ten pages; Justice McNamara's dissent, three. After outlining the main facts of the case, Rizzi wrote:

In the present case the State contends that it produced direct evidence that defendant was guilty because "the confession clearly proved defendant guilty of murder beyond any doubt." The State's reference to a confession is a voluntary acknowledgment of guilt after the commission of an offense, and it does not embrace mere statements of independent facts from which guilt may be inferred. In the present case, defendant never acknowledged guilt in relating his dream. Consequently, the State's attempt to elevate defendant's dream to a status of a confession fails because it ignores the very essence of a confession. It follows that the State did not produce any direct evidence of defendant's guilt.

We next address whether the State produced sufficient circumstantial evidence to prove that defendant is guilty beyond a reasonable doubt. When, as in this case, the State's evidence of guilt is entirely circumstantial, the defendant cannot be found guilty unless the facts or circumstances proved exclude every reasonable theory of innocence....

Here the State argues that in relating his dream, defendant stated facts which only the killer could have known.... We believe the State's conclusion that defendant had special knowledge of the crime is not supported by the evidence.

Defendant first told the police about his dream in a telephone conversation on Monday October 6, two days after the body was found. Between the time that the body was found and defendant first recounted his dream to the police, the police had canvassed the residential area asking neighbors for clues regarding the victim's death. It is reasonable to assume that the neighbors would have discussed it among themselves, and that whatever details they might have learned from the police would have been augmented by the news media accounts of the murder. Moreover, much of the information to which the State refers appeared in a newspaper report of the murder before defendant told police about his dream. The newspaper article described the victim as a twenty-four-year-old female, living alone and working as a nurse's assistant. The newspaper article used the word "bludgeoned," as did defendant in relating his dream. Also, the article indicated that the victim was struck by a blunt instrument and that she suffered a head wound. In addition, the newspaper article stated that the police suspected that the victim knew her attacker because there were no signs of forced entry into the apartment.

As for the other details which the State claims only defendant knew, defendant's account was either inexplicit or actually inconsistent with the facts.

Then Justice Rizzi highlighted the inconsistencies between the dream and the actual murder and concluded:

Finally, in determining whether the circumstantial evidence produced by the State is sufficient to prove that defendant is guilty beyond a reasonable doubt, we are mindful that no fingerprint evidence was introduced which connected defendant to the crime, or any object related to the crime. Nor was any evidence introduced to connect defendant with the tire iron that was found by the police. Also, no evidence was introduced to show that anything in defendant's residence or wardrobe related to the crime. In addition, no tangible evidence was produced to show that defendant was ever in Phillips's apartment. Defendant denied that he knew Phillips, and there was no evidence produced which rebuts defendant's testimony. We do not suggest that it was necessary for the State to produce any of this evidence to prove defendant guilty beyond a reasonable doubt. However, in determining whether the circumstantial evidence which was produced here was sufficient, we believe that it is proper to consider, in light of all the facts and circumstances of the case, not only the evidence which was produced but also the absence of evidence which could have proved or disproved certain matters in issue.

We conclude that the circumstantial evidence produced by the State merely raises a possibility, or suspicion, that defendant is guilty. The evidence is plainly not sufficient to exclude every reasonable theory of innocence, which includes the possibility that defendant simply had a dream similar to the occurrence and that he acquired knowledge of additional facts through the news media, or from neighborhood talk about the crime, after a police canvass of the neighborhood.

Under the circumstances, we believe that as a matter of law, the State did not meet its responsibility to present direct or circumstantial evidence which proves that defendant is guilty beyond a reasonable doubt. While it was the province of the jury to weigh the evidence and determine the credibility of witnesses, a reviewing court will not hesitate to reverse a conviction which, as in this case, rests solely upon circumstantial evidence that merely raises a possibility or suspicion that defendant is guilty. If we did not reverse such a conviction, we would indeed be derelict in our duty as a reviewing court.

Justice McNamara dissented as follows:

I believe that the State proved defendant guilty beyond a reasonable doubt. Defendant's statements to the police exhibited knowledge of the crime which only the killer could have.... His description of the killer strongly implicated himself.... I believe with the State that defendant's statements to the police were a confession.... Furthermore, head hairs found at the scene of the murder were consistent with defendant's head hairs, and defendant's expert witness agreed that the odds that two similar head hairs could have originated from different sources are one in 4500.

Defendant's pubic hairs were consistent with hairs found near the body of the victim and defendant's expert witness agreed that the odds that two similar pubic hairs could have originated from different sources are one in 800. The blood tests which were performed also failed to exclude defendant. I believe that all the facts were inconsistent with any reasonable hypothesis of innocence, and that defendant was proved guilty beyond a reasonable doubt. Since I do not believe that any of the other claimed errors warrant reversal, I would affirm the judgment of the Circuit Court of Cook County.

McNamara's opinion flies in the face of the Gaudette articles submitted with Decker's briefs. And it also ignores the 1981 *Giangrande* case involving hair evidence and other recent and significant decisions regarding physical evidence and the destruction of evidence by the State.

The decision received good news coverage over the next several days as Steve's release was anticipated. His release, on his own recognizance (a cashless bond) on August 21 was ordered by the Appellate Court and signed by Justices Rizzi and White. But the State strenuously objected. The *Chicago Sun Times* reported their position on Friday, August 16:

Illinois Supreme Court Justice Daniel P. Ward yesterday issued an emergency order temporarily halting the release from prison of Steven P. Linscott, whose murder conviction was overturned by the State Appellate Court. . . . Ward said he stayed Linscott's release on bail until the entire seven-member Illinois Supreme Court has an opportunity to review whether Linscott should be set free during the anticipated further appeals in the case. "The practical effect of the ruling will be to keep Linscott in custody until the Supreme Court has an opportunity to consider the State's motion to revoke bail," the justice explained. Ward said he gave Cook County prosecutors until Tuesday to file an appeal of the lower-court ruling reversing Linscott's conviction on what the Appellate Court called "entirely circumstantial" evidence.

The State acted quickly. It filed with the Illinois Supreme Court a "petition for leave to appeal" the Appellate Court decision. Clearly, the newspaper articles originally reporting the crime made the State jittery and defensive. The petition attempted to refute the argument that Steve's dream owed a literary debt to the *Chicago Tribune* article initially reporting the murder—it was far too close to reality for the State's comfort. The State argued:

The novelty and importance of the case lies in the fact that by its decision the Appellate Court has reversed the jury's verdict finding the defendant guilty.... In doing so the Appellate Court has relied upon matters, namely, newspaper articles, which are completely *dehors* the record on appeal and which the jury never saw. Moreover the Appellate Court has reweighed the evidence and erroneously held that the People failed to exclude every reasonable hypothesis of innocence despite the fact that the jury was properly instructed not to find the defendant guilty unless the People were able to exclude every reasonable hypothesis of innocence. The actions of the Appellate Court in going outside the record and substituting its judgment for that of a properly instructed jury who saw and heard the witnesses and observed the defendant, sets a dangerous precedent....

When asked to describe the victim, defendant gave a description which closely matched Miss Phillips. Defendant said that in the "dream," the victim was a woman who had *more than* a high school education and that she was very religious. In fact, Miss Phillips had a bachelor's degree in science from Aurora College, was studying to be a nurse at Rush Presbyterian, St. Luke's School of Nursing and was a member of the Kriya Yoga religion.

Throughout the trial and in its Appellate brief, the State argued that Steve had said the victim's education was *little more* than high school—a fact only the killer could have known. In earlier arguments the State had down-played her post–high-school and graduate education. Now, it changed its approach.

In his answer to the petition, Decker wrote:

The Appellate Court opinion reversing the conviction of Mr. Linscott because of insufficient evidence is factually based and involves no significant interpretations of law. It conflicts with no Appellate opinion. The decision also has no precedential potential. So far as has been determined, Mr. Linscott is the first person *in any country* against whom has been used what he said was a dream.

Then Decker lost no time in attacking the State's petition:

The petition cannot be described charitably. It departs wholly from the function recently described by Chief Justice Clark for such a pleading, that it present "the legal questions involved, not the factual situation, in a clear and concise manner . . ." The petition cites no decisions, no statutes.

Such legal positions as are presented by the petition are frivolous and unsupported by authority. But it is the "factual" account in the petition which offends most. It is drawn from the taped interviews of the defendant. The tapes are unambiguous, yet their content is ignored or badly misrepresented in the petition. Anticipating misrepresentations, the defense accurately described the contents of much of the tapes in its opening Brief in the Appellate Court. When the People did misrepresent the tapes in their brief, the defendant's reply brief pointed out each departure from the truth. . . .

The People's most serious deviation from the truth is the statement that a defense expert agreed at the trial that the odds that two similar head hairs could have originated from different sources are 1 in 4500 for head hairs, 1 in 800 for pubic hairs. The People *conceded* sub silentio in the Court below that the odds were inapplicable to the hairs tested in this case, but renew the claim now. At the trial a prosecutor argued the odds to the jury. On appeal, the defense argued that the argument was improper and prejudicial because the defense expert repeatedly disagreed that the odds were applicable if the People's expert did not conduct the same number of examinations as had Gaudette, who conducted the studies from which the odds came. (The People's expert did not run the same tests; he and another testifying expert inexplicably were not asked about the applicability of the odds.)

There was no evidence that the hairs were of "average commonness," nor that the proper number of the defendant's hairs were compared, both threshold factors established by Gaudette in determining his odds. Gaudette also warned that his odds were dependent on the inspection of *all* the hair characteristics he examined, numbering twenty-three for head hair and twenty-six for pubic hair. (The People's expert at the trial testified variously that he examined between seven and a dozen characteristics.) Nor did the People's expert examine hairs in cross section, which Gaudette warned was essential.

It was little wonder that the State, in essence, called "foul play"; Decker had secured permission to submit the Gaudette articles in support of his Appellate briefs. It was unfortunate that Justice McNamara ignored them, or else failed to comprehend their significance.

Decker then turned the focus on Justice McNamara:

The decision of the dissenting Justice is founded upon misconceptions of the evidence, evidently derived from the People's disregard for the record.... He wrote inaccurately.... Extracting the inaccuracies from the dissent, then, we are left with the residue that the defendant and the dream assailant were light-complected blonds and that the dreamed and real assaults caused blood-letting.

For those similarities Steven Linscott was convicted of murder and sentenced to forty years in prison!

Closing his answer to the petition for leave to appeal, and citing numerous cases, Decker argued that the point relied upon for reversal in the petition is meritless and that the Appellate Court properly took judicial notice of the newspaper article. He contended that

even assuming, *arguendo*, that it was improper for the Appellate Court to take judicial notice of the newspaper article, review by the Supreme Court is still not warranted....

267

The Appellate Court's reversal of the conviction on the ground of insufficiency of the evidence was proper despite the fact that the jury was properly instructed on the reasonable-doubt issue.

In conclusion, Decker argued:

The "point relied upon for reversal" is wholly devoid of merit. It was not the subject of dispute among the Appellate justices. And the State's arguments find no support in the record, in logic, or in case law. That this is the most substantial point that the State has to raise in regard to "error" in the Appellate Court's decision is, plainly, a testament to the validity of the Court's holding and analysis.

On October 2, 1985, the Illinois Supreme Court allowed the State's petition for leave to appeal, and they added, "The motion by the petitioner to revoke bond is allowed."

This means that Steve must remain in prison until the State Supreme Court announces its decision.

The fight to establish Steve's innocence continues. Three possibilities exist: the Supreme Court could uphold the Appellate Court decision, reverse it, or grant a new trial—in which case the process would begin all over again.

There is a long haul ahead.

The case against Steve Linscott is a strange one. There was no confession; no eye-witness testimony; no finger-prints; no physical evidence directly linking him to the scene of the crime or to the crime itself. There was no proof that Steve had ever met the girl who had been murdered. There was only a partially accurate dream.

The answer to the question "Did he do it or did he dream it?" is simply "Neither." Steve did not commit the crime, nor did he ever claim to have seen the actual murder in his dream; he merely believed the police, for a time, when they said it might have some relevance.

The chances that the real killer of Karen Ann Phillips will ever be caught are slim. The investigations by the Oak Park Police Department seemed to be inadequate: leads were not followed; those closest to Karen Phillips were never seriously questioned or investigated.

George R. Seibel, the investigator hired by Tom Decker in October 1982, concluded that it was highly likely that someone other than Steve Linscott had murdered Karen Phillips. Decker noted that substantial evidence exists that Karen Phillips was killed by someone she knew well. There were no signs of forcible entry into Karen's locked apartment. Since Karen was wearing only a nightgown when her body was found, it is unlikely that she would have admitted a stranger after midnight, which is what the State contended.

The State also made no attempt to explain the presence of the Negroid hairs that were found on the carpet beneath her body, on the bedsheets, and among the wood shavings near the jimmy marks on the outside of Karen's front door.

Researchers estimate that 80 percent of all murders are committed by people known to the victim. Many people among Karen's acquaintances were never eliminated as suspects. For instance, one friend of Karen's was known to have had a key to her apartment the week she was killed. Another friend moved away shortly after the murder. And the Aurora man, whose blood type matched Karen's, remains a prime suspect.

In spite of the many possibilities that had existed, Steve's dramatic recounting of his dream seems to have been the moment when the police began to bring their investigation of other suspects to a halt.

The Old Testament prophet Habakkuk once faced a problem too big for him to solve. He saw violence. He saw the law ignored. He saw justice ineffective and truth perverted. There was no response to his cry, no apparent answers to his questions. But Habakkuk knew that one day "the earth will be filled with the knowledge of the glory of the Lord, as the waters cover the sea" (Habakkuk 2:14), and that came as a great consolation to him. The Judge of all the earth would someday make his righteousness known.

With that assurance, Habakkuk could say, "I will rejoice in the Lord, I will be joyful in God my Savior. The Sovereign Lord is my strength; he makes my feet like the feet of a deer, he enables me to go on the heights" (Habakkuk 3:18–19).

Steve and Lois Linscott join in that chorus. They know God has a purpose and that one day that purpose will be revealed. Meanwhile, they accept God's will for their lives.

Steve is still on trial. But so are the police and the prosecutors and the lawyers and the judges and the entire American justice system.

And whatever the outcome, God is the final arbiter.

Epilogue

Steve and Lois were perplexed. After the Appellate Court's reversal of Steve's conviction and their decision to release him, things were looking up. God was working! Steve was jubilant. But then his bond was revoked, and Steve felt forlorn. Undaunted, he prayed for a miracle.

At about that same time, the First Baptist Church in Centralia inherited a house on the outskirts of the city—a first-time experience for the church. What was God telling them? What would they do with an empty house? As the church prayed for guidance, the answer came. Make it available to the Linscotts after Steve's release from jail. But when his bond was revoked, the excitement diminished. Had God misled them?

Tom Decker filed another motion for Steve's release before the Illinois Supreme Court. On November 1 came the miracle that Steve had prayed for. In a four-to-two decision—

with one abstention—the Supreme Court agreed to release Steve for the original amount of bail—$450,000. The paperwork and legal procedures began. Through the generosity of a Christian friend, $45,000 was immediately posted—the 10 percent bond required. Decker flew to Centralia, and the prison officials had courteously agreed to work overtime to ensure Steve's release that same day.

The December 1985 issue of the independent journal *The Chicago Lawyer* carried an article on the case and stated, "Prosecutors have appealed the reversal [of the Appellate Court decision], but their chance of prevailing is considered slim—the Supreme Court has freed Linscott on bond." Things *were* looking good for Steve.

Early on Friday evening, November 1, Steve Linscott walked out of the Centralia Correctional Institution. Waiting for him were Lois—who had faithfully remained with him throughout the ordeal—and Katherine, Paul, and Vicki. Tears rolled uncontrollably down their cheeks.

Steve was home.

A Final Note from the Author

On Friday, October 17, 1986, the Illinois State Supreme Court issued a stunning four-to-two decision to reinstate Steve's conviction. The majority opinion relied on similarities between the murder and the dream (particularly what they considered to be Steve's "knowledge" of the murder weapon and the victim's passive acceptance of the attack) and the forensic evidence. The dissenting justices accused the majority of giving undue weight to circumstantial evidence and of affirming a conviction on a mere suspicion of guilt. They strongly felt there is a reasonable doubt as to Steve's guilt.

On December 1, 1986, the State Supreme Court strangely agreed to keep Steve free on bond. Three weeks later it remanded the case back to the Appellate Court for a resolution of outstanding issues. A retrial is hoped for! The story is far from over.